YOU CAN'T MAKE THIS UP

YOU CAN'T MAKE THIS UP

Miracles, Memories, and the Perfect
Marriage of Sports and Television

AL MICHAELS
WITH L. JON WERTHEIM

WILLIAM MORROW

An Imprint of HarperCollins*Publishers*

HarperCollins books may be purchased for educational, business, or sales promotional use. For information please e-mail the Special Markets Department at SPsales@harpercollins.com.

A hardcover edition of this book was published in 2014 by William Morrow, an imprint of HarperCollins Publishers.

FIRST WILLIAM MORROW PAPERBACK EDITION PUBLISHED 2015.

Designed by Lisa Stokes

Library of Congress Cataloging-in-Publication Data has been applied for.

ISBN 978-0-06-231497-0

15 16 17 18 19   DIX/RRD   10 9 8 7 6 5 4 3 2 1

To the loves of my life—

Linda, Steve, Jenny and Jeff, Kaitlyn, Aidan, Nate and Emily

CONTENTS

PREFACE   ix

CHAPTER 1
Brooklyn   1

CHAPTER 2
California Kid   7

CHAPTER 3
The Rascal   13

CHAPTER 4
Cut by the Lakers   20

CHAPTER 5
Aloha   31

CHAPTER 6
Rose, Bench, Sparky, and the Machine   48

CHAPTER 7
The Giants of Candlestick, and the Wizard of Westwood   70

CHAPTER 8
Wide, Wide World   93

CHAPTER 9
Do You Believe in Miracles?   105

CHAPTER 10
Saturdays in the Fall   124

CHAPTER 11
The One and Only   135

CHAPTER 12
Roone, the Olympics, and the Fight Game 152

CHAPTER 13
Monday Nights   169

CHAPTER 14
Two for the Ages   183

CHAPTER 15
O.J.   205

CHAPTER 16
Diversions   217

CHAPTER 17
Monday Night Transformations   228

CHAPTER 18
Partners   246

CHAPTER 19
Links   261

CHAPTER 20
A New Home   270

EPILOGUE   285

ACKNOWLEDGMENTS   289

Don't Ever Get Jaded

IT'S JUNE 2012. AND I'm astonished that in my sixties, I can feel like I'm six.

I'm at center ice, fourteen rows up, at Staples Center in Los Angeles, and Game 6 of the Stanley Cup Final is about to start. To my left is my wife, Linda. To my right are my son, Steven, and my eight-year-old grandson, Aidan. The Los Angeles Kings are facing the New Jersey Devils, with the Kings leading the series, three games to two. Each of us has that same pit in our stomach. That pit only sports can give you.

There are actually nine members of the Michaels family in the arena. My brother David is here with his son Jake, my nephew, a few sections over. And my daughter Jennifer, her husband Jeff, and their son, my grandson Nate, are here, too. Three generations of the family. All in one place for a hockey game. More than fifty years ago, I grew up going to Rangers games with my father at the old Madison Square Garden on Eighth Avenue in New York. But in 1967, after my family moved to Los Angeles, I was at the first Kings game—it was played at the Long Beach Arena—and I've been a Kings fan ever since.

I've covered a couple of thousand sports events all over the world. I've called Super Bowls and World Series and NBA Finals, the Summer Olympics, the Winter Olympics—and have hosted the Stanley Cup Final. A number of years ago, a colleague at ABC figured out that I've appeared on live prime-time network television far more than anyone in history. But from day one, I've always tried to follow the advice the legendary sportscaster Curt Gowdy once gave me: *Don't ever get jaded.*

The Kings have helped take care of that.

Our family has had season tickets since the early nineties. I have no interest in sitting in a suite with twenty people. I just want to concentrate on the game. When I'm on the air, I'm deep into the production and the mechanics of the telecast—dispensing information, communicating with my producer and director and my on-air partners, and seguing to taped pieces or commercials. Here, I just want to absorb the game.

A lot of people know me for an Olympic hockey call, and I hosted three Stanley Cup Finals in early 2000s—but I've actually only announced a handful of NHL games. Still, hockey has a hold on me like no other sport. A friend once told me it's the only game where misery and euphoria dance the tango. No other sport can put you through the wringer and the range of emotions like hockey does. And the Kings are my connection to that.

I have nothing to do with them professionally. When I go to a Kings game, I don't bring a media credential—I bring a ticket. I don't have to prepare notes or try to gather nuggets of information in the locker room beforehand—I go straight to my seat. When I'm on the air, I work to be impartial. With the Kings, I can just be another fan who lives and dies with a team.

We've kept it in the family. The same way my dad passed down his love of sports, taking my brother and me to Ebbets Field and Madison Square Garden and then, when we moved west, to the Los Angeles Coliseum, the Los Angeles Sports Arena, and ultimately

Dodger Stadium when it opened in 1962. We took our kids to Kings games. And now our kids take their kids.

But still, countless times through the years, we would leave the arena after another Kings loss and say to each other, "Why can't *we* be the Red Wings?" Yes, Wayne Gretzky led us to the Stanley Cup Final in 1993—and then the Kings won only one playoff series over the next nineteen years. Five or six years ago, I joked with my son, "Steve, I don't think we're going to renew the tickets; we'll just renew the parking."

But in this playoff run, in the spring of 2012, the Kings have morphed into something else entirely. Suddenly, we've *become* the Red Wings. For the seven weeks since the playoffs began, the Kings have played game after game that they haven't just won—but dominated. Now, here we are, in the Stanley Cup Final.

It's the Kings and the Devils. (In a perfect world, for my own personal symmetry, I wish it were the Rangers.) As the series started, our goalie, Jonathan Quick, who'd been red hot throughout the playoffs—a hot goalie is the biggest key to any NHL postseason run—stayed dominant, and in every series, the Kings have gone up three games to none. Now they're one game away from hoisting the Stanley Cup.

Something like this really captivates any city. Almost everyone becomes a hockey fan. People who didn't watch are now fully invested. For Game 4, the Stanley Cup itself was in the building. But the Kings lost 3–1, and before I even got into my car, I was racked with nervousness. *We can't blow a 3–0 lead, can we?*

Now my son was making plans to take Aidan, the eight-year-old, to New Jersey for Game Five, so they could be there in person in case the Kings won the Cup there. But the Devils won that one, too, turning the whole Michaels family into a wreck. You know the feeling—it borders on paranoia. It's familiar to every sports fan. Your team is leaking oil. And you're wondering if they can somehow find a way to ratchet it up one more time. What you're really doing is praying.

So here we are, back in Los Angeles, in our seats at Game 6. When the Kings were leading three games to none, Steven asked me, "If we win, do you think it'll make up for everything we've been through over the last twenty years?"

"It might," I responded. "But I'll tell you this. If they lose this series, it will be *worse* than anything we've endured over the last twenty years!"

But halfway through the first period, the Kings get a big break. There's a five-minute major penalty against the Devils, and during that long advantage, the Kings score three times, and lead 3–0 after the first period.

In the second period, another goal puts the Kings up 4–0—at which point I would normally be thinking, *We're good as gold—the Devils would have to score five goals against Jonathan Quick to win the game.* But I don't want to think logically. The whole thing has been so surreal. The Kings had barely gotten into the playoffs as the number-eight seed in the Western Conference, and then had gone on this improbable run, and now are just a period away from winning the Stanley Cup. But here I am, only thinking about everything that can go wrong. I keep looking up at the clock—*why is it ticking down in slow motion?*

Finally, it's late in the third period, and the Kings now have an insurmountable 6–1 lead. The whole crowd is standing and bellowing. People in our section have their arms draped around one another. The Kings are about to win their first Stanley Cup in the franchise's forty-five-year history. And inevitably, someone near me turns and yells out, "Hey Al, do you believe in miracles?"

As the horn sounds, Staples Center is going absolutely wild. The streamers are coming down from the rafters, the fans are hugging complete strangers. Minutes later, the Kings are skating around the ice with the Stanley Cup. Pure exhilaration.

The ceremony concludes, and when it's over, we walk out onto the concourse and my grandsons spot each other. Aidan and Nate, who just turned six, both play hockey, and both are wearing their Kings jerseys. They run up to each other and hug.

I look at Steven and Jeff, laugh, and say, "You know, in sixty years, they'll say to each other, 'Remember when the Kings won that one Stanley Cup?'" Here *we* are after all these years, and *these* two kids are experiencing it at eight and six. I'm thinking, *If only they knew that this could happen just this once in their lifetimes.*

Of course, at that point, there's no way to know that the Kings will be right back here two years later, in the Stanley Cup Final—this time against the team of my youth, the Rangers. I couldn't possibly fathom that we'll be able to experience the same cardiac thrills, from the same seats, in an unforgettable double-overtime win in Game 5, when the Kings will do it all again.

But on this night, in 2012, I'm looking at the first time as the only time.

We go to the parking lot, and I think of Curt Gowdy. *Don't ever get jaded.* I think also of the great Jim McKay, and his line from *Wide World of Sports.* "The human drama of athletic competition." You just don't know what's going to happen. But so often, sports have the capacity to create these moments. The kinds of moments I've had the great fortune to broadcast throughout a career I dreamed of since I was six years old.

From minor-league baseball in Hawaii to the Miracle on Ice to *Monday Night Football* to *Sunday Night Football* and so much in between, if there's such a thing as reincarnation, and if you believe in the law of averages, in my next life I'll be working in a sulfur mine.

In Mongolia.

On the night shift.

I'm always remembering how lucky I've been. And I have this crazy, unscripted drama known as sports to thank for it all.

CHAPTER 1

Brooklyn

MY FIRST MEMORY IN life is going to Ebbets Field in the summer of 1950.

I was almost six, and the ballpark was a twenty-minute walk from our second-story apartment in the Flatbush section of Brooklyn. We walked in on the first-base side of Ebbets Field, and more than sixty years later, I can still see the colors vividly in my mind's eye. The grass was a stunning shade of green. The red-brown infield dirt. The uniforms that seemed almost too white to be real—what Vin Scully has described through the years as "wedding cake white."

I remember everything about Ebbets Field. I remember the signage at the bottom of the right field wall. And I remember the faces of the players. Jackie Robinson, taking infield practice. Duke Snider and Pee Wee Reese, walking out from the dugout to the batting cage.

But there was another image I remember from that day, above the field. From time to time I would turn around and look at an enclosure that was just below and attached to the upper deck. My father told me that was the Dodgers' broadcast booth.

The Dodgers were playing the Cardinals, and I really don't remember if they won or lost. It didn't matter. By the time we left, I was enthralled. I wanted to come back to Ebbets Field the next day, and the next day, and the day after that.

A few months later, my father took me to Madison Square Garden for a hockey game. It was a Saturday afternoon, and the New York Rovers of the Eastern Hockey League were playing the Atlantic City Seagulls. (I was too young to go to a Rangers game, since they only played on Sunday and Wednesday nights—school nights.) We got to the Garden early, before the teams had even come out to warm up. We took our seats in the corner of the lower part of the balcony, and again, just like when I walked into Ebbets Field, I was transfixed by the scene.

The combination of the lighting and the just-resurfaced rink made the ice shimmer. As was the case with my first baseball game, I don't remember who won, but it was the ambience, the environment, the whole package—that's what stuck with me.

More than sixty years later, it still does.

MY PARENTS WERE BOTH teenagers when I was born. They met at Midwood High School in Brooklyn and got married before they graduated. Our apartment in Brooklyn had one bedroom. When I was four, my brother David was born. He and I shared the bedroom and my parents had a Castro Convertible sofa bed in the living room that they opened up every night. We lived in that apartment for the first twelve years of my life.

We didn't have a lot of money but we never felt poor. Brooklyn was as vibrant, and as energetic, as any place in the world. Or so it seemed to me. Looking back, I can't imagine having grown up anywhere else. I've lived on the West Coast for the better part of my life, but I still consider myself a New York kid. Brooklyn is my DNA.

My mother, Lila Michaels, was a character. She was Joan Rivers and Phyllis Diller rolled into one. She had a tremendous sense of humor, and was a big prankster. Maybe because she was so young when I was born, she was a lot more lenient than other moms, and a lot more mischievous as well. She might have even been too young to have read Dr. Spock. How many other moms never insisted that their kids eat vegetables? To this day, I've *never* eaten a vegetable.

My dad, Jay, worked for a talent agency in Manhattan called General Artists Corporation. (Many years later, it would be bought out by ICM, International Creative Management.) At that time, my father was still working his way up as an agent, and represented a bunch of fringe entertainers, like a singer few people would remember by the name of Joni James. Eventually, my father moved up and worked with more mainstream acts like Pat Boone, who burst onto the scene in the mid-fifties as a singer notable for wearing white buck shoes. A couple of years later, when we had moved to Long Island, one day Pat Boone came to our house. The neighbors were flabbergasted.

My father was also a huge sports fan. He taught me the rules, the nuances, the history of sports—everything. I was immersed. I couldn't get enough.

At the time, there were sixteen big league baseball teams, with three of them in New York—the Dodgers in Brooklyn, the Giants in Manhattan, and the Yankees in the Bronx. So I was that kid, like so many others, lying in bed, tilting the transistor radio to just the right angle to hear the games. I would get transported to cities across the country. One night I'd be in Chicago, the next night St. Louis, another night Detroit. Listening to a game unfold through the words of the broadcaster. Red Barber. Russ Hodges. Mel Allen. Jack Brickhouse. Curt Gowdy. Every play, every anecdote, every insight.

There was also that magical box that sat in our living room around the time my dad started taking me to Ebbets Field and Madison Square Garden. Even if sports coverage on television back then was normally just a three-or-four-camera, black-and-white presentation, it was the next best thing to being there.

And it wasn't only baseball that absorbed me. I loved hockey and basketball and football, even though the NFL bore no resemblance to what it would become. I was an easy kid to shop for. When I was nine or ten, my grandparents bought me a gold-leafed book about the history of the Olympics. The history at that time included the most recent Olympics, 1952 Helsinki Summer Games. It must have been three hundred pages, but I remember going through every one of them, immersing myself in the stories.

I collected baseball cards, too—didn't just collect them, memorized them. I'd have other kids in the neighborhood quiz me. Batting averages, home runs, earned run averages, fielding averages, players' birthplaces. My father would take my brother and me to Army football games at West Point, and on the way home, I'd go through the plays that had been run in each quarter. My parents would go to the night harness races at Roosevelt Raceway in Westbury, on Long Island. On occasional weekend afternoons, my father would take my brother and me to the track, where we could go to the barn area and meet some of the trainers and drivers. But that was all we could experience, because in those years, even if you were accompanied by an adult, the law didn't allow a minor to go to the actual races. Still, I learned how to read the racing form, and really got into it. I even started my own tout sheet, which I titled *Big Al at Westbury*, and sold it to our neighbors for $1.50. One day I picked a horse named Algerine, who went off at odds of 75–1—and won. The next day, everyone in the neighborhood wanted to buy a copy of that night's *Big Al at Westbury*.

Years later, my brother would call it my "manic intensity." I still prefer to think of it more as passion combined with compulsion. Doing anything halfway, halfheartedly has never appealed to me. Or even three-quarters heartedly. Not getting something right has always been anathema to me.

* * *

I LOVED PLAYING SPORTS. But by the time I was a teenager, even though I had played little league baseball and some organized youth sports, and like any kid in Brooklyn in those years, punch ball, stickball, and a game only known inside the borough as ringolevio—I loved watching sports more. I would rather go to a Dodger game at Ebbets than play in a game in a park down the street. I just loved the big-time feel. It was thrilling.

In fourth, fifth, and sixth grades, our school, P.S. 139, because of overcrowding, was on a half-day schedule, and I was originally placed in the noon-to-four session. But that wasn't going to work, because how could I go to Dodger games if I was going to school in the afternoon? (In those years, most major-league teams played the vast majority of their games in the daytime, including the Dodgers.) So my mother wrote a note to the school principal with some nonsensical, fabricated excuse to get me switched to the eight-to-noon session. It worked. And so when I was twelve, I was at more than 50 of the 77 Dodger home games.

At Ebbets Field, I'd glance occasionally at the broadcast booth. At that time, the Dodger announcers were Red Barber, Connie Desmond, and a very young Vin Scully. All I could think was that had to be the best job in the world. A job where you'd go to the ballpark every day, and get in for free. A job where you'd get to meet the players, travel with the team, and, I assumed, get paid. That's what originally got me thinking about broadcasting. Most kids dream of playing Major League baseball. I dreamed of announcing Major League baseball.

In the summer of 1956, my father got a small raise, and we moved from Brooklyn to a modest tract house in North Bellmore, Long Island. My sister Susan would be born shortly thereafter. We now had a backyard, and I would practice calling games using the garden hose as a microphone. My brother David, then about nine years old, would pretend to be the athlete, and I'd announce whatever he was doing. I remember David picking up a large round rock and pretending he was Parry O'Brien, the Olympic champion and world record holder in the shot put. It was around the time of the 1956 Melbourne Olympic Games. So I called the reenactment in a backyard on Long Island.

We wouldn't live there very much longer. In the summer of 1958, between the eighth and ninth grades, I went to a summer camp in the Poconos. The bus back home dropped us in Manhattan, and my father picked me up. He took me to his office and told me he'd gotten a promotion, and that in a couple of months we would be moving to California.

I was stunned. But this was just a few months after the Dodgers themselves had moved from Brooklyn to Los Angeles. That had broken the hearts of every Dodger fan in greater New York. But now the Michaels family would be following the team, and its stars, out west.

Gil Hodges, Duke Snider, Carl Furillo. The emerging superstars Drysdale and Koufax.

And, of course, Vin Scully.

CHAPTER 2

California Kid

WE MOVED TO CALIFORNIA in October 1958. I was almost fourteen. We were too late for the Dodgers, but a week after we arrived, my dad took me to see the Los Angeles Rams play the Chicago Bears at the Los Angeles Coliseum. "Jaguar" Jon Arnett, who had played college football at the University of Southern California, had a monster performance, running the ball, catching passes coming out of the backfield, and returning kicks. The Rams won, 41–35. The crowd that day? 100,470. So many years later, with the NFL absent from the country's second-largest market, I hear the argument that Los Angeles wouldn't support a team anyway. Well, with the Los Angeles metropolitan area at that time 40 percent of the size it is now, more than 100,000 showed up for a game at the Coliseum. You really think you couldn't fill a 70,000-seat stadium today on a regular basis? Don't be ridiculous.

We lived on the west side of Los Angeles, in Cheviot Hills. I went to Alexander Hamilton High School, and as in Brooklyn, I was going to forty to fifty Dodger games each season. The team played in the

Coliseum until 1962. The tickets ranged from $1.50 for a bleacher seat to $3.50 for the best seat in the house. I was there—along with 93,102 other fans—when Roy Campanella, who'd been the Dodgers' regular catcher in Brooklyn, and had been paralyzed in an automobile accident in January 1958—was honored on May 7, 1959. They wheeled him out as they dimmed the stadium lights, and almost everyone in the stands lit a lighter or a match in tribute. A few months later, I was at the 1959 World Series when the Dodgers beat the Chicago White Sox in six games. Games 3, 4, and 5 were at the Coliseum. The crowds each day were 92,000 and change.

Meanwhile, when I wasn't at a game, Vin Scully was still taking me there on the radio. Scully was just twenty-two years old when he'd joined Red Barber in 1950, and then came with the team to Los Angeles, where he'd quickly become extremely popular in the land of the car—and the car radio. Now that I was a little older, I was paying closer attention to what made Vin different from all other broadcasters. I guess the best way to summarize it would be that at the time, a lot of announcing was black-and-white—here's what happened, and here's what happened next. Vin, though, was full-blown color, breathing life and detail into virtually every moment of every game.

When the Dodgers moved to California, owner Walter O'Malley had feared that putting the games on television—giving them away for free—would hurt them at the gate. Today teams make much more money on television contracts than ticket sales, but in the late 1950s, the thinking—and the economics—were different. In any event, no TV meant that my experience with Scully came almost entirely on the radio. I couldn't see the game, so he'd form the images in my mind.

I loved the Dodgers. I loved the Los Angeles Rams. Eventually, years later, I'd switch my NHL allegiance from the Rangers to the Kings, who started play as an expansion team in 1967. And when my teams weren't involved, I still watched every sports event I could on television—not necessarily to root, but instead to see what stories would emerge. I was fascinated by the competition. I was rooting for drama, a close game—and excitement. I loved the ebb and flow. I wanted extra innings. I wanted overtime. I wanted controversy, strategy, anything you could talk about with your friends for days afterward.

When I was seventeen, ABC launched a new show on Saturdays, *Wide World of Sports*. Years later, I'd become a regular on *Wide World*. There was Jim McKay's famous line, "the thrill of victory and the agony of defeat," as the ski jumper—a Slovenian by the name of Vinko Bogataj—careened down and then fell off the side of the jumping hill. It looked catastrophic. What you didn't see was that thirty seconds later, he walked away with only minor injuries. Still, I always found the next line to be even more poignant. "The human drama of athletic competition." That's what I could never get enough of.

Even now, when I'm in my car in Los Angeles, I'll turn on a Dodger game and still know I'm going to hear Vin Scully, well into his eighties, describe some of that drama. I used to dream about replacing Scully and becoming the voice of the Dodgers at some point in my life. That ship, of course, has sailed. A couple of years ago, I was at an awards luncheon with Vin and said to him, "Let me get this straight. How is it that *I'm* going to retire before *you*?"

We shared a wonderful laugh.

BY THE TIME I reached the end of high school, I may not have been talking into a rubber hose in the backyard anymore, but my dream of becoming a sportscaster had not wavered one iota. So as graduation approached, and I got set to choose a college, I had two criteria above all others: to stay on the West Coast, and to find a school with a radio and television program as well as a campus radio station (and maybe even a TV station) that allowed students to broadcast sports.

My father helped me research it, and we narrowed the choice down to two schools, the University of Southern California and Arizona State. And since another criteria was going away to college, and USC was a fifteen-minute drive from our house, the decision was pretty much made for me.

So, in September 1962, I flew to ASU in Tempe and registered for classes. Standing in a long line, I ended up talking with a kid standing behind me. He was from the Midwest, and he was there on a baseball scholarship. Not long after that, we'd run into each other again—him playing on the freshman team, and me calling games on the campus radio station for the varsity. And ten years after that, we'd find ourselves in the same place again—the visitors' clubhouse the day before Game 1 of the 1972 World Series. The kid's name was Sal Bando. And unbelievably, long before he was a four-time All-Star with the Oakland Athletics, and before anyone knew my name, there we were together, standing in line to register for classes at ASU.

Long before reality exceeded the dream, I discovered that Arizona State was the perfect school for me. The Sun Devils baseball team played about forty home games, and I called the majority of them for the campus radio station. The team was coached by Bobby Winkles, who would later go on to manage the Angels and A's. Our broadcasts were live, and I also recorded some of them on reel-to-reel tape so that at some point I'd have a compilation for future auditions. I called most of the games by myself, but every now and then another kid would show up and work a few innings, but only if he didn't have a class conflicting with the game. For me, though, calling the games was the priority. Even if the campus radio station could only be picked up within a radius of seven blocks, I loved it.

By my junior year, Bando had become a standout third baseman on the varsity, but the biggest star was a sophomore outfielder named Rick Monday. There was also an outfielder on the freshman team. The following September, he was a cornerback on the football team, and then when the baseball season began, he was the starting right fielder. There was nothing to indicate any outsize personality—he was just another one of the guys on the team. His name? Reggie Jackson.

And let me tell you something—had he chosen football, I think Reggie would have been good enough to play in the NFL.

By the time I finished my four years at ASU, I had called at least 150 baseball games. I was the sports editor for the school newspaper and wrote a column called "The Hot Spot." Year-round, I also announced football, basketball, and some track meets as well. I would walk across campus from one class to another and dream of doing the World Series and the Olympics. The dreams were as big as they could be.

Back then, Arizona State was in the Western Athletic Conference, playing the vast majority of its football games at night and in the Mountain Time Zone. The teams were usually very good, but because the games would end past the deadlines of eastern newspapers, not much national attention was paid to the program. My sophomore year, the fall of 1963, the Sun Devils were supposed to play a ten-game schedule. But we ended up playing only nine, because on November 22, President Kennedy was assassinated in Dallas. Our game against Idaho the next night, one in which ASU would have been a huge favorite, was canceled.

As it turned out, Arizona State only lost one game that season: their opener at home against Wichita State. ASU took a 13–0 lead, but then Wichita ran off thirty-three unanswered points and won the game in a stunning upset. One of the Wichita State starters? A linebacker named Bill Parcells.

Sun Devil Stadium had just opened up, and the locker rooms hadn't been completed, so the team dressed at the old venue, Goodwin Stadium, about a half mile away, and then bused up to the new place. Well, after that game, I went back down to Goodwin to interview the players. Except that when I walked inside the locker room, no one was there. Where was everyone? Well, Frank Kush, who would coach the team for twenty-two seasons before a brief run with the Colts in the NFL, was the classic drill sergeant. Most of the players feared him—a few even despised him. Losing a game to Wichita State, to say the least, did not sit well with Kush, so when the team got off the bus at the old stadium, he had the field lights turned on. "Don't even think about changing clothes," he told the players. "You didn't play at Sun Devil Stadium, so you're going to play *now*." And the team stayed in their full uniforms and went through a full-contact scrimmage that didn't end until almost midnight.

Years later, in one of my dozens of meeting with Bill Parcells before a Monday or Sunday night game, I reminded him of that night. Bill has a steel trap for a memory and remembered everything about the game. "Well, here's something you probably don't know," I said. "While your team got dressed and out of there, Frank Kush had the whole ASU team stay out on the practice field in their uniforms for a full-contact scrimmage."

"Don't know it?" Parcells said, laughing. "Listen. We got dressed that night and headed to the airport in a bunch of school buses. We looked out and the lights were on at the stadium. So when we drove by the field, we pushed down those half windows, all screaming at the team we just beat, 'Screw you!'"

Classic Parcells.

CHAPTER 3

The Rascal

WHEN I WAS GROWING up, Vin Scully and my father were my two most important broadcasting mentors. Vin, through all the listening I did on the radio. And my father, through advice, guidance, and encouragement along the way.

By this time, my dad was becoming quite successful in his own work. Not long after we'd moved to Los Angeles, he'd switched to another agency, MCA, and they'd asked him to start a sports division, brokering deals and buying rights to sporting events. My father was instrumental in writing the original American Football League television contract with ABC—parts of which were drafted on my kitchen table in 1959. The league started in 1960, and as a high school kid, I met Lamar Hunt, Ralph Wilson, and Bud Adams, all original owners, as well as Barron Hilton, who was the original owner of the Chargers, when they started in Los Angeles. (Barron was the son of the legendary Conrad Hilton, but is probably best known today as the grandfather of Paris Hilton.)

Around that same time, my father, on behalf of MCA, began to make deals with a Cleveland sports entrepreneur by the name of Mark McCormack. McCormack was representing the then-emerging young golf stars Arnold Palmer, Jack Nicklaus, and Gary Player, and my father was involved in the deals for *Shell's Wonderful World of Golf, Big Three Golf,* and other golf television specials. He and McCormack were in frequent negotiations. By the mid-sixties, as McCormack's management company, International Management Group (IMG), was growing, he asked my father to join with him. McCormack's idea was to take out the middleman and develop and produce his own programming. And that's how the man who represented Joni James, and moved his family to Long Island after a nominal raise, ended up founding and running Trans World International (TWI), the television arm of IMG, which is still around today (it's now called IMG Productions). My dad always recognized the enormous potential of sports on television, and he was very excited that my dream was to get into the business.

My father crossed paths with all kinds of sports figures, and at one point, he met Curt Gowdy, already a broadcasting legend, then the voice of the Boston Red Sox. The Red Sox were in Scottsdale, Arizona, for spring training—about five miles from the ASU campus. My father had mentioned to Gowdy that he had a son at Arizona State who wanted to be a sports broadcaster. Gowdy told my dad to have me give him a call, and that he'd be happy to listen to a tape.

So when I called Curt, he invited me to the ballpark. I brought my tape recorder, and suddenly there I was, nineteen years old, sitting next to Curt Gowdy in some little room adjacent to the Red Sox clubhouse underneath Scottsdale Stadium, as he listened to my tape. Curt gave me some advice and some tips and a good deal of encouragement. Over the years to follow, our paths would cross and crisscross in all sorts of ways. But I'd never forget that first meeting, and that first act of kindness.

At ASU, broadcasting games was at the center of my college experience, but of course there was also time for fun. I had a journalism professor, Gordon Jones, who was a horse racing aficionado—believe it or not, he eventually became the racing writer/handicapper for the *Los*

Angeles Herald Examiner. I'd show up for class ten minutes early, before the other students filed in, and he and I would talk about that day's races, going over potential daily double bets. If there was a combination we liked, Professor Jones wasn't above wrapping up class twenty minutes early so he and I could drive the thirty miles to Turf Paradise in northwest Phoenix in time to get a bet down on the first race.

Gordon Jones—first ballot, unanimous choice for the Professor Hall of Fame.

In another journalism class, on the first day of school in my sophomore year, a few buddies and I were sitting in the back, and, nineteen-year-old boys being nineteen-year-old boys, we ranked the fifteen girls in the class, 1 through 15 in terms of who we wanted to ask out on a date most. This was our own goofball version of the NFL Draft. Well, talk about a jaw-dropping moment: fast-forward to the following September, and get this—our consensus number-four pick in a classroom with fifteen girls at Arizona State University is walking down the ramp wearing a tiara with Bert Parks singing "There she is, Miss America." *What?* Her name was Vonda Kay Van Dyke, and she had blown the judges away in the talent portion because she was a tremendously skilled ventriloquist. Her dummy's name was Kurley-Q.

But talk about dummies. How about my buddies and me drafting her fourth in a class of fifteen? Can you imagine drafting Tom Brady in the sixth round? Oh wait . . .

IN 2001, I WAS in Miami doing a *Monday Night Football* game, Jimmy Johnson was in Key West, and we were doing what's known in the TV business as a two-way—a satellite interview. This was eight seasons after Johnson had led the Dallas Cowboys to back-to-back Super Bowl titles in the nineties, and then abruptly left the team after clashing with the team's owner, Jerry Jones. In the months before our interview, a number of people were speculating that Jerry had had some plastic surgery. Meanwhile, the Cowboys were 4-8 and in last place in their division. And as we discussed his old team's travails, Jimmy couldn't help himself.

"If Michael Jackson—I mean, Jerry Jones—would have kept Troy Aikman, they'd be in first place," he said with an impish gleam.

Then, as soon as we got to the commercial, I could hear the guys in the truck still laughing.

The next day, I called Jimmy to thank him for doing the interview and told him I couldn't believe what he'd said.

"You know what," he said. "You gotta have a little rascal in ya."

Rascal? Absolutely.

When I was a kid, my mom was the first to cultivate my mischievous side. Then came Arizona State. I took my broadcasting training seriously, but I was in college. My inner rascal had to find its way out whenever it could.

I was in the Sigma Nu fraternity, where I met a guy named George Allen (no relation to the NFL coach), who became a good friend. Like me, George was a city kid—he was from New York. Like me, George enjoyed pranks. And together in what in our minds was then a small, Podunk town, we were always on the lookout for a prank.

At the time, Phoenix had no major sports teams, so any pro event felt like a big deal. One night, the just-opened Veterans Memorial Coliseum booked an exhibition minor-league hockey game between Tulsa and Oklahoma City—the first hockey game ever played in the new building. We wanted to go, but of course had to figure out a way to get in for free.

Our solution? A few hours before the game, George and I called the box office and made up a name, pretending to be a Tulsa player with a far-fetched story. "Hey, I missed the original flight to Phoenix and my wife just gave birth and everything got messed up. Can you leave me free tickets for two close relatives." Two hours later, we showed up at the box office just before the game and—what do you know?—two tickets were waiting. Eighth row, center ice.

On another night we were bored and decided to see if we could put one over on the sports desk at the Phoenix newspaper, the *Arizona Republic*. So we created a high school baseball player: Clint Romas from Fredonia, Arizona—and pretended to be the stringer calling in with the line score from this tiny town just north of the Grand Canyon with a population of about a thousand. "Fredonia beats so-and-so, the score was four to nothing, and Clint Romas not only pitched a two-hit shutout—he hit two home runs!"

Well, we picked up the paper the next day and there it was—the line score. We were hysterical—and a few days later, we called back. "Hey, it's the Fredonia stringer again. Remember Clint Romas?"

"Oh, yeah."

"Listen to what this kid did today: he played the outfield—the coach wanted him to rest his arm before his next pitching start—and he hit four home runs!"

Sure enough, the newspaper arrived the next day, and there it was again.

A few more days later, we called in again, upping the ante. "You're not going to believe this, but Romas pitched a perfect game, struck out twenty in a seven-inning game, and hit five home runs!"

The next morning, we couldn't wait for the paper to be tossed into the fraternity house driveway, so we could see if we had pulled it off again. We had. The whole fraternity house exploded in laughter.

Now we had to go for the grand slam. We came up with a new idea that included Danny Murtaugh, who had managed the Pittsburgh Pirates to the World Series title in 1960, and then had left the dugout for health reasons, and had become the Pirates' super-scout.

"Clint Romas pitched *another* perfect game, struck out *every* batter, and hit *six* home runs. And—get this—Danny Murtaugh flew in from Pittsburgh and offered Clint a hundred-thousand-dollar contract right after he stepped off the mound!"

The whole fraternity house couldn't wait for the paper to come the next day. But as we thumbed through the sports section, there was nothing in there about our legend.

The next week, a local columnist, Dave Hicks, wrote about how his paper had been duped, and that there really was no high school baseball star named Clint Romas. But the prank had gotten solid mileage—and we were never fingered as the perpetrators.

In 2002, I got invited back to Arizona State to receive the Cronkite Award from the newly named Walter Cronkite School of Journalism and Mass Communication. Walter Cronkite himself—the most respected figure in the history of television journalism—was there to present the award to me in person, and in my speech, I had to ask him if he was sure he had the right guy.

You know, the guy who spent a month of school calling in stories to the local paper about the great Clint Romas.

ONE OTHER THING ABOUT high school and college. I met Linda Stamaton in the tenth grade when we were in the same large circle of friends at Hamilton High in Los Angeles. We were in these social clubs that interacted a lot—hers was called the Carousels and mine was the Imperials. My house at that time was like a neighborhood clubhouse—my mom loved hosting and entertaining—so Linda was at my house with dozens of other kids all the time. In a school that was probably 90 percent Jewish, she was Greek Orthodox—one of the few shiksas.

She wound up going to what's now California State University, Northridge, then known as San Fernando Valley State University, and we stayed in touch. Occasionally, during the school year, I would fly home for a weekend, and since Linda was going to school in Los Angeles, we would get together. In my junior year I took her to a Los Angeles Blades Western Hockey League game at the Los Angeles Sports Arena. As I took her home that night and went to say goodbye, suddenly it went from two friends who had regularly hugged good night to . . . *whoa*! We started dating and pretty soon, it was clear it was serious.

But there was a problem. Linda's father was a prominent figure in the Greek community of Los Angeles, a good-looking guy, successful in business with a lot of social panache. He fashioned himself a Zorba the Greek type—and he had designs of his daughter marrying a descendant of Socrates. Or Aristotle. Or at least Aristotle Onassis. As we got serious, this became an issue. It wasn't so much that I was Jewish. It was that I wasn't the purebred Greek he wanted.

But in the summer of 1965, before our senior year, Linda and I decided we were going to get married. Of course, we had to tell her parents. Her mother liked me, but the whole key was to find a way to win over her father. Finally, I gathered the courage to approach him and lay out my intentions. My heart was beating like a jackhammer as I—aspiring broadcaster—got right to the point. "Mr. Stamaton, Linda and I are going to get married—with or without your blessing—and we both fervently hope that it's *with*."

He was speechless, and didn't react or respond immediately. If it was a cartoon, and you'd put a caption next to his image, it would have read "Holy $%#." Then finally he said to me—How do you expect to take care of my daughter?

I told him that my goal, and my dream, was to become a sports announcer. Mr. Stamaton knew so little about sports that his perception of a sports announcer was the guy who tells the fans on the way out of the park, "Thank you for coming, and drive carefully on your way home. Good night." But when I explained the difference between a public address announcer and what I wanted to do—broadcast games on radio and television—I think he started to understand. Ultimately, he realized how serious we were, and that this was really going to happen. Within a few weeks he gradually and wholeheartedly embraced me and set his sights on throwing a wedding the Greek community of Los Angeles would always remember. He succeeded.

He became a huge sports fan, and we wound up having a wonderful relationship until his death in 2002.

Linda is still the love of my life. How's that for a way to get there.

CHAPTER 4

Cut by the Lakers

I GRADUATED FROM ARIZONA STATE in 1966 with a degree in radio and television, a minor in journalism, and somewhere in the range of two hundred live baseball, football, and basketball broadcasts on my résumé. I was ready to break into the business. All I needed was a shot. Looking back now, I was naïve, but that was valuable. At that age, naïveté can be a good thing. Everything is still possible.

The fact was, teams weren't exactly eager to hire a twenty-one-year-old kid right out of college. I had written letters to every franchise in Major League Baseball. Every NBA franchise, too. No responses. Teams in those days had flagship radio stations, but there was no real television presence—no cable, certainly no regional networks. Which meant there was usually just only two play-by-play jobs per team. And not a lot of "churn," as we say today. Once you got one of these jobs, you'd normally hang on to it for years. All I could do was go to the mailbox every afternoon and hope that I'd hit the lottery.

Right around graduation, the city of Phoenix was awarded an NBA team that would start play in 1968. The new team had hired a general manager by the name of Jerry Colangelo, a bright young Chicago Bulls executive. *Perfect opportunity,* I thought—I knew the Phoenix market, and maybe I could connect with this GM who wasn't much older than I was. I made an appointment to meet with Colangelo. I drove back to Phoenix from Los Angeles to interview with him at his office, which was actually a trailer outside the Veterans Memorial Coliseum. Jerry couldn't have been nicer, or more encouraging—we still run into each other to this day, and reminisce about that meeting. But in 1968, he didn't have that job for me. The new team needed an established voice, someone known in the area.

Ironically, the announcer Colangelo hired was also an Arizona State–affiliated broadcaster who called ASU games on local radio. He'd often be in an adjacent booth—me broadcasting to a seven-block radius, him to most of the rest of the state of Arizona. His name—Al McCoy. Al turned eighty in the spring of 2013, and as I write this, he's still calling the Suns games on KTAR. Colangelo always had a great eye for talent on and off the court.

Meanwhile, back in Los Angeles, I needed a job. When I was home from college a couple of summers, I'd worked as an office boy for a Hollywood television production company. And before I left to go back for my senior year, I had to train a new office boy. He'd go on to become one of the most successful writer/producers in television history, with shows like *The Rockford Files* and *The A-Team* on his résumé. But back then, I was just teaching him how to answer phones. His name was Stephen Cannell.

Anyway, at that job, working at a game show called *Seven Keys,* I met someone who knew someone who knew somebody who knew Chuck Barris. Chuck had started out in the music side of the TV business, working on *American Bandstand* with Dick Clark. He even wrote a hit song called "Palisades Park." Eventually he'd move into game shows and start his own company to produce them. His first show was a hit—*The Dating Game.* And he offered me a full-time job in the summer of 1966, shortly after my graduation, to help procure potential contestants. The salary: ninety-five dollars a week.

I was getting married to Linda within three months, and in fact, Chuck would wind up hiring Linda shortly thereafter to be an assistant prize coordinator. But there I was in a small room in an office just two blocks south of Sunset on Vine Street in Hollywood, with about five other production assistants, basically cold-calling women—and men—and then interviewing them on the phone, seeing if they wanted to be considered as contestants. I'd also ask if they had friends who might be interested—that's how we got the call lists. And this was in a world of rotary-dial phones and no answering machines. For twelve hours a day, I called strangers and hoped they'd pick up.

If you've seen *Confessions of a Dangerous Mind* or know anything about Chuck, you know he's a character. As a boss, he was also a great motivator. After I was in the office for all of four days, he came in and said with all the enthusiasm on the planet, "You're doing an incredible job! I'm giving you a raise to a hundred bucks!"

A week later, "Al, you're doing a fantastic job! I'm bumping you up to $105 a week." I went back to work feeling like a million bucks.

Then another week went by. "Just fabulous work you're doing. I'm giving you *another* raise to $110."

Within a few months, my starting salary almost doubled, getting up to something like $160. Which was terrific, except for one thing: that's probably what I should have been making from the start. Chuck was a master psychologist.

I started working at *The Dating Game* in late June, and got married on Saturday, August 27, 1966. As I've said, the ceremony was beautiful, and the guests had a great time. Chuck was invited, and in the receiving line he sidled up to me. I figured he was going to congratulate me, or maybe offer another raise. Instead he leaned in and said, "So, when are you coming back from your honeymoon?"

"Thursday, Chuck."

He paused. "Are you back in town Thursday—or back to work Thursday?"

"Yes, Chuck, I'll be in the office Thursday."

BEFORE THE 1966 FOOTBALL season, after years of competition, the NFL and AFL reached an agreement to merge. The complete merger wouldn't take place until 1970, but in the meantime, the champions of each league would meet in a title game at the end of every season. As a big AFL fan, I couldn't wait.

My brother and I had been following the renegade league since its founding in 1960, and were planning to go to the inaugural championship game at the Los Angeles Coliseum in January 1967. My dad wound up with two fifty-yard-line tickets for us. Tremendous.

The tickets read "AFL-NFL World Championship Game"—the term *Super Bowl* had been tossed around by football executives, but not officially coined yet. The Coliseum held nearly 100,000 people—but on that day, there were more than 30,000 empty seats. And with the Green Bay Packers and Kansas City Chiefs matching up in Los Angeles, for the most part the crowd consisted of mainly neutral observers, and was relatively absent of passion. Today at NFL games, you might have catering by Bobby Flay or Wolfgang Puck. But that afternoon, it was just your basic hot dogs and Cokes at the concession stands.

The game was televised on two networks: CBS, which held the NFL rights, and NBC, which had the AFL package. Because a lot of the details of the game hadn't been worked out until late in the season, rather than negotiate the leagues basically said, "Here, you both televise it." CBS had Ray Scott, Jack Whitaker, and Frank Gifford in their booth, while NBC had Curt Gowdy and Paul Christman. The cost of a thirty-second commercial on either network? Forty-two thousand dollars.

Meanwhile, with regard to the competition, a lot of people still considered the AFL a minor league. And the Chiefs certainly weren't intimidating to the Packers, who had Bart Starr at quarterback and Vince Lombardi roaming the sidelines. The first half was competitive, though. The Packers led only 14–10 at halftime, and I remember talking to another Chiefs fan and speculating that Kansas City had a chance to win this thing after all. So much for that. Green Bay outscored KC 21–0 in the second half, and won the game, 35–10.

No one then had any inkling that the Super Bowl would grow to become an unofficial national holiday. That the thirty-second commercial spot that cost $42,000 in 1967 would balloon to $4 million by 2014. More people now watch the game than vote for president. Ironically, for as wildly as the NFL has grown, Los Angeles—with its huge population and good weather and all those ties to the media and entertainment communities—doesn't have an NFL team. The reason in a nutshell: no first-rate football stadium.

There wasn't much traffic as David and I drove out of the stadium that day. And how in the world could I have possibly imagined that forty-eight years later, in February 2015, I'd be getting ready to call my ninth Super Bowl on national television.

WHILE WORKING FOR CHUCK Barris, I continued my search for a sports broadcasting job. I wrote to dozens of team owners, general managers, and individual announcers—some of whom, like Ernie Harwell in Detroit, actually took the time to write me encouraging and gracious letters in response. The advice was generally to just keep knocking on those doors. And a few months later, in the summer of 1967, I thought I'd gotten my big break.

I knew someone who knew someone at California Sports Inc., the company that had purchased the Los Angeles Lakers. The company was building a state-of-the-art arena in suburban Inglewood, which would be called the Forum, and the Lakers would move there from the Los Angeles Sports Arena by the end of 1967. In addition, the National Hockey League was expanding from six teams to twelve, with one of the new franchises awarded to Los Angeles. CSI owned that team as well, and named them the Los Angeles Kings. I interviewed for a job in the public relations department, which would at least give me a small toehold inside the company, and who knows what could happen from there.

Well, I got the job, and let people inside the company know that I was dying to get into broadcasting. The Kings had hired a play-by-play announcer but were still looking for a color man. Back then, a color announcer was a number-two voice doing minimal analysis, bearing very little semblance to the role that today's analysts typically fill. They had hired a young announcer, Ken McDonald, as their number-one announcer—but the president of CSI, one Jack Kent Cooke, who took the term *bombastic megalomaniac* to new levels, decided that Ken McDonald wasn't a distinct enough name. Cooke wanted everyone to have a nickname, and he asked McDonald if he had one. McDonald told his new boss they used to call him Jiggs when he was younger. And that was the start of Jiggs McDonald's forty-year Hall of Fame career calling games for the Kings, Flames, Islanders, Olympics, and more.

In mid-September, with the Kings already in training camp, and no partner for McDonald yet hired, I got a call at home from Cooke on a Saturday morning. He wanted me to meet him at the airport around five that afternoon. He was flying up to San Francisco, where the Lakers were playing a preseason game against the Warriors at the Cow Palace, and wanted me to join him. Hours later, I was on the plane with him and confused about exactly what was happening. The mysteriousness, though, was exciting. We flew back to Los Angeles after the game, and I was still confused. Then, at the end of the following week, my boss in the PR department told me I was going to be the new radio color announcer for the Los Angeles Lakers.

What? A few months earlier, I'd been trying to convince people to try out for *The Dating Game*. Now I was going to be the color man for the Los Angeles Lakers! Jerry West!! Elgin Baylor!! I was twenty-two years old.

Now it was October. The Lakers' preseason schedule was winding down, and Cooke wanted me to join the team immediately. So I flew to Salt Lake City, where the team that night was playing the Baltimore Bullets. It was the first stop of a three-game, three-night trip, and right off the bat, I was going to be on the air alongside Chick Hearn, the team's extremely popular, eventually iconic announcer. This was too good to be true.

And you know what? It was. Chick didn't want to work with *anybody*, least of all a twenty-two-year-old.

So when I arrived in Salt Lake City, I didn't exactly get the warmest greeting from my new partner. Chick put up a virtual wall. And when the radio broadcast started, my role as "color announcer" for the Lakers turned out to be something that was neither color, nor announcing. I was consigned to reading the halftime stats. That's it. And during the actual game, I did nothing but keep statistics for Chick.

So that was my debut. And then we flew to Boise, Idaho, and drove to the small town of Rupert for another game the next night against the Bullets. Then on Sunday, we flew to Seattle for a game with the Warriors that was a part of a doubleheader, with the Sonics, who were in their inaugural season, meeting the St. Louis Hawks in the other game. On each broadcast, all I did was read the halftime stats. No color, no analysis, nothing else.

We flew back to Los Angeles after the Seattle game, and Monday was an off day. Tuesday we flew to Fresno for a game with the San Francisco Warriors. That game was on television as a simulcast—the same broadcasting crew, with one call for both radio and TV. But that night, Chick didn't even mention my name on the air except when he impassively turned it over to me for the halftime numbers—which by the way, didn't include an on-camera appearance. He didn't talk to me much anywhere else, either—before or after the games, on the bus, at the hotel. Instead I wound up becoming a little friendly with some of the players who were closer to my age, and much more welcoming. Mel Counts, the seven-foot center, and I had two or three meals together on those first couple of road trips. I quickly developed a nice vibe with Archie Clark, a second-year guard. West and Baylor were the big stars and I was in awe of them, but they were friendly enough.

The regular season was starting, and I was beginning to get a little nervous. On the one hand, I had this great job title: color announcer for the Los Angeles Lakers. But really, what was I other than a stat reader? Meanwhile, I'd been given another duty that had nothing to do with broadcasting. I was basically a quasi–traveling secretary, which meant getting to the airport early—these were the days when NBA teams flew commercial—and handing out the tickets to the players. Yes, I'd been looking for expanded duties, but on the air, not at the airport.

Now it was on to the regular season, which opened with a road trip. We started in Chicago, and then flew to Philadelphia, where the Spectrum had just opened. Next, St. Louis, then still the home of the Hawks. (The Gateway Arch was being built at the time, a thrilling sight.) From Philly to St. Louis, the flight had stops in Pittsburgh, then Columbus, then Louisville. Three stops to go eight hundred miles. It was the Greyhound bus in the skies. Finally, the trip ended in New York. Overall, five flights with eight total stops, five nights, four games. And my sole on-air function was still to read the halftime statistics. Sure, my friends thought it was cool. But I was now getting very nervous about the immediate future. If Chick didn't want me, what was the endgame?

After four games back in Los Angeles, the fourth of which was against the Knicks on a Wednesday night, another road trip was on the docket. We were leaving the next day for a Friday night game in Boston, and then would go on to Cincinnati for a game against the Royals the next night. I got to the airport, checked in and checked my bag, and then went to the curb to hand out the tickets to the players as they got out of their cars and cabs. I gave Jerry West his, I handed Elgin Baylor his—and then the team's rookie head coach, Butch Van Breda Kolff, pulled in, got out of a cab, and told me to hand him the rest of the tickets. Don't get on the flight, he said. And I should immediately call Alan Rothenberg at the CSI office.

Rothenberg would go on to help launch professional soccer in the United States. But in 1967, he was a young lawyer/hatchet man running Jack Kent Cooke's day-to-day operations. Getting an order to call him under these circumstances couldn't be a good thing. When I reached him from an airport pay phone, he told me to come immediately to the team offices, which were in a wing of the Beverly Hilton Hotel, on Wilshire Boulevard in Beverly Hills.

At that point, even if I wasn't sure what was going on, the embarrassment was beginning to envelop me. But first I had to go to the United Airlines counter and ask if they could get my bag off the plane before it took off. Try doing that at LAX today. After a long, lonely wait at baggage claim, it came down an empty carousel. I then got in a cab to see Rothenberg, a guy I hadn't trusted from the beginning.

Rothenberg was direct. "Look, this isn't really working out. We've hired Hot Rod Hundley to be the new color announcer. And we're letting you go."

And I wasn't even offered a job to stay with the company.

Right then, it became clear. I'd been set up. Hot Rod Hundley had retired from the Lakers four years earlier. But before hiring him, the Lakers had used me as a wedge to get Chick to work with *somebody*. Hearn had always worked alone. Instead of moving Hundley in immediately—which Chick would have resisted—I became the sacrificial lamb. With Hundley, Chick could take solace that at least his new partner had played in the NBA, and wasn't twenty-two years old. I was angry and upset, and most of all, embarrassed. And I had to turn on the television the next night and watch Chick introduce Hot Rod Hundley, standing right next to him on camera at Boston Garden in a way that I never did.

Dejected and upset, but still naïve, I called Cooke's secretary and asked if I could see him. A few days, I'm there. He started in, "Oh, Alan"—that was his "nickname" for me, Alan, my given name, something that no one other than my mother ever called me—"this will be the best thing that ever happened to you. You'll have a good career."

I muttered something to the effect of "No thanks to you." And I walked out.

Hundley, of course, would go on to become a longtime NBA announcer. He also had one of the great sports quotes of all time. "My biggest thrill came the night Elgin Baylor and I combined for seventy-three points at Madison Square Garden. Elgin had seventy-one of them."

Meanwhile, years later, Chick Hearn and I would eventually reconnect in Los Angeles, become friends, and often share laughs about the whole episode. For my money, Chick and Marv Albert are the greatest basketball announcers of all time. And deservedly, there's a statue of Chick outside the Staples Center. When he died in 2002, I was asked to write an appreciation piece for the *Los Angeles Times*, which I was honored to do. Suffice to say, when Jack Kent Cooke died in 1997, I wrote no such column. It would have been a beauty.

CHUCK BARRIS STILL HAD a job for me. In fact, his empire was growing. *The Newlywed Game*, another Barris production, had become a hit. Chuck was now also overseeing a pilot for a series based on variety shows at military installations. I made a trip with the production crew to Eglin Air Force Base, near Pensacola, Florida, and a couple of weeks later we went to Fort Gordon outside Augusta, Georgia.

So here I am in Georgia on that trip, and Linda calls. Two months earlier, I'd gone with her dad on a trip to Hawaii. He had a vending machine business in Honolulu, and had gotten to know an advertising executive named Frank Valenti, who knew a man named Jack Quinn. Quinn ran the local minor-league baseball team. So my

father-in-law asked Valenti to try to set up a meeting for me. I met
with Quinn in February and left a tape with him, though he didn't
have a job opening at that point. But he was friendly, and said that he
would stay in touch if anything opened up. I flew back and went back
to working for Barris.

Now, two months later, Linda was on the phone telling me that
Jack Quinn had called our apartment in Los Angeles asking for me. I
was in Georgia, almost five thousand miles away, and when I reached
him, he asked if I could fly over ASAP and call a few games on the
radio for the Hawaii Islanders.

"A few games?"

"I have some issues," he said. "I'd like you to fill in."

It turned out his "issues" were that the Islanders announcer, Marty
Chase, was in a military reserve unit that had been called to active
duty. It wasn't entirely clear what Chase's commitments would be,
but Quinn was giving me an opportunity to announce some games.

I was so excited I could have flown home without a plane. I immediately called Chuck in the hotel—he had always known what my
dream was, and he was very excited for me. Then I flew home on
the first flight the next morning, Augusta to Atlanta to Los Angeles,
packed my bags, went to sleep, and flew to Hawaii the next day. Linda
would join me a week later. I would never work in an office again.

CHAPTER 5

Aloha

JUST SOUND LIKE VIN SCULLY. That's what I told myself on the flight to Hawaii. I had heard Vin's voice in my ears since I was six. The authority, warmth, knowledge, creativity, and maybe most important of all, the rhythm.

I think it's the same in most artistic fields. When you're young and starting out, there are people you idolize, and you are going to imitate their style until you more clearly develop your own. For me, that model was Vinny. Early on, I sounded like him. Similar cadence, similar delivery.

I was beyond excited for this chance, but there were a few challenges. At the top of the list: In 1968, you couldn't exactly go on the Internet (which didn't exist) and immerse yourself in all things Hawaii Islanders. Who are these guys? What's the manager like? What are the team's strengths and weaknesses? Jack Quinn, the general manager, understood this, and told me to take a couple of days to watch three or four games in the stands and familiarize myself with the team before I made my on-air debut.

And if I needed a reminder that this wasn't quite the big time, all I had to do was look around Honolulu Stadium—which was separated from glamorous Waikiki by the fetid Ala Wai Canal. Termite Palace, as it was called, was a ramshackle stadium that seated about 22,000 and had been jerry-built through the years. They would add 2,500 seats in one section one year, then a thousand more seats down the right field line a few years later. Nothing fit. And it was an all-purpose stadium. Baseball in the summer. University of Hawaii football in the fall. Tons of high school football games, too. Occasional concerts. It was in constant use. There was one deck and the broadcast booth was a wooden cubbyhole up behind home plate.

But the conditions didn't matter to me. It was thrilling—the golden opportunity. I was a lot like many of the players: hoping to get to the majors one day, but for the moment, happy just to be there, getting paid to do something I would have done for free. My Islanders salary was $15,000 a year, but shortly after I started, the Islanders gig led to me getting another job at local television station KHVH (the ABC affiliate), where I made another $15,000–$18,000.

Linda and I started out in a modest apartment. Then, when it became clear that we were going to be there awhile, we got a much nicer apartment at the foot of Diamond Head, owned by an undertaker in Spokane, Washington, who was renting it out for four hundred dollars a month. The undertaker hadn't been there in years, and didn't realize he could have rented it for three times as much. It was tiny, but it was on the eleventh floor and came with a wraparound lanai and a view of the Pacific Ocean and Waikiki. There was a swimming pool downstairs, and just beyond the pool you could climb down a ladder into the ocean. It was heaven. The air smelled like a flower garden. There were these perfect evening breezes. We were barely in our mid-twenties. I suggested to Linda that when we had children, we should give them Hawaiian middle names. We laughed when we thought that even if we would wind up in the majors, it might seem we'd be going downhill. Life was fabulous.

My radio partner was Dick Phillips. He was an infielder who had played parts of four seasons in the majors with the Giants and the Washington Senators. And when he was available, Marty Chase—the announcer who'd been called up to active duty—would join us in the booth as well. Because of the distance to away games—and the expense of airplane tickets—we only worked the Islanders' home games. When the team was on the road, we would do re-creations of the games, beginning the broadcasts roughly ninety minutes after the first pitch and relying on someone, normally a sportswriter, in the visiting press box to give us the rundowns of each at bat. They'd call in with updates every half hour or so, and then we'd go from there—occasionally taking some creative license. Since there was a considerable time delay, if it was 10–1 in the eighth inning, and we got an account of an inning where every batter had taken a full count, sometimes our audience heard a nice, crisp three- or four-pitch inning. A decade earlier, Les Keiter had done almost real-time re-creations of Giants games for a New York audience after the team moved to San Francisco. We didn't use a drumstick against a wooden block to simulate a batter connecting like Les did, but we did have the engineer pipe in crowd noise that was appropriate in the flow of the game. Another connection I had to Keiter: His career started when he was in the service in Hawaii in the 1940s, and in 1970 he would move back to Honolulu to run an advertising agency. But shortly thereafter, he would up becoming the sports director at KHON (the NBC affiliate) and eventually replacing me as the Islanders announcer.

The Islanders were in the Pacific Coast League, with the seven other Triple-A clubs located on the mainland. Visiting teams would come to face the Islanders once or twice a season, and the series usually spanned seven games and would last an entire week. Our big rival was the Los Angeles Dodgers' farm team, the Spokane Indians. In 1970 the Indians came over to Hawaii with a lineup that included Steve Garvey at third base, Bill Buckner at first base, and Bill Russell and Davey Lopes in the outfield. And the team's manager was a rotund, charismatic Italian by the name of Tommy Lasorda. At the time, the Dodgers' general manager was Al Campanis and, after every game, Lasorda would call Campanis in Los Angeles to give him a status report.

Well, six games into that series, Lasorda made his ritual postgame call to Campanis. Garvey had three hits, Buckner had two. Then Tommy added something else: "By the way, the Islanders have this kid who does a great job announcing the games. I know that Scully's the best, but you might want to keep this kid in mind if there's ever an opening. His name is Michaels—Al Michaels."

Then Lasorda went back to his recap. Davey Lopes did this. The pitchers did that. He finished, and just before they hung up, suddenly something occurred to Campanis. "Wait a second, Tommy," he said. "This Michaels guy—the announcer."

"Yeah," said Lasorda. "What about him?"

"How do you know that he's any good?"

"Well, I've been thrown out of the last four games and I've been in the clubhouse listening to him on the radio."

It was only a slight embellishment. Lasorda had been thrown out of one game in around the fifth inning. Then he got thrown out of the next game while presenting the lineup card because he was still so flipped off from the night before. He managed to last the entire next game, but the following night, the Indians were getting blown out early, and Lasorda was so crazed, he got ejected from that game, too.

And in Termite Palace, the visiting team's clubhouse was maybe a hundred feet beyond the center-field fence. So it's not like if you got thrown out, you could walk back from the clubhouse through a tunnel and sneak peeks at the action and relay instructions from just behind the dugout. Here you had to walk across the field to the center-field fence—which was 430 feet from home plate—and then walk another hundred feet, with the crowd serenading you the whole way. It was the reverse of a relief pitcher coming in from the bullpen. Oh, by the way, the umpiring crew that threw Lasorda out all those nights included Bruce Froemming, who would go on to have a thirty-seven-year career in the majors, the longest tenure of any umpire in history.

Spokane's best player in 1970 was not Buckner, Garvey, Lopes, or Russell. It was a young, tremendously gifted shortstop with speed and power and a dash of panache who'd been such a great all-around athlete that he'd been recruited to potentially replace O. J. Simpson as USC's tailback. His name was Bobby Valentine. In 1970, Valentine would be named MVP of the Pacific Coast League. As the season wound down, he was neck-and-neck for the league batting title with Islanders outfielder Winston Llenas (pronounced YAY-nuss).

With the regular season drawing to a close and the team playing well, I went on the road for the first time that year, joining the team in Tucson and Phoenix, where the Islanders—several days before the end of the season—clinched the PCL South Division title. Spokane had clinched the North Division title as well, setting up a matchup in the league championship series. It was Hawaii's first-ever appearance in the PCL playoffs, and because the team was so popular and drawing so well, the league decided to extend what would normally have been a best-of-five-game series to a best-of-seven. But first, as the regular season wound down, there was still the suspense of the batting title.

Coming down to the last day, our guy, Llenas, and their guy, Valentine, were in a virtual tie. I was now back in Honolulu, again re-creating the final regular season games that had no impact on the standings. On the very last day of the season, we had heard from Spokane—and remember, this is through rudimentary communication—that Valentine had gotten two hits with the help of very liberal hometown official scoring. When I heard about this, I made a big deal of it during our re-creation. "Llenas should have won the batting title, but because of some local-yokel scoring decisions, Valentine has won the batting title!" So to everyone listening in Hawaii, I had helped turn Valentine into a major villain.

A couple of days later, in the championship series to decide the Pacific Coast League title, the Islanders opened in Spokane, and we were televising the games back to Hawaii. The production was so cheap that we had only four cameras, and two of them went caput early in the game. Apollo 11 had sent better-looking pictures back from the moon fourteen months earlier. We lost both games, 5–3 and 12–4.

So the Islanders headed back to Hawaii, down two games to none. The fans were already upset and booed Valentine vigorously every time he came up to bat. Spokane won Game 3, 5–0. Now the bloom was almost entirely off the rose and the Islanders, this team that was so good during the regular season, were about to get swept. And who leads off in Game 4? Bobby Valentine. The crowd continued to take all of its frustrations out on him. We had a pitcher, Greg Washburn, who had appeared in a few games for the California Angels the year before. On the first pitch of the game, Washburn threw a fastball and hit Valentine squarely in the face. To this day, I can still hear that sound in my mind's ear—it was just sickening. Valentine was splayed in the batter's box and ended up in a local hospital for several days.

I remember trying to tell myself, *I didn't create this.* But I felt an overwhelming sense of guilt. I had helped make Bobby Valentine this monster. And now he was laid out in the dirt. Fans would always talk about Bobby's star-crossed career, and the injuries that cost him the chance to become the player most people thought he would be. This was the start of that. He was twenty years old at the time. I was twenty-four. It made me think about getting everything I would say on the air *exactly* right. It's so much easier today to collect and validate facts. I had based an assumption on hearsay—there was no video (or other proof) that the official scorer in Spokane had really done anything odious. I had embellished without verifying. It would turn out to be a career lesson for me. Get it right.

* * *

ON THURSDAY, FEBRUARY 12, 1970, I had a very nervous wife. Linda was pregnant and though she was three weeks short of her due date, she felt like she was ready to go into labor. She was also superstitious. She either wanted to give birth right then, or hold off until Saturday. She didn't want to have her baby born on Friday the Thirteenth. But nature ran its course and Steven Scott Michaels—I wanted a Hawaiian middle name, Linda didn't; as any husband knows, you pick your battles—was born on Friday, February 13, 1970, at Kapi'olani Hospital in Honolulu, the same hospital where Barack Obama had been born about a decade earlier. (Whenever the Obama "birther" debate arises, I remind Steven that we *do* have his birth certificate.)

Becoming a father for the first time was incredible. I'd come home and just stare at this infant in the crib. In April, after the baseball season had started, I invited my boss, Jack Quinn, and Chuck Tanner, the Islanders' manager, to the apartment for dinner. I can still see Chuck, who at that time was forty-one years old, had played in the majors for eight years, and would go on to manage the "We Are Family" 1979 world champion Pirates, cuchee-cooing Steven. We took the baby to the ballpark as well. It's ironic to realize how much fatherhood and parental norms have changed. If a ballplayer was on the road in those years, and his wife went into labor, the player almost always stayed on the road. Steven was born at 8:30 A.M. that Friday, and ten hours later, I called a high school basketball game. Thank God I wasn't away. My daughter's birth, however, would turn out to be a different tale—more on that later.

Then, as now, to make it in broadcasting it was important to get "reps"—to get on the air as much as possible. It's like a baseball player getting at bats. Simulated games aren't the same as real games. The more you're out there—under the lights, in real game situations—the more comfortable you get, the more nuances of the trade you learn, the more skilled you get at handling curveballs—literally for a ballplayer, and figuratively for a broadcaster.

In Hawaii, I got plenty of reps on radio and television. The Islanders played seventy-three home games each season. I did five high school and/or University of Hawaii football games a weekend for three months in each of my three years there. That's around 180 games. If you were working for an NFL team, that's a decade's worth of work. And when you factor in high school, University of Hawaii, and Armed Forces League contests, I called roughly seventy-five basketball games a year as well. I often worked by myself, but worked from time to time with a popular figure in Honolulu, Chuck Leahey.

There were times I would call four straight games during the Hawaii state high school basketball tournament. We would stay on the air between games and during halftimes, so when I was on my own, I would yack for ten straight hours. Invariably, Ephraim "Red" Rocha, the University of Hawaii head basketball coach, would be at the games, scouting local prospects. He was a former NBA player whom I remembered watching when he was on the Syracuse Nationals (who in 1963 became the Philadelphia 76ers). He was also a nonstop talker who could give a woodpecker a headache. So when I needed a bathroom break or wanted to get a hot dog, I would grab Red, have him put on a headset, and tell him to keep talking until I came back to the table. Couldn't have done it without him.

One night in 1969, Long Beach State was in town to play the University of Hawaii and they had a young coach on the rise. Before the game, the coach came up to me and introduced himself. "You're doing a great job," he said. I was thrilled, but wondered how he had any idea. How did he know about me? It turned out he had been driving around the island the night before and happened to tune in to a high school game on the car radio. It was a reminder—you *never* know who is listening or watching. The coach's name: Jerry Tarkanian.

I was also working at a local television station, KHVH, the ABC affiliate in Honolulu, delivering the sports report on the six and ten o'clock news every night. I would do the six o'clock show, race to the stadium or arena, depending on the time of year, to do baseball, football, or basketball, and then head back to the studio for the late news.

Hawaii natives have an expression for Californians, "dumb coast haole" (HOW-lee), which basically translates to "outsider." I didn't want that to be me. One thing I did to win favor with the locals: I went to great lengths to pronounce every name correctly. You lose credibility with the audience if you call LeBron James *Lee Bron,* or Robert Griffin III *Robert Griffith III.* But lots of Samoan or Filipino or native Hawaiian names aren't that easy or obvious to pronounce correctly. So I'd often call a parent of a high school player to have them pronounce the name for me. When you're doing a McKinley High School basketball game, with turnovers galore and possessions changing every few seconds, and you can identify five Samoan players running a fast break—and get it right—it's a beautiful melody. What I learned was if you screwed it up, you'd often hear from the family. On the flip side, they would really appreciate that you took the extra effort to get it right.

Looking back on my work schedule in Hawaii, it was crazy, and should have been exhausting. But I loved every minute of it. I got reps. I got experience. I was getting a nice reputation. I got better. And while talent is important, it helps to have good fortune. I thought the job with the Lakers was my Big Break. It turned out to be a mini-disaster. But ultimately, I wound up in the right place at the right time. One call from Hawaii and next thing I knew, I was not only with Islanders and working for a great boss, Jack Quinn, but also announcing dozens of other basketball and football games and appearing on television twice a day. I was getting the equivalent of five years' experience for every one year on the calendar.

Some other opportunities came my way, too. In 1969 the show *Hawaii Five-O* was in its second season and starting to gain widespread popularity. The exteriors were filmed all over Oahu and many of the interior scenes shot at Diamond Head Studios. CBS had to consider the expense of flying cast members back and forth between Hawaii and the mainland. Jack Lord and James MacArthur were in Hawaii the majority of the time. To fill other small roles, though, they would often "borrow" members of the local media.

One day I got a call from someone involved in the production of the show. They were asking if I would be in an upcoming episode, playing the role of a young public defender. A number of my colleagues at KHVH had played bit roles and they had fun. "Sure," I told them.

I got a copy of the script and, being the perfectionist I am, I made sure I had every line right, every nuance down impeccably. I practiced in front of a mirror. I practiced in front of Linda a hundred times. On the day of the shoot, I checked in at Diamond Head Studios. (I thought nothing of it at the time, but another guest star on the episode was a young actor named Christopher Walken.) Jack Lord was going to be in my scene but I didn't see him when I arrived. A production assistant greeted me. They put some makeup on me, and I went onto the set. My scene was going to take place inside a jail cell. As local public defender Dave Bronstein, I was going to visit my client, the inmate, who was charged with murder.

Finally, Lord appeared. He was a big man physically, with a larger-than-life persona. He didn't so much as *acknowledge* me. He said something to the cameraman. He said something to the director. I might as well have been invisible. No "hello," no "aloha," no "welcome," no nothing.

Then it was lights-camera-action, the scene began, and I had the first lines. I said about five words and all of a sudden, Lord looked toward the camera and in this booming voice, he yelled, "Cut!"

I was panicked. I must have screwed up. What did I do? How did I piss Jack Lord off so quickly? I tried to figure out what I had done wrong. Then Lord spoke again. Glaring at a production assistant behind the camera, he barked, "I need more hand makeup!"

What the . . . ? Hand makeup?? How could he even *know* he needed hand makeup?

Lord got his hand makeup in a flash. We then did the scene in about five takes. Then I left, still without a shred of off-the-set interaction with Lord. The episode ran a few months later. (You can check it out on the Internet—the episode is from season two and aired January 14, 1970, titled "Run, Johnny Run.") I got paid scale—in those days, as I recall, around eighty-five dollars. Hooray for Hollywood.

THE HAWAII ISLANDERS WERE located more than twenty-five hundred miles from the closest major-league market. When I arrived in 1968, the team was the Triple-A farm club of the Chicago White Sox. Then, in 1969, Jack Quinn made a deal to become the California Angels' Triple-A affiliate, and also decided to change the business model. There would still be young Angels prospects on the roster, but he was going to surround them with veteran players—former big leaguers at the tail end of their careers. As a fan, and a senior in high school, I saw Bo Belinsky pitch a no-hitter for the Angels on May 5, 1962, against the Orioles at just-opened Dodger Stadium. Bo wound up with the Islanders while I was there, and I called a no-hitter he pitched for Hawaii against Tacoma.

We signed a pitcher who had appeared in three World Series for the Yankees, Jim Coates. We signed Dennis Bennett, who was then in his thirties, and had had some productive years for the Phillies and Red Sox. Bennett would win eighteen games in 1970 for the Islanders. Elroy Face, a pitcher who was approaching his fortieth birthday, but who in 1959 had been an astonishing 18-1 as a reliever for the Pittsburgh Pirates, became a Hawaii Islander. Quinn also bought the contract of former All-Star Juan Pizarro, who went 9-0 in nine starts for Hawaii in 1970 and then was sold to the Cubs.

We had some promising prospects from the Angels organization

as well. Marty Perez was the Islanders' shortstop in 1970, and then
was traded to the Braves in 1971, and spent most of his six seasons in
Atlanta as a starter. We had a young second baseman, Doug Griffin,
who'd wind up winning a Gold Glove in Boston in 1972. Overall,
we had a number of players with some name recognition—but not
as many up-and-coming prospects as the Angels would have liked.
It was more important to the parent team that we developed young
talent. But it was more important to Quinn to draw fans, win games,
and make money.

Despite this push and pull with the parent club, around the baseball industry the Islanders were seen as a model for what a minor-league
team could be. Outstanding attendance (approximately 450,000 fans
in 1970—a huge number in those days), good management, an entertaining product on the field. When that happens, a lot of people in
the organization benefit by association. It happens in all sports, and
is still the case today. If you work for the San Antonio Spurs or the
St. Louis Cardinals, that's a good connection. And in Hawaii, I knew
that my name was getting out there and circulating among major-
league teams—at least in part because I was with the Islanders.

In the late summer of 1970, the Angels' farm director, Roland
Hemond, whom I'd gotten to know well, and who was Jack Quinn's
brother-in-law, was going to be named the Chicago White Sox' new
general manager. And as soon as the PCL playoffs were over, he was
going to hire Chuck Tanner to be the White Sox manager. Roland
told me he wanted to bring me to Chicago to be the number-one announcer for the White Sox, and that he and Chuck would begin to
lobby for me as soon as they got to Chicago. He thought he could
get the deal done, and just needed to convince the White Sox owner,
John Allyn.

I was over the moon. The big leagues were looming. The Islanders'
season ended and I waited about six weeks. "It's coming along, we're
working on it," Hemond kept telling me. The job was open. Then, in
late October, I picked up the phone and I could tell from Roland's

voice it wasn't good news. "Allyn loves your tape and feels you have a great future," he said. "But he just can't bring himself to hire someone in his mid-twenties and bring him into a market as big as Chicago as the number-one announcer."

Too young for a big job *again*?

The White Sox wound up hiring Harry Caray, who'd been a popular figure in St. Louis broadcasting Cardinal games before getting fired, and then had spent a year in Oakland. He'd wind up spending eleven seasons as the White Sox announcer, and then of course move across town in 1982 to finish his iconic career with the Cubs.

ON SEPTEMBER 21, 1970, I had lunch with Don Rockwell, the news director of KHVH. I remember the date because we talked about a show that the ABC network was debuting that night: *Monday Night Football.*

The show was in good measure the brainchild of Roone Arledge, the president of ABC Sports. In the late 1960s, the NFL had played a handful of random games on Monday nights. The ratings were ho-hum. NFL games were as much a part of Sunday as going to church, so pushing the last game of the week to prime time on Monday was a gamble. Pete Rozelle was the commissioner, and had experience with night football games when he was the publicity director of the Los Angeles Rams in the late fifties. The Rams had played some night games when he was there, and he believed that televising a game *every* Monday night could work.

ABC was a distant third behind CBS and NBC in a three-network universe. So ABC had the least to lose by doing this.

Arledge knew that. But Rozelle preferred that the games not necessarily be on the (distant) third-place network in a three-way race. Rozelle asked the others first. NBC passed, fearful of letting football supplant its popular *Movie of the Week* program. CBS passed, too. They weren't going to bump their Monday night hit *Mayberry R.F.D.*

So almost by default, the slate of Monday night football games went to ABC, which replaced two shows—*The Survivors* and *Love, American Style*—to make room in the lineup.

When the rights went to ABC, Arledge felt it was very important to pick his own announcers. This was uncommon. In those days, if a league didn't actually handpick the broadcasters, they had a strong influence on whom the networks could use on the games.

What's more, for the *Monday Night Football* games, Arledge didn't want to utilize just two announcers on the telecast, as was customary. He wanted a three-man booth. And one of the hires he had in mind was a former lawyer turned boxing analyst, an iconoclast who used words like *supercilious* and *bellicosity* on the air. That, of course, was Howard Cosell.

The NFL agreed. The New York Jets played the Cleveland Browns in the first Monday night game in 1970. Keith Jackson was the play-by-play announcer/straight man. And Cosell and Don Meredith, the folksy, recently retired Cowboys quarterback, were the color commentators. Don Rockwell, the news director, who was not a sports fan, said the network was making a disastrous decision and that the ratings would be embarrassing. I, on the other hand, thought it would be a phenomenal success, which was mainly due to my wishful thinking. Network sports in prime time? Yeah!

Meanwhile, in mid-November, while I was still getting over the rejection from the White Sox, came a call from the Cincinnati Reds. They were looking for a new radio play-by-play man. Would I fly to Cincinnati for an interview? Of course.

After another weekend of doing five football games—two Friday night high school games, two Saturday high school games, and a University of Hawaii game—I went to the airport to take a red-eye flight to Cincinnati with a connection in Los Angeles, where my mother met me at the airport to bring me my father's overcoat and scarf so I'd have something to wear in Cincinnati, where I arrived early Sunday evening.

The next morning, I was picked up at the hotel by Gordy Coleman, the former Reds first baseman then working for the team in community affairs. The Reds hadn't even met with me or made an offer, but Coleman was assigned to show me around town and drive me around some neighborhoods where I might want to settle if they offered me the job. Even if nothing was explicitly said, it seemed like a good sign for my prospects. We started in Kentucky directly across the Ohio River from downtown Cincinnati. I couldn't say this to him, but the truth was, I had grown up in Brooklyn and then moved to Los Angeles. Now I am living in Hawaii. How could I possibly tell my family and friends: we've just moved to Kentucky! Our new address is in Kentucky! I couldn't wait to get back on the other side of the river.

At around three thirty that afternoon, I arrived at the Reds' team offices in the Central Trust Tower. (Riverfront Stadium had opened in the middle of the 1970 season, but the team offices were still under construction.) I met with the team's general manager, Bob Howsam; his second-in-command, Dick Wagner; and the team's director of broadcasting. Broadcasters didn't have agents in those days. We talked for about an hour and a half, and they offered me the job. Two weeks earlier, I was told, in essence, that I was a little too young to be the Chicago White Sox' number-one announcer. What a difference a fortnight makes, huh?

It turned out that Dick Wagner had called Chet Simmons, the number-two executive at NBC Sports. My father had known Chet, and Simmons had been to Hawaii on a few occasions for the Hawaiian Open golf tournament, where I'd visited with him. Chet had occasionally seen and heard my work. Simmons told Wagner that yes, he knew me, and I'd be someone they should interview.

The offer from the Reds was a three-year deal: $24,000, $27,000, and $30,000. I was disappointed. It was 162 regular season games, all thirty spring training games, and even some duties in the off-season. It was more money than the Islanders were paying me, but less than I was making in Hawaii all put together. In Cincinnati, I wasn't going to be supplementing my income by working at a local television station. Then again, it was the Cincinnati Reds—the big time. I told them I would give them my decision after speaking with my wife.

A million thoughts were rocketing around in my head. One of them: as far as I could tell, the city of Cincinnati had two dominant colors on that November day, gray and brown. It had been a dank 41-degree day (82 in Honolulu that afternoon), with the streets looking like Warsaw at rush hour. I walked from the meeting back to my hotel, and was waiting for a light to change. I glanced to my right, and in a ground-floor window of the Terrace Hilton Hotel was a travel agency. And as I was standing on the corner, bundled up in my father's scarf and overcoat well before Christmas or even Thanksgiving—what do I see in the window? A huge poster of Diamond Head. Not only that—as I looked a little closer, I could see the apartment building that Linda and I had called home.

Marbles were shooting out of my brain.

In no way could I pass up the Cincinnati Reds, the team that had just won the National League pennant, to go back to the Hawaii Islanders. I called Linda. Then I called my boss in Hawaii, Jack Quinn.

"What do you think," I asked.

"A fabulous opportunity. You have to take it," said Jack.

I had dinner that night with Wagner at the Maisonette—a longtime world-renowned restaurant, may it rest in peace—and told him that I wanted the job, but that the money was an issue. We'd just had a baby. Sooner than later, we would want another. This was less than what I was making in Hawaii. He came up a little. And I accepted. (Of course!) Before we left the table, Wagner made arrangements for a press conference the next morning to announce my hiring. I would fly back to Hawaii in the early afternoon. My partner would be Joe Nuxhall, a former pitcher best known for being the youngest player in major-league history, having debuted for the Reds when he was fifteen years, ten months old in 1944. Nuxie, as everyone called him, a beloved figure in Cincinnati, had already been a part of the broadcast team for four years.

Back at the hotel after dinner that night, I spoke to Linda for almost two hours (a very expensive call in those days—I was already eating well into the $24,000). I tried to sleep but couldn't get a wink. I was up all night rolling around in bed, pacing by the window, thinking about this wonderful existence in Hawaii I would be leaving behind. I couldn't back out of the Reds job. But I was so exhausted that I even had thoughts about going through with the press conference, then flying back to Hawaii and calling Howsam and Wagner in a few days to say I'd had a change of heart. It's not like they would fly five thousand miles to reel me back in.

I went through with the press conference in a sleepless fog. I flew back across the mainland and then half of the Pacific. My brain was still going in a thousand different directions. Could I *really* call back and say I had changed my mind? Or was I just a victim of Polynesian fever? I got off the plane and saw a copy of the *Honolulu Star Bulletin* at the airport newsstand. And there it was—me staring back at me from the front page—the headline, "Voice of Islanders Off to Cincinnati."

When minor league players get called up to the majors, they're ecstatic. No one would agonize whether to stay in Triple-A. This was my call-up to the bigs. But I was all over the map. The Hawaiian Islands were an elixir. Still, in the end, there was *absolutely* no decision.

It was on to Cincinnati, the Big Red Machine, and the big time.

CHAPTER 6

Rose, Bench, Sparky, and the Machine

AT THE END OF January 1971, Linda, Steven, and I moved to Cincinnati and settled into a townhouse (on the Ohio side of the river, of course). On one very cold night a couple of weeks later—only two weeks removed from wearing aloha shirts in Honolulu—it was time for our fireplace to make its debut. Having spent years in Southern California, Arizona, and Hawaii, I had never lit a fire before. No problem. There were some logs already in the fireplace, and I covered them with paper and threw in a match. Five minutes later, the room was filling with smoke. Fortunately, one of our new neighbors smelled smoke, came over, assessed the situation, and said to me, "You *do* know you have to open the flue, right? It lets the smoke out."

I had no idea what a flue was.

Acclimating to other parts of our new life went more smoothly. The Reds had an annual off-season regional tour known as the Reds' Caravan. In mid-February, as the new voice of the Reds, I would join this off-season's edition. Several of the team's players lived in the area full-time, and on the Reds Caravan, which included some of

those players and manager Sparky Anderson, we visited cities like Indianapolis, Lexington, Louisville, Columbus, and Huntington, West
Virginia, among others over a three-day span to meet and greet fans
and talk up the Big Red Machine. On that swing, I got to know the
guys and began to get a sense of the fan base. I'd always loved geography and maps, and this was a brand-new part of the country to
explore. Apart from the November trip when I was hired, I'd never
been to that part of the country.

I had seen Joe Nuxhall pitch when I was a kid. He was also a local
legend, and couldn't have been more gracious, introducing me around
town and making sure people knew I had his stamp of approval. In
Cincinnati, where the Reds are almost like a public trust, his support
made a huge difference.

Each of the three network television affiliates in Cincinnati had
a local daily morning talk show. The ABC show was hosted by Phil
Donahue, but he was based in Dayton. I was a guest a couple of times
on the NBC show, hosted by Bob Braun. But the man who was most
helpful in getting me accepted quickly was the host of the CBS show.
His name was Nick Clooney. He had a young son named George. A
few years ago, I was playing in a charity golf tournament in Las Vegas,
and at the tournament dinner, my wife noticed that George Clooney
was in the room. "You have to go and say hello to him," Linda said
excitedly. Of course *she* wanted to meet him—what else is new? "I
can't do that," I told her. "I don't know him." A couple of minutes
later, Clooney spotted me and came straight over to our table—in
what I thought must be a case of mistaken identity. The first thing he
says is "I've always wanted to ask you. *Why* did you leave Cincinnati?"
George was one of those kids who went to bed with a transistor radio
pressed to his ear, listening to Reds games, much like I had done with
the Brooklyn Dodgers. For the next hour, we reminisced about the
Big Red Machine. He couldn't get enough stories.

In early March 1971, it was on to spring training in Tampa. Ironically, the first game I was to call was our exhibition season opener

against the White Sox in Sarasota—in other words, the team I was with, versus the team I was almost with. We had a pregame show that began a little after 1:00, followed by an opening segment for the game itself at 1:30, then a commercial break, with the game itself scheduled to start at 1:34. Except on this day, the umpires were ready to begin at 1:31. It was my first broadcast and I was nervous enough—now we were going into a commercial break with the first pitch about to be thrown. I'm in a mini-panic. *What am I going to do—make my big-league debut three batters into the game?*

Fortunately, Harry Caray, who had gotten the White Sox job that six months earlier I thought would be mine, was in the adjacent booth and his station's format was the same as ours. Harry had been around for years, and knew the umpires. So he stood up, and in that unmistakable bellowing voice of his, yelled down to the umps, "Hey, you gotta hold it up for us! You gotta hold up the game!" And they did.

Harry had a different broadcasting philosophy than I. My approach was based on Vin Scully and Red Barber's philosophy of neutrality—while Harry was an out-and-out homer. But I always respected him, and viewed him as an announcer who understood and fit in well with his audience, since at that time, sports were more regionalized, and what worked in New York or Los Angeles might not work as well in the Midwest—and vice versa. Harry knew his market, embraced the fans in his own inimitable way, and will always be remembered as one of the most popular announcers ever. Now, there's a fine line between overwhelming the situation with force of personality, or being someone who doesn't take himself too seriously and appeals to the fan base. Harry was on the right side of that line. He got it. And to this day, I think back to that spring training game and thank God Harry made sure I had a clean break out of the starting gate.

SPRING TRAINING IS OVER and we head back to Cincinnati. Opening Day was April 5, 1971, a Monday afternoon. By tradition, because the Reds were the first professional baseball franchise, founded in 1869, they were annually accorded the honor to open the season first. The Reds had won the pennant in 1970, and lost to the Baltimore Orioles in a World Series that will always be remembered for Hall of Famer Brooks Robinson's brilliance. Now a new season was starting against the Atlanta Braves. And who's playing shortstop and batting eighth for the Braves? My man, Marty Perez from the Islanders. I saw him before the game and we both had the same thought. *Holy mackerel*—the last time we saw each other was at Termite Palace in Hawaii. Now we're both in the big leagues.

A lot like a player making his major-league debut, I felt a mix of excitement and nervousness and Oh-My-God-Look-Where-I-Am awe. Riverfront Stadium was packed. Gary Nolan was the Reds' starting pitcher, and the first batter to come to the plate was Sonny Jackson, who had been Joe Morgan's double-play partner with the Astros for a number of years. More on Morgan shortly. Jackson hits the first pitch of the game on the ground well to the right of second baseman Tommy Helms, who makes a backhanded stop and throws Jackson out in a bang-bang play. I say, "One pitch, one great play, one out." The second batter was Ralph Garr, who would win a batting title two years later. And the third batter: Henry Aaron. It was a one-two-three inning. Then the Reds come up, and the leadoff hitter is Pete Rose. So my major-league broadcasting career starts with the longtime home run leader and the to-this-day major-league hit king among the first four batters. And Tony Perez, Johnny Bench, and Orlando Cepeda were in the game as well. And Phil Niekro started for the Braves. Five Hall of Famers—plus Pete Rose.

It was the first full season of the new ballpark in downtown Cincinnati, Riverfront Stadium. Cincinnati was beginning to feel like home. In the birthplace of baseball's first professional team, you could feel the tradition of the sport woven throughout the fabric of the city. The fan base was special. And while I *know* the Internet and ESPN can be valuable, in the days before their existence getting information was a much different exercise. I'd comb over box scores in the newspapers and read everything I could—but mostly, the way to get information was to build relationships with players, managers, coaches, and executives.

It was easy to become close to Sparky Anderson. Each day before every spring training and regular season game, we would tape a ten-minute pregame show called *The Main Spark*. And those ten minutes would often lead to anywhere from another five to thirty minutes where I had a private audience with the man who was such a great manager that he'd be inducted into the Hall of Fame in 2000. I was receiving a Ph.D. in baseball. I was also developing close relationships with the coaches, including Alex Grammas, George Scherger, Larry Shepard, and the hitting coach, Ted Kluszewski. I remembered watching this huge first baseman, Big Klu, playing for the Reds when I was seven or eight. Now I'm with him nearly every day for six months. And you know what he was? A big, giant teddy bear.

I also became good friends with a number of the players. Most of them were around my age. First baseman Lee May was the player who lived nearest to me, and I would often drive with him to the ballpark. Johnny Bench became a good pal. So did Tommy Helms, Bernie Carbo, Gary Nolan, Tony Perez, and a utility infielder by the name of Jimmy Stewart who had been with the Hawaii Islanders in 1968.

And I became fast friends with Pete Rose. When spring training opened in 1971, Pete didn't report on time. Why? He was holding out. The team was offering him $105,000 and he wanted $110,000. They eventually settled on $107,500, which sounds like a joke now. There are players today—a lot of whom couldn't carry Rose's luggage—who make fifty times that.

Pete and I hit it off right away. After he'd reported for camp, the Reds had an off day, but Pete being Pete, he wanted to go out to the facility to take extra batting practice in the morning. Then, Pete Rose being Pete Rose, he had arranged that we would make the thirty-minute drive over to what was then Florida Downs (now called Tampa Bay Downs), near Clearwater, for a day of thoroughbred racing. Bob Hertzel, the Reds beat writer for the *Cincinnati Enquirer*, came with us.

When the races concluded in late afternoon, we got back into the car and drove the twenty-five minutes to Derby Lane in St. Petersburg for a full card of greyhound racing. (The Cardinals and the Mets both trained at the same facility in St. Pete, and the Phillies were up the road in Clearwater, so the place was often filled with major-league ballplayers, coaches, front office people, and broadcasters on any given night.) After the last race, we drove back across the Gandy Bridge to Tampa. At the other end of the bridge was a jai alai fronton. The fronton featured a late daily double. So where do you think we ended up? We were pulling off a pari-mutuel trifecta.

By the way, as a newspaper guy, Hertzel wasn't exactly flush with cash. In fact, he had only $7 in his pocket when we left the greyhound track. At the jai alai fronton, he then had the option of boxing an exacta for $6—giving him three separate combinations—or getting a cocktail for $1.75 and then splitting the box by picking only two combinations. He opted for the cocktail and the split box. And you guessed it—the third combination came in.

Rose had had a big day and night and won around a thousand bucks. Hertzel got dropped off back at the hotel with $1.25.

The Reds lost their first four games in 1971, and never made it above .500 the entire season. It was the one bad year in the Big Red Machine's run. But I was having the time of my life. Driving to work for home games, I'd come around the last bend of Columbia Parkway—an insanely dangerous road, which had been a WPA project, and ran parallel to the Ohio River leading into downtown Cincinnati—and see Riverfront Stadium. It was a beautiful sight—and a daily reminder that I was in the big time. Then the Reds would go on the road, and I'd get to explore all of these great American cities. One night I could be looking out at Lake Michigan in Chicago. The next day, I would be standing next to the Liberty Bell in Philadelphia. A week later, I'd be gazing at the Golden Gate Bridge in San Francisco.

A week and a half into the season, we flew to Montreal for a weekend series against the Expos. I had never been to Canada before. As it turned out, the Boston Bruins were in town to meet the Montreal Canadiens in the first round of the Stanley Cup playoffs. Game 6 was scheduled for that Friday night while the Reds would be playing the Expos at Jarry Park. When I woke up that morning, it was snowing. The Expos called that night's game off by noon, which meant if I could somehow get a ticket, I could go to the hockey game. Pete Rose loves all sports, but had never been to a hockey game. I saw him in the lobby around noon and said, "This is something you *have* to see."

A couple of other players also wanted to go, including Johnny Bench, and somehow, someway—I don't remember how—we wound up getting six or seven single tickets that were scattered around the Forum. Montreal had brought up a goalie at the end of the regular season, a rookie by the name of Ken Dryden. Dryden had gone to Cornell, where he'd led the team to a national championship. Now he'd been called up for the last six regular season games, had won the starting job for the playoffs, and had become an overnight sensation. And there I was, in the balcony at the Montreal Forum behind one of the nets, staring down at this six-foot, four-inch goalie with his chin on the knob of his stick, in the middle of the Stanley Cup playoffs. What could the odds have been that nine years later in Lake Placid, New York, that same Ken Dryden and I would wind up partners on a broadcast that would be the most impactful and exhilarating of my career?

Meanwhile, Pete Rose was sitting by himself in the balcony as well. In the prime of his career, having just played in a World Series, having bowled over Ray Fosse in the All-Star Game the previous season, on his way to eventually breaking Ty Cobb's hit record—there was Pete at his first hockey game. If he was recognized or asked to sign an autograph, who knows? That was Pete. It was also a different time. No Instagram. No paparazzi. No iPhones. Pete was a star, but not a celebrity to the point that he couldn't be comfortable sitting by himself in the upper reaches of the Montreal Forum. Of course, as I'd find out years later from Dryden—leave it to Johnny Bench to get himself into the Canadiens' locker room that night, and get a picture with the goalie himself.

Another Pete story: Two nights earlier, the Reds played in Atlanta. During the broadcast, Joe Nuxhall and I had made a big deal about it being Pete Rose's thirtieth birthday. *Can you imagine Charlie Hustle—thirty years old?* After the game, we were on the bus going back to the Marriott hotel in downtown Atlanta. Pete was sitting across the aisle from me and I said to him, "When we get back to the hotel, let me buy you a drink for your thirtieth birthday."

Rose looked at me and said, "If you wanted to have done that, you would've had to have been here last year."

I looked at him and started to laugh. And he shot back, "And don't you say *anything* about that."

Again, it was a different time. A kid would say he's eighteen, and you'd assume he's eighteen—no one would go digging to confirm. But remember, too, before 1965 there was no draft. When kids were signed out of high school by a scout, it was a fairly common practice for them to say they were a year younger than they really were. At the time, careers typically ended much earlier, and if you were in your early thirties, you were considered washed up. Thinking ahead, in order to buy a possible extra year at the end of their careers, players would commonly lie about their ages. The scout would often be in cahoots with the player, to do whatever was necessary to sign him. So on that night in Atlanta, Pete Rose was actually a year older than everyone thought he was.

It was obvious then, too, how much Pete loved to gamble. Apart from going to the horse races and the dog track and the jai alai fronton, he and I played a lot of gin rummy on team flights. It was just Pete and the all-out way that he approached life. He loved action. He *craved* action. Did I ever see it manifesting itself in the way it did—that he would manage a team and bet on their games and wind up with a lifetime suspension from baseball? No. Never. That was shocking to me, because I figured Pete could always find enough action apart from baseball to satisfy his gambling jones.

I'm often asked by people who know how close we were at that time my feelings about what happened to Pete. The word I always use is *sad*. Not tragic—that's an overwrought description. But sad. To this day, he's the athlete I most loved covering. I watched his every at bat for three years. His work ethic was out of this world. He was a terrific teammate, embraced by almost everyone on the team. When you were around him, you always felt more alive.

I've read and heard it said, "Pete was selfish because he paid so much attention to his own statistics." That's flat-out nonsense. He paid attention to *everybody's* statistics. I loved being around him because I would always learn something new about the game. He would see nuances and subtleties no one else did. I'd sit with him on the bus leaving a stadium and he could recite the box score from his brain. The entire box score. He literally remembered every pitch of a game. *In the third inning, Torre fouled off a fastball, took a called strike on another fastball, and then lined out to shortstop on a slider.* Selfish? Terrible description. Pete was into everything.

And the record he would wind up setting was beyond comprehension. Breaking Ty Cobb's record for career hits? When I was a kid, 4,192 hits was one of those records you assumed could never be broken. Who could possibly have the equivalent of twenty-one seasons of 200 hits? Cal Ripken Jr. breaking Lou Gehrig's "Iron Man" record for consecutive games? I get that. It takes a lot of good fortune because you have to avoid serious injury—remarkable, but in my mind, it still doesn't compare to what Rose did.

A few years ago, Pete and I happened to wind up on the same cross-country red-eye flight from Los Angeles to Tampa. Pete had already been banned from baseball for several years. We switched seats so that we could sit together and we talked for the entire flight, reminiscing and getting caught up. As the flight landed, he didn't directly ask me for advice, but as I reached into the overhead bin for my carry-on luggage, I said, "Pete, you just have to tell the truth." He was either in a state of denial or had reached the point that he couldn't backtrack on what he'd been contending for years. Maybe it had been too hard for him to admit an error. It wasn't that it was never his fault—but I felt that he never wanted to admit a lapse in judgment. In the years since that flight, from time to time, Pete has gradually come closer to admitting culpability.

It shouldn't be like this. Pete Rose was one of the greatest players ever, and it's a shame that this is a major part of his legacy. Again, I go back to the same word. Sad.

THERE WAS A VERY interesting dynamic between Pete Rose and Johnny Bench. Even though he was from rural Binger, Oklahoma, Bench had a cosmopolitan, somewhat sophisticated, and occasionally regal air about him. Johnny was entrepreneurial, and in the year I arrived, 1971, he had signed to do a syndicated television show, which would include interviews with celebrities from all walks of life. It was produced by a man by the name of Doug Schustek, who was based in New York and sold the show to various television stations around the country. In my first season on the job, before spring training had ended, Johnny came to me and offered me a role on the show as his Ed McMahon. So for the next two years, in addition to broadcasting Reds games, I made a few extra bucks as the sidekick on *The Johnny Bench Show*. It aired weekly during the baseball season. We would tape it in a local studio when the Reds were at home. If we were on the road, we'd tape it in that city the morning or early afternoon of a night game. And Johnny was able to get some big-name guests. For example, on one trip to San Francisco, Bob Hope came to the studio.

While Johnny had polish and sophistication, Pete was Charlie Hustle, the hometown, rough-around-the-edges kid who squeezed every ounce out of his talent. By the fifth inning on any given night, his uniform would almost always be dirt-stained or caked in mud. He was also as street smart as they come. Baseball was like a ballet to Johnny—he always made everything look so easy. Pete always looked like he was swimming upstream, churning and chugging. No one worked harder at his craft than Pete. Bench and Rose were never that crazy about each other. But unlike some other examples of two superstars in the same clubhouse or locker room, nothing in their relationship would ever become detrimental to the team. Me? I liked them both very much.

It was a special group. We had Pete Rose and Tony Perez in their primes. Johnny Bench heading into his prime. And that off-season, Joe Morgan would be traded from Houston to the Reds as part of a five-for-three deal that would, in 1972, restore the Big Red Machine to its glory. Sparky Anderson was a terrific manager, and a great guy. It was a remarkable clubhouse—and that included everyone: players, coaches, trainers, equipment men. There was this beautiful, state-of-the-art new ballpark, and a city whose identity was inextricably linked to its baseball team. Linda and I had overcome the culture shock of moving from the tropics to the Midwest, and had made a lot of good friends. We were looking at what could be a very long run.

The Reds also allowed me to take on an outside assignment after the 1971 season. I talked about Chet Simmons, the NBC executive who had recommended that the Reds interview me. In November 1971, I got a call from a producer at NBC Sports who worked with Chet. NBC would be covering the Winter Olympics three months hence in Sapporo, Japan. They wanted to know if I'd be available.

Absolutely! So I flew to New York and they didn't even put me through a formal audition. They simply talked about their plans, and the next thing I knew, I was headed to the 1972 Olympic Winter Games in Japan. Today, of course, NBC has thousands of staffers working on its Olympics telecasts, and more than a hundred on-air personnel. For instance, at the Sochi Games in Russia in February 2014, I was a daytime host (Bob Costas was the prime-time host, a role he's brilliantly filled since 1992), but NBC had seven other hosts and dozens of other commentators spread over its various platforms. In 1972? There were only nine on-air broadcasters. Total. And one of them, Curt Gowdy, my mentor, was the sole host.

I wound up covering some speed skating, biathlon, ski jumping, and an array of other events. That gold-leafed book that my grandparents had given me as a child was sure coming in handy. Then, on the final day of the 1972 Games, the Soviet Union would meet Czechoslovakia for the gold medal in ice hockey. Who gets assigned to it? Me. Why? Because of my extensive experience? Hardly. It was because Curt Gowdy was in the studio and the other two play-by-play announcers in our group, Jim Simpson and Jay Randolph, were assigned to other events.

I had *never* called a hockey game. But having grown up loving hockey, I was minimally fit for duty. So here I am, calling the gold medal game of the 1972 Olympics. Live. On national television. By myself with no analyst. The Soviets won, 5–2. I had a blast, but I figured calling a hockey game would be a one-time deal. A few weeks later, I'd be starting another baseball season with the Reds. Little could I imagine how profoundly my career would be impacted by calling this one game at the 1972 Winter Olympics.

IN MY SECOND SEASON in Cincinnati, the team bounced back from a 79-83 record and a fourth-place finish in their division, and won the National League West. The Big Red Machine was again in full throttle. Bob Howsam had concluded that with more and more artificial turf ballparks coming into baseball, a player like Joe Morgan—who

hit for power, but could also run, too—would be increasingly valuable. Sure enough, Morgan hit sixteen home runs and led the team in
runs scored with 122 and stolen bases with 58.

At that time, NBC had the exclusive rights to broadcast the
World Series—and they had the following setup: Curt Gowdy and
Tony Kubek, who were doing NBC's *Game of the Week,* would handle
the play-by-play and analysis of the World Series. In addition, Curt
and Tony would be joined by the lead announcers for the two teams
that had won the American and National League pennants. Those
announcers would work the games on NBC television in their home
parks, and move over to NBC radio with Jim Simpson for the road
games. So I go into the playoffs that year knowing that if the Reds
win the pennant, *I'm* going to be calling the World Series on NBC.

In the National League Championship Series, the Reds faced the
Pittsburgh Pirates, the reigning World Series champions, in a best-
of-five series. The teams split the first four games. So it came down to
one game for the pennant. And one game to determine if I would be
working the World Series. If the Reds lost, the season would be over
for all of us—see you at spring training. If the Reds won, it would be
on to the World Series—meaning the following Saturday afternoon,
at the age of twenty-seven, I would be calling the action on NBC.

I had always taken my cue from Vin Scully and Red Barber and
shied away from being a "homer." I wanted to be impartial and call
games in a straightforward fashion. If the opponent did something
well, I praised them. If the Reds didn't do something well, I addressed
that. But for this fifth game, I had an undeniable rooting interest—
and I think I might have been more nervous than any of the players.

Going into the bottom of the ninth inning of Game 5 in Cincinnati, the Reds trailed 3–2. Johnny Bench led off and hit a home run
over the right field fence. Bench was a dead pull hitter, so an opposite-
field homer was rare. In my call, I think I reached an octave I'd never
struck before. Now the game is tied. Tony Perez singles, and George
Foster comes in to run for him. Denis Menke singles. The pennant

is at second base with no one out. Cesar Geronimo flies out to deep right field, deep enough to get Foster from second to third, despite one of the most hellacious throws I have ever seen. A laser one hop from the wall to third base. It will be the last play of the right fielder's career. Roberto Clemente would die in a plane crash that New Year's Eve. Darrel Chaney pops out, but then, with pinch hitter Hal McRae at the plate, Bob Moose uncorks a wild pitch, sending Foster home with the winning run. The Reds have won the pennant. The Reds are going to the World Series. And I am going with them. At twenty-seven. In my second year in Major League Baseball.

Driving home from the game with Linda, we were glowing. And giddy. Not that long ago, I was a kid glued to the World Series on television. Now I would be *announcing* the World Series on NBC. I was thinking, *I can now die and go to heaven. Just wait until after the World Series.*

We were still waiting to find out who the opponent would be—the Oakland A's and the Detroit Tigers would be playing their decisive Game 5 to determine the American League championship the next day. In Game 5, Reggie Jackson walked in his first at bat, and wound up scoring the A's first run by stealing home. But in the process, he pulled a hamstring, and though the A's won the game 2–1, Reggie was done for the rest of the postseason. So my fellow Arizona State Sun Devil, whose exploits I had covered just a few years earlier, wouldn't be playing in the World Series.

The A's flew to Cincinnati to work out at Riverfront the day before Game 1. I walked into the Oakland clubhouse and the first player I ran into was Sal Bando, the A's starting third baseman. When we saw each other, we didn't even have to say a word. If our eyes could have spoken, they would have said, "Can you believe *this*?" Ten autumns ago, we were these two freshmen at Arizona State standing in a long line to register for courses. He wanted to be a major-league ballplayer and I wanted to be a major-league broadcaster. Now, it's the fall of 1972, and we are both a part of the World *Freakin'* Series. I *still* get goose pimples when I think about that day. Fantasy had become reality. Delicious.

What followed would become a watershed moment in my career. The country, in effect, was going to be seeing and hearing a lot of me. It was a wonderful opportunity to make an impact. But I was also living in fear of making an egregious mistake. Even in the days before YouTube and viral video clips, if you made a terrible mistake on the air, it could become a scarlet letter that you wore for a long time. You could do irreparable damage to your reputation with one bad performance. On live television, there are no second takes.

Older and more experienced, I'm now to the point where I don't even think about that. What's the worst thing that can happen to me now? I make a terrible mistake, and I say, "Folks, I don't know what to tell you. I had a complete brain cramp." But you don't have that luxury at age twenty-seven, so I felt enormous pressure.

Before Game 1, I was beyond nervous. This was the *World Series*. There was the red, white, and blue bunting. A buzz throughout the city. A television audience of many millions. Fifteen minutes before the game, we rehearsed the open. Now we're on the air live. Gowdy opens up the telecast, sets the scene, and then turns to bring me in. "We now welcome in the young Cincinnati Reds announcer, Al Michaels."

The camera pulls back for a "two-shot," which means we're now both on camera. I had one subconscious thought I couldn't get out of my brain: *Please, God, when I open my mouth, let* air *come out.* That's how exhilarated and nervous I was. I wasn't sure *what* was going to happen when I began to move my lips. But fortunately, words did come out and I think they even made sense.

The Reds lost that Series to the A's in seven games. I didn't make any glaring mistakes. I'm sure I made a couple of minor ones, but making none is like asking a hitter to bat 1.000. Despite the Reds losing, I still had an afterglow when it ended. The national exposure and the entire experience was a dream come to life. At about that same time, I was learning that the San Francisco Giants were interested in signing me, but I was under contract with the Reds through the 1973 season.

After the Series, as he did when I was in college, Curt Gowdy again took me under his wing and said, "Kid, you're gonna have a good career. Just do me a favor. Don't ever get jaded." Which at that time was unthinkable. I was in my twenties and living the life and everything felt fresh and new. But as my career continued on, and even to this day, I can still hear Curt's words in my ears.

THERE ARE BLOOPERS, AND then there are *bloopers.*

In May 1973, Joe Nuxhall and I bused with the Reds to Indianapolis, where we would play an exhibition game that night at the old Bush Stadium against our Triple-A affiliate, the Indianapolis Indians. In that era, in-season exhibition games between parent clubs and their minor-league affiliates were common. Per usual, I taped my pregame show, *The Main Spark,* with Sparky Anderson in his clubhouse office. Our standard procedure was for me to tape the Sparky show with a cassette recorder, and then hand the recorder to Joe, who would tape his pregame show, called *Turfside,* in one of the dugouts with a player. We had a regular engineer who worked every game at Riverfront, and on the road there were regular engineers who worked with different teams, and were experienced in dealing with different formats and workflows.

So, that night, Joe taped his *Turfside* show with one of our minor-league prospects in the Indians dugout. I was out by the batting cage and as he taped his segment maybe ninety minutes before the game, I noticed several of the Reds' players gathered in front of the Indians dugout. There was a little commotion, and a lot of laughter. I thought nothing of it—but as I look back now, I remember one of the players tossing pebbles in Joe's direction to distract him.

I took the tape machine back from Joe, went back upstairs to the broadcast booth about an hour later, and gave it to the engineer, whom we'd never worked with before—he was on loan from a local station in Indianapolis. I told him each of our segments began on tape the same way—with Joe or I saying "Five, four, three, two, one" as a cue to let him know he could then hit playback. Then I went out on a catwalk behind the broadcast booth to get the last rays of the afternoon sun. I had in my hand a transistor radio to listen to the show and make sure everything went smoothly. Indianapolis is barely one hundred miles from Cincinnati and our station, WLW, came in clear as a bell.

I listened to *The Main Spark,* and everything sounded fine. But when Joe's pregame show came on, this is what I heard out of my transistor radio: "Hi everybody, this is Joe Nuxhall. The Reds are in Indianapolis tonight playing their Triple A—get out of here, get out of here—you son of a bitch, you cocksucker . . . Five, four, three, two, one. Hi everybody, this is Joe Nuxhall . . ."

I looked down at my radio as if it were a hand grenade that had been tossed into a crowd.

Joe had forgotten to erase the original recording before starting over. I thought and hoped I was dreaming. Now Joe comes bounding up the stairs to the broadcast booth, and as he sits down, I have to break the news. "Joe, we've got a big problem."

I explained what had happened. Joe turned bedsheet white. Remember, Joe had started his career pitching for the Reds in 1944 when he was fifteen years old. Now he was sure he was going to get fired. On the broadcast that followed that night, he might as well have been catatonic. We bused back to Cincinnati after the game. The players, who'd all heard about it from their wives, were in hysterics—but poor Joe looked as if he was ready for his own memorial service. Back home the next morning, we both got calls from Dick Wagner. The Reds that night would be playing at Riverfront Stadium, and Wagner wanted us both in his office in midafternoon. Nuxie was preparing for the worst.

When we entered Wagner's office together, Dick had a very stern look on his face, but he also had a slightly perverse sense of humor, and I could sense that deep down, he understood the other side of this. But at this juncture, this was not exactly a laughing matter.

"Tonight," he told Nuxhall, "when you go on the air, you're going to apologize."

At this point, it was clear that Joe was *not* going to be fired—and he was relieved beyond comprehension. That morning, a local newspaper columnist had written, "How about that Reds broadcast team? Al Michaels does the play-by-play. Joe Nuxhall handles the off-color." We left Wagner's office and started getting ready for the broadcast. Nuxie went about his regular pregame routine. The players were still ribbing him, but he was in decent spirits—he'd avoided death row. Still to come, though, was the on-air apology that Wagner had demanded. And when Joe got up to the broadcast booth, about twenty-five minutes before the game, I could tell he was extremely nervous—in fact, he was sweating profusely. I looked over at him and asked what was wrong. With the clock ticking down, he explained, "I have to deliver this apology. I don't have any idea what to say."

I tried to get Joe to relax. I wanted to lighten the mood, so I said, "Look, Joe, it's simple. Just say, 'Ladies and gentlemen, I'm very sorry I said 'cocksucker.' And it won't happen again.'"

My attempt at humor was an abject failure. I thought Joe was ready to pop me. But then I was able to get him calmed down, and help him work out what to say. He got through it, and we moved on. And he'd keep his job with the Reds another three decades, until 2004—*sixty* years after his pitching debut.

IN MY THIRD SEASON in Cincinnati, the Reds won 99 games during the regular season and again finished atop the NL West, and faced the Mets, who had won only 82 games, in the National League Championship Series. In Game 1 at Riverfront, Tom Seaver took a

1–0 shutout into the eighth inning, but then Rose homered with one out to tie it, and in the ninth, with Seaver still on the mound, Bench won it with another homer. The Mets came back to even the series the next day on a Jon Matlack two-hit shutout. And then the series went back to New York, and Shea Stadium.

Bud Harrelson, the Mets' light-hitting, five-foot-eleven, 160-pound shortstop, had been quoted as saying that against Matlack, the Reds "all looked like me." Joe Morgan had some sharp words with Harrelson during batting practice before Game 3. Then, in the fifth inning, with New York on its way to a 9–2 win, Rose barreled into second base on a potential double-play grounder the only way he ever did—at full speed. Harrelson was in the bull's-eye and in a flash, punches started flying. Both benches quickly emptied. There were no ejections. But then it got ugly.

When Rose went out to his position in left field, the fans pelted him with beer cans, batteries, and whatever else they had access to. In response, Sparky Anderson pulled his entire team off the field. The National League president, Chub Feeney, along with the umpires, prevailed upon the Mets to send a "peace party" out to left field to get the crowd calmed down. Simultaneously, the public address announcer was warning that the game could be forfeited to the Reds. So manager Yogi Berra, Seaver, Rusty Staub, and a forty-two-year old Willie Mays headed out to left field and were instrumental in restoring order. The game resumed and after the final out had been recorded, the Mets led the series, two games to one, and were one win away from the World Series.

We bused back to the Roosevelt Hotel in Manhattan. Several cops would be brought in to stand guard outside, with extra security in the hallways. Pete Rose was a marked man and the number-one villain in Gotham City. Early that evening, everyone in the traveling party got a note slipped under their doors from the team's traveling secretary instructing us to have our luggage in the lobby in the morning and be ready to leave town after Tuesday's Game 4. The organization was trying to save a night's worth of hotel bills in the event the Reds lost. Not exactly an inspirational message. But a couple of hours later the edict was reversed. Someone had figured out that that would have been a terrible signal to send to the players.

We all boarded the bus to Shea for Game 4 at around eleven o'clock the next morning. The bus ride was by far the quietest I'd witnessed in my three years with the Reds. With so many outsize personalities on the team, someone—even if the team was struggling a bit—was always talking. But on this day—near absolute silence. As we pulled into the Shea Stadium parking lot there were three or four hundred Mets fans at the gate, holding placards, chanting, screaming, cursing at Rose, throwing rocks, eggs, and whatever else they could get their hands on at the bus. Rose, who was sitting near the front, got up, stood in the aisle, looked back at his teammates, and yelled out, "Do or die, boys! Do or [bleeping] die!" He'd have a ton of extra security at the stadium. And later that afternoon, in the twelfth inning of a 1–1 game, he'd homer off Harry Parker to win it for the Reds, and send the series to a decisive fifth game.

I sat across the aisle from him on the bus ride back to the hotel. I said, "Pete, try to put into words exactly what you're thinking when you know the ball is gone." Rose says, "I was rounding first base. And when you round first base at Shea, you can look directly into our bullpen in left. And I was thinking, 'Sparky, better get Tom Hall [a lefthander] up, because the Mets have Staub and [John] Milner [left-handed batters] coming up in the bottom of the twelfth.'" Pete had just hit the home run every kid dreams of—and barely a second later, he was already thinking about the lefty-lefty matchups his team could get in the bottom of the inning. Again, there is no one who's ever been more totally into a baseball game than Pete Rose. For the record, Sparky would go with Pedro Borbon, a right-hander, in the twelfth, and he retired the side in order.

Still, despite all that drama, my shot at doing back-to-back World Series on national television went down the drain the next day in

Game 5 when Seaver and the Mets beat the Reds, 7–2. It was clear, though, this was an extraordinary team—and the question was not whether Big Red Machine would win a World Series, but how many.

Even if I knew that my days in Cincinnati were numbered.

LATE IN THAT 1973 season, the Giants had been expressing interest in me again. Their longtime play-by-play announcer, Lon Simmons, was only fifty years old, but he was retiring because of the death of his wife. (Lon would eventually unretire and we would work together in 1976.) Now the question would become, did I want to go to San Francisco, and work for a station group owned by Gene Autry? My three-year contract in Cincinnati was coming up for renewal and the Giants were offering me the chance to do television as well as radio. They were also offering me more time off so I could accept potential network assignments, like regional NFL games. Oh, and they were going to more than *triple* what the Reds were paying, with a starting salary in six figures.

In August, with a sense that the Giants were going to come after me following the season, and with the Reds leading the National League West, we had a Saturday night game at Riverfront Stadium against the Cardinals. The atmosphere was electric. There were fifty thousand fans in the stadium on a pristine summer night. You had Bench, Rose, Morgan, Perez, and Dave Concepcion in the lineup, and Sparky in the dugout. Earlier that day, the Reds had called up the top prospect from their Triple-A farm club. He was the starting right fielder that night and went 2-for-4. His name? Ken Griffey. Senior. And I'm thinking, *Oh my God—here comes* another *Reds superstar. And I'm also thinking, am I* really *going to leave this behind?*

The season is over and in comes the offer from San Francisco. Linda and I talked about it and tried to figure out what it would take for us to stay in Cincinnati. We had grown very comfortable with the town and had a lot of good friends. We decided that we would probably stay in Cincinnati if the Reds came up to $70,000 or $75,000. It would mean more than doubling my salary. But it would still be considerably below what the Giants were offering. I still didn't have an agent, so I went into a meeting with Howsam and Wagner for the renegotiation. They offered me $40,000, and felt that a 33 percent raise was more than fair. I remember saying to Howsam, "I'm sorry, but we're not really even close. If that's the final offer, I have to go to San Francisco."

There was one slightly messy postscript. Several months later there was a column in the *Sporting News* detailing my departure and questioning the wisdom of the Reds in letting me get away. Dick Wagner took issue with the article and wrote a letter to the editor in which he implied that I'd signed with San Francisco prior to negotiating with the Reds and questioned my "maturity." He also released the salary I was earning with the Giants. I had to respond. I wrote my own letter to the editor that read in part: "I negotiated in good faith with the Reds. I have known Dick Wagner for years now, and have come to the conclusion that his definition of maturity is total subservience." Today, I can look back and laugh. But this was before the days of media agents and the Internet and Twitter battles. These were the days of dueling letters to the editor. And by the way—now you know what I said to George Clooney when he asked me why I had ever left Cincinnati. He understood.

In any case, while the Big Red Machine went on to win the World Series in 1975 and 1976, I would be in San Francisco. It was a very hard decision—I was walking away from what I knew would be one of the great teams in the history of baseball.

But San Francisco had made me the offer I couldn't refuse.

CHAPTER 7

The Giants of Candlestick, and the Wizard of Westwood

BY THE EARLY 1970S, the marriage between sports and television was evolving and strengthening. More and more games were being televised—on the three networks and local TV as well—and the fit was working. Fans could see their favorite teams more often— without fighting traffic, or paying for parking, or waiting in line at a concession stand, or having their view blocked by someone who wouldn't get down in front. Instant replay and other innovations were enhancing the experience. And television sets were improving. The pictures were sharper, and in 1972, for the first time, more Americans bought color TVs than black-and-white sets.

Television networks and local stations were adding more sports programming. And they were paying for it. By the seventies, the broadcast rights fees for leagues, primarily the NFL and Major League Baseball, were steadily increasing. Same for the Olympics. ABC had paid $1.5 million to air the 1964 Summer Games in Tokyo—and then for the Munich Games eight years later, the rights fee multiplied by six to $7.5 million. That was a lot of money then, but also provided a lot of inventory—dozens, sometimes even hundreds of hours of airtime. And sports programming was still generally cheaper than developing original shows that might or might not become hits. Local stations were carving out more and more deals with teams in their markets.

On a personal level, I loved it. There would be more sports programming to watch, more jobs in the industry. But as far as my particular job was concerned, I would be doing play-by-play for the Giants both on radio and television. At that time, television play-by-play wasn't radically different from radio play-by-play. Replays were generally just slowing down the same few seconds of action that we had just seen live. And graphics would be added. In the seventies, there were a number of team broadcasters, for instance Vin Scully with the Dodgers and Chick Hearn with the Lakers, who regularly did TV and radio simulcasts—the same audio was being provided simultaneously by the same announcer for both mediums. (To this day, Vinny still simulcasts a couple of innings for the Dodgers.)

I've always subscribed to the philosophy that on television less is usually more. What I mean by that is that on radio, verbs are very important, because the audience can't see the game. But on television, the viewers are absorbing the action with their own eyes and in effect, the verbs are being played out visually in their brains. If an announcer says, "he swings and *rips* one into right field for a base hit" but at home you see it as more of a soft line drive, it's disconcerting. What I try to do on TV instead is strike the right tone, and match the words to the action without necessarily using a lot of verbs. Often, ellipses or captions can suffice. You don't have to be nearly as descriptively complete as you do on radio.

One distinct difference since the advent of television: You can only appreciate the exploits of athletes from the pre-television age through written accounts and stories that have been passed down. There's little or no archival visual coverage. It's almost impossible to go back and look at more than snippets of what somebody like Jim

Thorpe did. From time to time, you might see a grainy film clip, but that's it. When I'm asked to name the greatest athlete of all time, I've long answered Thorpe. Here was a man with so much talent and skill and durability that he played professional football and baseball, and won Olympic medals. How differently would we think about Jim Thorpe today if his whole career had been played out on television?

WE MOVED FROM CINCINNATI to the Bay Area in late November 1973, and before I had even announced one game for the Giants, an additional opportunity came along. Dick Enberg had been the play-by-play man for UCLA basketball on KTLA, a local station in Los Angeles (the same station where I'd worked during a couple of summers in college). Under John Wooden, the Bruins had become the greatest dynasty in the history of college basketball. Enberg was being hired to work for NBC full-time and would no longer be able to do UCLA games on local Los Angeles television. KTLA was owned by Golden West Broadcasting, the Gene Autry enterprise that also owned KSFO—the station in San Francisco for which I'd be announcing the Giants games in the spring. With Dick leaving, suddenly the UCLA job was open. A Golden West executive called me and asked if I'd be interested in that job. UCLA basketball? John Wooden? A team that would enter the season with already the longest win streak ever? I said, I'd love it.

For me, it worked very well logistically. Because of the team's popularity, UCLA played the majority—and nearly all of its non-conference games—at home, primarily on back-to-back Friday and Saturday nights. With that schedule, I could fly down from the Bay Area on Fridays around noon, work the game, stay overnight (my folks were living in Los Angeles, so I could see them as well), work the Saturday night game, and then take a midnight flight back home. I could do two games with only one night away from the family. And the travel to road games typically kept me on the West Coast and

included a weekend when the Bruins would visit Stanford and Cal—
games I could drive to from home.

Sports television was growing, but there was still concern in some
quarters that if games were televised live, the gate would suffer. So
even though Pauley Pavilion, UCLA's home gym, was packed for
every game, the home games were televised on tape delay. I would do
the games live to tape, but the broadcast wouldn't start until 11 P.M.
Still, even at that hour, the ratings were spectacular. We once saw research that UCLA Friday night home games were outdrawing Johnny
Carson and *The Tonight Show* by something like five-to-one. On the
road, the games would air live.

But before I could officially inherit the job, I had to get the bless-
ings of UCLA athletic director J. D. Morgan and Coach Wooden
himself. A month before the season would begin, I flew to Los Angeles to go to a practice and meet Morgan and Wooden. I met Morgan
in his office, and then he walked me over to Pauley Pavilion, where
the Bruins would be practicing. We sat down in the second row of the
bleachers. The team had just come onto the court to limber up, and
drills would begin in a few minutes. At that point, Coach Wooden
came over and sat down next to me. We hit it off right away. Wooden
was a huge baseball fan and knew my background. And as a southern
Indiana native, he knew all about the Cincinnati Reds. So, while his
players continued to loosen up, we sat there talking not about basketball, but mostly about Pete Rose, Johnny Bench, Sparky Anderson,
and the Big Red Machine. I got the job.

UCLA came into the 1973–74 season with a 75-game winning
streak. The team's roster included Keith (later to change his name to
Jamaal) Wilkes, Dave Meyers, the freshman Marques Johnson, and a
very free-spirited center—Bill Walton. You can't overstate the great-
ness of that group. And it all began with the man who, for my money,
was the greatest coach in the history of sports, John Robert Wooden.

In early January 1974, UCLA made its annual trip to the state of
Washington. The Bruins beat the University of Washington Huskies

on a Saturday night in Seattle, and the next day we took a commercial flight across the state to Spokane, which was followed up by a ninety-minute bus ride to Pullman, the home of Washington State University. The following night, the Bruins would play the Cougars. When the bus rolled into Pullman but before we would check into the hotel, Coach Wooden had the driver head straight to the Cougars' arena. He wanted the players to stretch their legs and go through a light practice. After about twenty-five minutes on the court, the players went back to the locker room to shower and change back to their street clothes. The weather that early evening was miserable—rain was turning to sleet. I was leaning against the wall in a corner of the locker room when Coach Wooden gathered the team, laid out what the following day's schedule would be, and said, "Boys, now it's very cold and damp outside. I want you to make sure you dry your hair very thoroughly. I don't want anyone to get sick."

I laughed to myself. Coach Wooden was clearly a father figure to so many of the players in that room. But at that moment, he wasn't just their father. He was also their mother.

The Bruins beat Washington State, but that night Bill Walton injured his back. Walton has said that game, and that injury, was the start of a lifetime of back issues. UCLA won the game and would go on to defeat California, Stanford, and Iowa to run their record that season to 13-0, and their overall winning streak to 88 games. The Bruins had not lost in nearly three years, with that last defeat coming at the hands of the Notre Dame Fighting Irish.

The next stop, ironically, would be South Bend on Saturday, January 19, 1974. Though Walton played with a back brace, UCLA led by 11 points with less than four minutes to play. Then Notre Dame reeled off 12 straight points and won, 71–70. The longest winning streak in college basketball history was over. It was a nationally televised game on NBC, which meant I didn't call it. Behind the mic, in one of his first NBC assignments, was Dick Enberg.

In an odd schedule twist, the Bruins would play Notre Dame

again the following Saturday night at Pauley Pavilion. The Irish were coached by Digger Phelps. I broadcast that game not only locally in Los Angeles, but on the TVS Network, run by Eddie Einhorn. Eddie ran what turned out to be a very successful operation, later became an executive at CBS Sports, and then along with Jerry Reinsdorf, bought the Chicago White Sox in 1981. So the Bruins were attempting to start a new winning streak, and did, rolling to a 94–75 victory. My broadcast partner on that game, by the way, was one Tommy Hawkins, who'd been with the Los Angeles Lakers during my ill-fated twenty-minute adventure as Chick Hearn's sidekick. Meanwhile, Einhorn was a real character. He reminded me a lot of Chuck Barris. In fact, on that night, with a huge national television audience tuned in, Eddie decided that I would interview *him* at halftime. Why? He wanted to announce the recent birth of his daughter. When you own the store, you can do whatever you wish.

I had also done some TVS games for Einhorn in a couple of the off-seasons when I was with the Reds. In fact, on two games, both in Olean, New York, on back-to-back weekends at St. Bonaventure University, my partner was Butch Van Breda Kolff, the Lakers coach who, a few years earlier, had been the man assigned to tell me at Los Angeles International Airport that I was not to board that flight to Boston. Bill was dabbling in broadcasting in between coaching jobs with the Phoenix Suns, in the NBA, and Memphis Tams, in the American Basketball Association. One unforgettable memory I have about working with Van Breda Kolff was the fact that on both weekends the temperature hovered around zero. We went out to dinner, and Butch had no parka, no overcoat, no scarf, and no hat—just a sweater. I'm shivering to death, and looked at him and said, "Are you kidding?" And he said, "Why travel around with a coat? You can go right from the car to the arena or the restaurant to the hotel. You're outside for fifteen seconds." You never know where your life lessons will come from.

In March 1973, I went to South Bend to broadcast a Notre Dame–

South Carolina game for TVS. One of the stars for the Gamecocks was Mike Dunleavy, who'd go on to coach four NBA teams. Forty years later, he'd be a frequent golf partner of mine in Los Angeles. And who did Einhorn pair me with for *that* game? None other than Hot Rod Hundley, the man who had succeeded me as Chick Hearn's partner with the Lakers. People in my career (and life, too) keep coming and going and coming and going. And then reappearing. I love it.

I worked two years of UCLA basketball for KTLA, and the 1974–75 season turned out to be John Wooden's last. The coach had not shown his hand all season in regard to possible retirement, and in fact said nothing until after the Bruins had won another national championship, Wooden's tenth, defeating Kentucky, 92–85, in the NCAA Tournament Championship Game. John Wooden was one of the most remarkable people I've had the great pleasure to know. He was honest, moral, encouraging, and inspiring. When he died in 2010 at the age of ninety-nine, he had left an indelible mark. I can't tell you how many people I've run into through the years—and not just his players—who have talked about the everlasting impact he had on their lives. In 2003, when UCLA named the court at Pauley Pavilion in John and his late wife Nell's honor, the Nell and John Wooden Court, I was asked to emcee the luncheon that preceded the dedication. Coach had insisted that Nell's name precede his. Of course. He was the quintessential gentleman. Always, "Ladies first." I said to the gathering, "For my money, he's the greatest coach in any sport, *ever*—but don't just take my word for it. The *Sporting News* named him the greatest coach of all time as well." I looked at John, and he had his head bowed. For a man of such singular accomplishment, he was always genuinely modest. He was remarkably humble and rarely comfortable with praise, which came often. Looking down at his table that day, I continued. "Coach," I said, "it's *your* own fault. You didn't have to go out and win those ten national championships."

* * *

NOW IT'S MARCH 1974. The San Francisco Giants are about to go to spring training, and I'm going back to baseball. Linda, Steven, and I had moved into a home we loved in Menlo Park, not far from the Stanford campus in Palo Alto. Linda was pregnant with our baby due in July. We were living in the middle of Silicon Valley during its nascent days.

The Giants were a mediocre team playing in one of the worst stadiums ever constructed, Candlestick Park. And it seemed to me early on that there was a malaise that was affecting the whole franchise. The owner was Horace Stoneham. He'd moved the team west from the Polo Grounds in New York sixteen years earlier, and now it was pretty clear he was beginning to run out of money. The team was so-so, attendance was terrible, and it affected almost everyone in the entire organization. I would spend too many nights in the broadcast booth at Candlestick, freezing my butt off, announcing a game with a crowd that would often number less than five thousand. Meanwhile, the Reds were in contention, playing to packed houses, and on their way to consecutive World Series titles in 1975 and '76, while Marty Brennaman had succeeded me in Cincinnati. In a way, how could I not think about what I had left behind? By the way, Howsam and Wagner wound up hitting the jackpot. Marty Brennaman is in the Baseball Hall of Fame, and has now been the voice of the Reds for more than forty seasons.

The Giants had some good players. The outfield consisted of Gary Matthews, Garry Maddox, and Bobby Bonds. Solid. Also, the team had been experimenting for a couple of seasons with Dave Kingman at third base. Kingman would go on to hit 442 home runs over the course of his career with several teams, though never quite living up to the incredibly high expectations that accompanied his perceived potential.

Anyway, by the middle of that April, the Giants were compelled to make a change at third—because it was becoming too dangerous for fans to sit behind first base. Night after night, Kingman would field a ground ball and wind up uncorking a throw into the fifth row behind first. He would be moved back to more comfortable roles at first base and the outfield by the end of April.

Very quickly, I could sense the difference between the Reds and the Giants in terms of chemistry and energy. The contrast was stark. Before the season was a week old, the Reds came to Candlestick Park—my old team against my new team. Before the game, when I walked into the Reds clubhouse, the players treated me like a long-lost brother, which felt great. In the second game of that series, Tony Perez came to the plate. Having watched his every at bat for three years, I obviously knew his strengths and weaknesses. The Giants didn't. Scouting wasn't what it is today. Cronyism prevailed. Some teams, like the Giants, would have a scout behind the plate with a notebook in one hand and a beer in the other.

So Perez comes up. In left field, Gary Matthews is playing him toward the line. In center, Garry Maddox is playing in the left center field gap. And Bobby Bonds is shading Perez toward the right field line. There was this enormous gap in right center. On the air, I said, "Well, the Giants are playing Perez exactly the opposite of the way they should. Perez's primary power is to right center field." As if on cue, he hits a home run over the right center-field fence.

Two months later, with the Giants at around .500, we ended a road trip in Philadelphia. The Giants led 3–0 going into the bottom of the eighth inning, when the Phillies scored four runs and won the game, 4–3. You can't lose in much more dispiriting fashion.

When the Reds would suffer a loss like that (which was not often), the bus ride out of the stadium would be a quiet one. Winning was too important to the Reds. Now, following *this* game, I witnessed how much the approach to and importance of winning could vary. The Reds' bus would have had a collective mute button on, but on this day, when the Giants filed onto the bus, an outsider would have had no idea whether they had won or lost. The guys just wanted to get out of Dodge and fly back to San Francisco. I was still upset about the way the game had unfolded. And I then came to the realization that I cared more about whether the team had won or lost than most of the players did.

I had received my baseball master's and Ph.D. degrees at the knees of Chuck Tanner in Hawaii and Sparky Anderson in Cincinnati. I remember telling a friend it was like having Socrates and Aristotle tutoring you in philosophy. Now I'm in San Francisco, and the manager is Charlie Fox.

In mid-June, we started a road trip with a weekend series in Pittsburgh, and in the Friday night opener, Fox wanted to make a pitching change with one out and a Pirates runner on second in the bottom of the sixth. He also wanted to bring in a new left fielder who could bat third in the top of the Giants' seventh since the 7-8-9 hitters would be due up and he could insert the new reliever in the six spot. In other words, your basic "double switch." He signaled to the bullpen to bring in the new pitcher, Elias Sosa. I immediately sensed a problem. We went to commercial during the pitching change, and I then watched as Fox proceeded to get into an argument with the plate umpire, Nick Colosi. I knew exactly what was going on. Thank you, Chuck Tanner and Sparky. Charlie had forgotten to tell Colosi that he was inserting two players simultaneously—the double switch. When he had signaled for Sosa alone, Sosa was immediately placed in the nine slot. He had forgotten to tell Colosi he was also making the change in left. Moments later, when he went back to the umpire to tell him what he had meant to do, the ship had left the harbor. He'd blown the double switch. The argument that followed was pure histrionics. Back from commercial, I'm all over it. "Here's what Charlie meant to do. Here's what happened. Here are the rules." I remember thinking I'd been spoiled. I'd been with Tanner and Sparky and now I'm with . . . ? Okay. Whatever.

I was off in the seventh inning and went over to the writers' area in the press box to check in with our beat reporters. "Can you guys believe how he messed that up?" I said.

"Messed up what?" came the response. "What happened?"

"Charlie blew the double switch. He lost track of the rule."

They were still clueless. Our three reporters had been their beats for a long, long time and riveting their attention on any game's nuances was not necessarily a priority. Sometimes an in-game nap would be in order.

After the game, on my way to the bus I stopped by the press box again and saw one of the writers. "Did you ask him about it? What did he say?"

"He said that he really didn't want to make the double switch," the writer responded.

Charlie probably figured the writers really didn't know what was going on, and that answer could help him avoid being pressed any further. Of course, I knew it was total bull. Then I got on the bus. Fox was already in the front seat where the manager typically sits. I said to him, "What happened in the sixth inning?"

I had felt that Charlie was always a little uncomfortable with me, knowing that I had spent three years with Sparky Anderson, and that I understood a lot of things that might otherwise have gone unnoticed. That night, though, Charlie acknowledged to me that he had blown it. At least he owned up to his mistake.

Still, the team was slogging along and he'd be fired about two weeks later.

FOX'S SUCCESSOR, WES WESTRUM, was another player I watched as a kid in Brooklyn—he played for the New York Giants. In fact, he was on the cover of the inaugural issue of *Sports Illustrated* in 1954, crouched behind the plate with Eddie Matthews batting in Milwaukee. Now in 1974, he had reappeared, another baseball card from my childhood come to life. He was an okay manager and a very decent man with some idiosyncrasies. Then again, who doesn't have some? Years before kids would text "OMG" to each other on iPhones, he always used the phrase "Omigod." Omigod, we have to go the bull-pen early. Omigod, I hope he gets out of his slump. It was his favorite expression, so much so that among several of the players, it became his nickname.

Westrum also had to deal with Dave Kingman. That was not necessarily easy. Kingman could be very off-putting, even with team-mates and the coaches, and almost always with the media. But for whatever reason, he liked me and we got along very well.

By August, the seeds had been sown—the Giants were destined to finish well down in the National League West standings. In the mid-dle of a twelve-game road trip, we flew from Philadelphia to St. Louis on an off day. A three-game series with the Cardinals would start the next night. It was one of those stretches of oppressive summer days in the Midwest—a thousand degrees by noon with 99 percent humid-ity. In those years, I was playing a lot of tennis. On the bus from the airport to the hotel, I casually mentioned to no one in particular that I was looking for a tennis game. As it turned out, Kingman would always bring a tennis racket on the road. Dave overhears me and says, let's go. I'll meet you on the court at one thirty. We were staying at Stouffer's Hotel downtown, next to the Mississippi River, with an outdoor court on the property.

Playing in intense heat had never bothered me. We played three sets. The next day, I run into Kingman at breakfast, and he says, you want to play again this afternoon? I say sure. We meet at the court at one. Our game with the Cardinals that night would start at around seven thirty. Westrum had recently chosen to platoon Kingman with the left-hand-hitting first baseman Ed Goodson. For several days, Kingman had been limited to a couple of pinch-hitting appearances, and knew he wouldn't be in the lineup that night against Bob Gibson.

So, on that sweltering afternoon before the game, we played for two hours, and at about three o'clock, we stood in the hotel lobby waiting for an elevator, holding our drenched shirts and our rackets and looking as if we'd just escaped a car wash. And when the elevator door opened, who would come out along with a couple of his coaches? You got it—Wes Westrum. Busch Stadium was a couple of blocks away, and they were walking over to the ballpark. Westrum looked at Kingman and—seeing his now part-time first baseman covered in sweat, without a shirt, holding a racket—did a double take. Eyes wide open, he exclaimed, "*Omigod. Playing tennis?*"

As Westrum was getting off the elevator, Kingman and I were getting in. Dave waited a beat and responded with perfect timing as the elevator doors were closing in front of him.

Looking straight at Westrum, he said, "Hey, got to get my exercise somehow."

I WAS NEVER SHY about criticizing the Giants on the air when I thought it was deserved. One night, after *another* dispiriting loss, I actually said, "Folks, you should come on out to Candlestick to see for yourselves how badly the Giants are playing. It's just too hard for me to describe."

From time to time, my broadcast partner Art Eckman and I had to have some fun. One night late in the season, with the Giants well out of contention, and with again tens of thousands of empty seats at Candlestick Park, I was handed an attendance figure that once more was embarrassingly low. The number was around three thousand. And then I thought—*why not?* So I said something to the effect of "Tonight's attendance—well, why don't I just tell you *who's* here: Jim McAlpine has driven in from Atherton. Steven and Sue Waxman and their three kids have come up from San Jose. Harvey Faloukian and his cousin have driven down from Mill Valley. . . ."

The Rascal was back.

Joey Amalfitano—the Giants' third base coach at the time, and a very funny guy—had my favorite line about the team's dismal attendance. In early 1974, Patty Hearst had been kidnapped—as, it later was discovered, by the Symbionese Liberation Army. For a number of months, no one had any idea where she was or if she was dead or alive. It was front-page news every day. So, one night in early July, I'm standing by the cage during batting practice, and Amalfitano looks toward the upper deck and says, "You know, I wonder if anyone's checked there for Patty Hearst. Nobody's been up there for at least five years."

Obviously, I wanted the Giants to do well and I wanted the team to sell tickets. But an announcer who's too much of a homer and overlooks obvious mistakes can lose credibility. The hitch is that, even today, some owners and team executives see negativity as an act of disloyalty and are reluctant to give their broadcasters much latitude. In Cincinnati, I understood how far I could and couldn't go, but the team was generally so good that the positives vastly outweighed the negatives. The Giants and KSFO, to their credit, rarely interfered or tried to censor me. I was fortunate in that regard because across San Francisco Bay were the Oakland Athletics, owned at that time by one Charles O. Finley. He had a different philosophy. He would have cut the microphone cord as I was talking.

One everlasting memory from that season: Linda was pregnant and due to deliver our second child in late July. Four years prior, our son Steven had been born about three weeks early, so I felt comfortable about being home from July 11 through July 24, when the Giants had a long home stand leading into the All-Star break. But July 24 comes along, and the baby still hasn't been born, and now my dilemma was that the Giants were going on an eight-game, seven-day road trip. Linda still didn't appear ready to go into labor, and I figured if I was on the road, and she sensed that she would be ready to go to the hospital, I could get back quickly enough.

So we get to our first stop—Cincinnati—and I'm on the phone with her every couple of hours, glad to keep hearing that everything is copacetic. I figure if we can get through the weekend series in Houston, I can miss the following two games in Atlanta and make sure I'll be home by Monday night the twenty-ninth. Everything was good through the twenty-seventh, and I was counting down the forty-eight hours until I was scheduled to fly home.

But sure enough, as I get into bed after that Saturday night game in Houston, the phone rings at about 2 A.M. Linda is already at Stanford Hospital with her sister Diana, and delivery is imminent. Our daughter, Jennifer Elaine Michaels, arrived in the wee hours of Sunday morning, July 28. And there I was—for crying out loud—at a Marriott hotel about a mile from the Astrodome.

Today, the vast majority of professional athletes wouldn't think twice about missing a game to be present for the birth of a child. At that time, though, expectations were different. Most professional athletes who would have been in my circumstance would still have been on the road—in uniform—playing the game as scheduled.

Forty years later, it's so different. Conventional thinking has changed. Either way, I'll never stop wishing I could have that one day back for a do-over.

THE GIANTS FINISHED 72-90 in 1974. It was time for a shakeup. So, shortly after the season ended, the Giants and Yankees effected a blockbuster trade. Bobby Bonds would be shipped to New York, and Bobby Murcer—who had become a regular in 1969 and was heralded to become the next Mickey Mantle—would come to San Francisco. The Giants didn't get much better, but the trade brought me a great buddy.

I used to call Bobby Murcer "the Pig Farmer." Bobby knew how to play the cornpone role, but he was smart as a whip. He was not unlike Don Meredith in that regard. Candlestick was a terrible place to play. Where else could you have a number of frigid nights in *July*? So Murcer would often try to keep his bat warm by placing it in the sauna in the Giants' clubhouse. Then just before he'd come out to the on-deck circle, Murcer would send the batboy back to fetch it. Though he later became an anti-tobacco activist, Bobby always had a chaw of tobacco in his cheek. Bobby and Kay Murcer and their kids came over to our house in Menlo Park for a barbecue on one off night, and my son Steven, then five years old, was mesmerized by Bobby and the cup he carried around to collect the tobacco juice that he'd spit into it. When the Murcers left, I remember saying to Steven, "I know you like Bobby, but don't *ever* do that."

One of my favorite Murcer stories: In August 1976, already well out of the playoff race, we had an eleven-game road trip that took us to Atlanta, Montreal, and then Philadelphia. In Montreal, Bobby sustained some sort of nagging injury that looked like it would keep him out for at least the first game or two of the Phillies series. He didn't play the Friday night game, and then he didn't play Saturday, either. Well, after the Saturday night game, in which the Giants got trounced, 13–2, in between multiple and interminable rain delays, we got back to the Bellevue Stratford Hotel after 2 A.M. The hotel bar was long closed, but the guys knew of an after-hours joint down the block that was open all night. Bobby and I went there with a number of other players, and around four o'clock the place starts to thin out, except for half our roster. Once again, the Giants with proof positive they're not the Reds. Now it's almost five o'clock. The rest of the guys start to leave. "Bobby, I'm out of here. I'm on the air seven hours from now. I'm working and you'll be out of the lineup again." He says, "Just one more." I say "no" and he says, "Stay for one more and I promise you I'll be in the lineup today." I say, "You'd better be." Twenty minutes later we walk the one block back to the hotel and I say to him, "Listen, you bum, you know you're ready to play, and you better be in the lineup." Bobby promises me again.

I toss and turn with the sun coming up through the windows and sleep for about an hour, and by nine, everyone's luggage had to be in the lobby. It was a getaway day, and the bus would be leaving for the stadium at nine thirty. I felt as if a rail had been rammed through my head. Bobby came down looking like a bag lady, totally disheveled and completely hungover. On the bus, I said to him, "Listen, you pig farmer. Thanks to you, I'm sick as a dog. Don't even think you're *not* going to play today. Your ass is in there or I'll murder you." Bobby just chuckled.

We got to the stadium, and an hour later the lineups are announced, and Bobby is in there, batting fourth and playing right field. I'm ready to go on the air with a humongous headache and a roiling stomach. It's a road I've never been down before, and will never go down again. I am miserable. I could only imagine Bobby's state. Then a couple of minutes before the start of the game comes an announcement on the press box PA: "There's a lineup change for the Giants. Bobby Murcer is still battling his strained muscle and Gary Thomasson will be batting fourth and playing right field."

I began to think what price I might have to pay for assault and battery.

I announce the first two innings. With our format, I was off in the third and seventh innings. In the top of the third, I turn the microphone over to Bill Thompson, who was working a number of games with us that season. I leave the broadcast booth and take the elevator down to the visitors' clubhouse at Veterans Stadium. I barge in, and there's only one person in the clubhouse. And there he is, laid out on the training table, sound asleep and snoring.

"I'm going to kill you," I yell, as I made a beeline for the trainer's room. He sits halfway up, looks at me, and with a goofy smile says, "I'm sorry."

"Strained muscle, my ass," I bellow.

And then as I turn the table over on its side, he slides off onto the floor and starts laughing.

I went back up to the booth to fight my way through the rest of the game in my compromised state. Bobby spent the rest of the day going beddy-bye in the clubhouse.

In 2008, Bobby Murcer died of brain cancer at the age of sixty-two. Linda and I are still friendly with a fabulous lady, his widow, Kay. I miss the Pig Farmer dearly.

* * *

WHEN MY SECOND SEASON with the Giants ended in 1975, I had made a deal with CBS to work a number of regional NFL games, most of them going to 10 to 15 percent of the country. I recall covering around ten games with five different partners, including one game with Johnny Unitas. Unitas had retired two years earlier and was just getting his feet wet in broadcasting. In November, Unitas and I were assigned to a game between the New Orleans Saints and the Raiders at the Oakland Coliseum. I was living in Menlo Park, so this was a home game for me, and a couple of days before the game, I drove over to the Raiders' practice facility in Alameda to meet with the Raiders head coach, John Madden.

It was the first time I had met him, and as I sat with John in his office for about a half hour it was immediately apparent that he was so much more than a football coach. He was an immensely curious man, and at one point that day, he mused about how when he was done with coaching, he wanted to get into a motor home and travel all over the country and explore everything. We then started to talk about the fabled John Steinbeck classic, *Travels with Charley*, which, of course, is about a trip around America with a dog. John was also a huge baseball fan and had heard me on the Giants' broadcasts, and we talked about that as well. I remember thinking, *Here's a guy who'd be terrific company on a regular basis.* He was interested in everything. Twenty-seven years later, that chance would come.

I also worked three or four games with Hank Stram. At the end of the previous year, Stram had been fired as the head coach of the Kansas City Chiefs. The first time we were paired was in November in Atlanta, and the following week, wouldn't you know it—we were assigned to a game in Kansas City, with the Chiefs facing the Detroit Lions. Hank coming back to Kansas City was huge news—a picture of Hank in the booth would wind up on the front page of the *Kansas City Star* the day after the game.

Before that, though, it was customary, as it is now, for the broadcast team to meet with the home team's head coach a day or two before the game. So, our meeting was set up for Saturday afternoon with Paul Wiggin, Hank's successor. I had known Paul because prior to his getting the Chiefs job, he had been an assistant coach for the 49ers and lived in my neighborhood. Stram, meanwhile, was still chafing over his firing by the Chiefs, and had no interest in going to that meeting. I met with Wiggin alone. That night, Hank and I were going to dinner, and as we drove to the restaurant, he grilled me on everything Wiggin had to say. But the one thing Hank obsessed over was if Wiggin had redecorated his old office. Had he moved the furniture? Had he gotten new furniture? What pictures were on the wall? And what about that Tiffany lamp?

As the season wound down, Hank and I were assigned to a game in New Orleans between the Los Angeles Rams and the Saints. We were supposed to have dinner the night before the game, but Hank called my room at around six to say he had to cancel because John Mecom Jr., the owner of the Saints, had called to ask if he could join him for dinner at eight.

I knew immediately that the Saints, whose record was 2-10 at the time, would almost certainly be looking for a new coach at the end of the season. So it was abundantly clear to me why Mecom was meeting with Stram. The next morning—game day—with a scheduled noon start, Hank and I were going to have breakfast together at nine o'clock. But at 6:45, my phone rings. I pick up the phone. "It's Hank. We have to have breakfast *right now*." Bleary-eyed, I drag myself out of bed, put some clothes on, and go downstairs to meet him in the hotel restaurant.

Stram is already there, and before I can even sit down, Hank says, "Do you think I have a future in the broadcasting business?"

"Absolutely," I told him.

"I'm enjoying this, but I have to tell you, last night John Mecom asked me to consider becoming his next head coach. I have to think about it."

"Hank, to me, it's very apparent that you still want to coach. I think you have a lot of coaching left in you," I told him. "I think you should take the Saints job because broadcasting will always be there for you. And at some point, you'll come back to this."

"You think so?"

"I know so."

Sure enough, Stram took the job and coached the New Orleans Saints in 1976 and 1977. He went back to coaching for only two years, and then—no surprise to me—had a long and very successful run at CBS Television and Radio.

THE GIANTS HAD FINISHED a game below .500 in 1975. Horace Stoneham was going bankrupt. Attendance was terrible. At the end of the season, Stoneham—the man who had moved the Giants from New York to San Francisco—announced that the team was for sale. There appeared to be no local people interested in buying. The group that was most interested? Labatt's Brewery—based in Toronto.

I had a three-year contract with Golden West Broadcasting. So I was not employed by the team itself—as I was in Cincinnati—but by a broadcast entity with the tacit approval of the team. In November, with the Giants now in limbo, I got a call at home from someone at Labatt's saying, "We're going to buy the team, and if we do and move the team to Toronto—which is our plan—we want you to come here as well. Are you interested?" I had to choose my response carefully. I gave him an amorphous answer, but when I hung up, what I really wanted to do was *throw* up. We had come back to California and settled into a beautiful home on the San Francisco Peninsula; a move to Toronto was an absolute nonstarter.

It would never come to that. The American League would soon

expand, and Toronto would be granted its own franchise, starting play in 1977. Also, the National League president, Chub Feeney, had been a Giants executive, and had moved the league offices to San Francisco. Chub loved the West Coast and there was no way he wanted to leave, either. If there was no team in his market, he would have to move. Still, at this point, *everything* was up in the air. Spring training was not that far away, and it was no certainty that the team was going to remain in San Francisco. Then a local buyer emerged— Bob Lurie, a native San Franciscan and a real estate magnate. Bob was a big Giants fan. He was in attendance frequently at Candlestick. I'd gotten to know him. I liked him. The problem for Lurie was that he was willing to come up with only half the money and needed to find other investors. The asking price for the San Francisco Giants in 1976? Believe it or not, $8 million! Think about that. Today there are dozens of *players* making $8 million *a year*.

Lurie was willing to invest $4 million. The question became, where was he going to get the other $4 million so that the Giants could remain in San Francisco? Out of nowhere at the eleventh hour came a cattle rancher from Arizona by the name of Arthur "Bud" Herseth, who was willing to put up the difference. Lurie and Herseth had never met, had only spoken by phone, but the deal got done almost overnight and a press conference was set up on the eve of spring training at the Mark Hopkins Hotel on Nob Hill to announce that, jointly, Lurie and Herseth were buying the team. The two men shook hands for the first time literally twenty minutes before they sat down at a dais to meet the press. Herseth came out wearing this gigantic cattleman's hat. He took it off and didn't say much. All of us in the room were thinking: *This is going to be the greatest co-owner ever. He's going to stay out of the way. He's in the cattle business—he lives out of town, but just wants to come to a few games and have some fun with his grandchildren. In the meantime, he's just saved the Giants for San Francisco.*

Well, he turned out to be too good to be true. The Giants for years had trained in Phoenix, Herseth's hometown. Soon, Herseth would be at almost all of the Giants' spring training games. And it became clear by the end of March that what all of us saw in San Francisco that day bore little semblance to what we were seeing in Arizona. Herseth would sit in the ballpark next to the dugout in Phoenix, and was loud and often obnoxious. One afternoon, Von Joshua, the Giants' center fielder, who is black, trotted back toward the dugout after an inning had ended. Herseth shouted out to him, "Hey, boy, get over here and sign some autographs for these kids." What we thought we had originally seen in San Francisco that day, we didn't quite get. By then Lurie, too, had been taken aback, but a deal was a deal, and there was nothing that could be done immediately. A year later, however, Lurie would wind up buying Herseth out for $6 million. So the cattleman made $2 million, a 50 percent profit in one year. Meanwhile, Bob was now in for $10 million—but it would work out well in the end for him, too. First he became a major local hero by helping to save the franchise for the city. Then, in 1992, Bob sold the team for over $100 million—with part of the condition being that the team stay in San Francisco. History had repeated itself. Today the Giants, in good measure because they moved in 2000 from perhaps the worst stadium ever constructed to what some consider be the best stadium in baseball, AT&T Park, are now valued at around $800 million.

PRIOR TO THE 1976 season, Lon Simmons would unretire and become my broadcast partner. Lon is in the broadcasting wing of the Baseball Hall of Fame, and has a Hall of Fame sense of humor. We had a million laughs—during a season that for me, turned out to be a crazy adventure when ABC hired me to be the play-by-play announcer for *Monday Night Baseball* concurrent with my job at KSFO.

Much more on ABC in a moment. Meanwhile, once Lurie had helped save the Giants for San Francisco, he brought back his old buddy Bill Rigney as manager. Rigney had managed the team when they had first moved to the Bay Area in 1958. We had one great char-

acter on the team—a full of life, irrepressible pitcher by the name
of John "the Count" Montefusco. The Count had been called up at
the end of the 1974 season, and in his major-league debut at Dodger
Stadium, had walked in his first plate appearance and then homered
in his first official at bat. In addition, he'd pitched brilliantly in relief
of Ron Bryant and proclaimed on our postgame show that night,
"Mark my words—next year, I'm going to win twenty games!" On a
team with more than its share of dullards, hopelessly out of the race,
Montefusco was the all-time breath of fresh air.

In 1975, he'd lead the pitching staff in wins with 15, and in 1976,
with another 15 wins already under his belt, he'd make his final start
of the season in a meaningless game on September 29 in Atlanta. The
Giants were twenty-seven games out of first place. An hour before the
game, as I walked from the field up to the broadcast booth, I passed
through our clubhouse. Montefusco was the only player in there, and
he was hunched over in front of his locker. I walked over and said,
"Count, are you all right?" He looked up with watery eyes said, "I feel
like I have the flu." I started to walk away and said, "So you'll probably go out there and pitch a no-hitter."

Three hours later, Montefusco was being mobbed by his teammates. He'd faced twenty-eight batters, walked one, and struck out
four and had pitched a no-hitter. On the postgame show, the first
thing he blurts out to me is "You called it. You called it!"

Hardly. It was something I'd probably said fifty times to various
pitchers through the years. A goofy little pep talk. And then it actually happened! Go figure.

CHAPTER 8

Wide, Wide World

AT MY LUNCH WITH KHVH news director Don Rockwell in Hawaii in September 1970, he had been certain that *Monday Night Football* would be a failure. No sports fan he. Well, it was an instant hit—in fact, it was an instant phenomenon and a huge success for the NFL and ABC. Football fans were used to watching games on Sundays, and now Monday nights became a bonus—a wonderful way to end the first day of the workweek. And the audience extended well beyond a rabid fan base. Roone Arledge's decision to go with a three-announcer booth—including the polarizing Howard Cosell—had made the show more than just a football game. It made it a national communal sports experience. After that first season, Arledge replaced Keith Jackson with Frank Gifford, creating—along with Don Meredith and Cosell—a booth with three disparate characters. The suave, good-looking former New York Giants icon. The folksy, likeable, witty ex–Dallas Cowboys quarterback. And the nasal, pontificating, nonpracticing lawyer from New York. All sitting there together in these hideous yellow blazers as a football game was being played out in front of them.

By 1976, *Monday Night Football* had been on the air for six seasons, and Arledge would try to replicate its success in the spring and summer. So *Monday Night Baseball* was conceived. At that pre-cable time, there was only one nationally televised Game of the Week— Saturdays on NBC. If you lived in Denver or Phoenix or a market without a team, that was your only chance to watch a Major League Baseball game. So *Monday Night Baseball*—a second national baseball telecast—was a big deal. Even if it wasn't going to draw ratings comparable to *Monday Night Football*, it would still be significant. And Roone Arledge's plan was to pattern the baseball show after the football show: three diverse men in the booth—no classic "pure" analyst, but a play-by-play man, a former athlete with a good sense of humor, and a provocateur.

In March, just as all the turmoil surrounding the San Francisco Giants ownership situation was transpiring, I got a call from Herb Granath, an executive at ABC Sports, asking me to come to New York to audition for *Monday Night Baseball*. I immediately went to my bosses at KSFO, Bert West and Herb Briggin, to run it by them, because if I got the job, I would have to miss ten to twelve Giants broadcasts during the season. They gave me the go-ahead, feeling it would be good for them, too, if their local announcer had national exposure.

ABC's plan was to televise two games each Monday. An "A" game would go to the majority of the country, and then a "B" game would be broadcast to 20–30 percent of the country—while also providing insurance that there would be a telecast if the "A" game got rained out. I was interviewing for the play-by-play role on the "B" game. The network had already decided that their No. 1 team would be Bob Prince, Bob Uecker, and Warner Wolf. Prince was the longtime voice of the Pittsburgh Pirates. Uecker was laugh-out-loud funny, a former player who had made a smooth transition to become part of the Milwaukee Brewers' broadcast team. (Lots more on Uecker later.) And Wolf was a sports anchor in the Washington, D.C., market at the time. I later learned that Ben Bradlee, the longtime *Washington Post* executive editor, had grown smitten with Wolf and had called Roone Arledge, touting him as "the next Howard Cosell." A talent scout Ben Bradlee was not!

At my audition in New York, I went into a little audio booth with a monitor where they rolled a tape of a game and I did three or four "pretend" innings. It was a tough way to try to re-create what I'd normally be doing live. I thought my audition stunk. But everyone understood the deal and I was offered the job a few days later. My broadcast partners would be Norm Cash, the former Tiger All-Star first baseman, and Bob Gibson, the future Hall of Fame pitcher who had just retired from the Cardinals. That 1976 season—at least logistically for me—would be absolutely insane.

Monday Night Baseball would debut on the first Monday of the season and run through late August, when *Monday Night Football* would take over the time slot. From Tuesdays through Sundays I would call the Giants' games and then fly to the Monday night game. One time, the Giants played a Sunday afternoon doubleheader at Candlestick, and I caught a red-eye flight to New York. I arrived at JFK at dawn, checked into a hotel, slept a couple of hours, broadcast the Monday night game at Yankee Stadium, and then got back on a plane the next morning to call Giants games Tuesday night and Wednesday afternoon in San Francisco. Thursday, we left for a series in Montreal. And the next *Monday Night Baseball* game was back on the West Coast. Naturally, the Giants were still back east so the next morning it was back to thirty-seven thousand feet for another five hours. Sadly, these were before the days of frequent flier miles.

By this point in my career, I'd called more than a thousand games. I know little about playing music, but I was still perfecting how to use my voice as an instrument. You always want to match the crowd. You don't want to be shouting while the crowd is quiet, and you don't want to be whispering when the crowd is screaming. I always try to be in sync with the action, and in the more dramatic moments, it's particularly important to be in lockstep with the game. The game is the melody and the announcer provides the lyrics. When it all flows as one, it's wonderful. But if you're off-key, to the audience, it's cacophony.

When I anticipate something very important or particularly relevant to the game is about to happen, I will try through my inflection to let the audience know that. Pay close attention, because this is something that could truly determine the outcome of the game. It may only be the third inning or the second quarter, but you know what, folks? This is an important juncture.

Crowds also differ. For instance, the New York crowds and the Philadelphia crowds have always been very sophisticated in terms of understanding nuances and subtleties. When an outfielder throws to the wrong base, they know it—collectively, you can hear a throaty groan, and a moment later, the booing starts. In Chicago, the fans can often be that way, too. In other cities, generally those with expansion or relocated franchises, the fans might not be as attuned to the finer points of the game. As a broadcaster, I'm always conscious of this.

I spent that whole 1976 season crisscrossing the country. Bill Rigney, John "the Count" Montefusco, and Giants six days a week, and the ABC telecast on Monday. I was the King of the Redeye. But I was young and my body could take it and I was thrilled for the opportunity. I couldn't have done this without Linda Michaels. Linda and I had two young children at home, and while I was on the road, which was often, she held down the fort. There was a nice payoff as the calendar year wound down—ABC offered me a full-time network job.

AS WITH THE REDS, I felt I could have stayed with the Giants for a long time. We loved the Bay Area and the team finally seemed to be heading in the right direction with Bob Lurie as the owner. But the ABC offer came very close to mirroring what I had in mind when I first dreamed of becoming a sportscaster. I'd continue to do baseball, and then get to do all sorts of other events—from college football to the Olympics to *Wide World of Sports*. And I could remain in the Bay Area, where our family was very comfortable. After what felt like a series of early career milestones—getting the Reds job, doing the World Series and Olympics in 1972, doing regional NFL football and the "B" game on *Monday Night Baseball*—this would be the capstone. So at the end of December 1976, I parted ways with KSFO and the Giants and started full-time at ABC.

At ABC, I was the new kid in town. It was like becoming a junior partner at a prestigious law firm and looking up to the titans of your profession. When I arrived, ABC had a murderers' row of talent: Howard Cosell, Jim McKay, Frank Gifford, Chris Schenkel, Keith Jackson. The network was pegging me as their up-and-comer. I wanted to be that guy a little faster than they did. It wouldn't be a straight line to my goal of reaching the apex. There were some bumps and bruises along the way. For example, I now had an agent—the high-powered Ed Hookstratten. There was little question that when I was signing full-time that I'd be elevated to the *Monday Night Baseball* "A" game. Bob Prince had been fired in August. It wasn't specifically written into the deal but Hookstratten said don't worry—it was obvious. Along the way, at some point in the negotiations, Hookstratten had gotten into a hissing contest with Arledge. I didn't find out about it until months later when the production schedule came out and I was still on the "B" game and Keith Jackson would be doing the "A" game. I was beside myself. It would be a great life lesson. Pay strict attention to every detail when it involves a contract or prepare to get blindsided. Shortly after that, I hired a new agent.

Overall, though, in the grand scheme of things at ABC, it was still very, very exciting. In my first year, I would continue to do baseball; college football, which at the time, was monopolized by ABC; and a potpourri of events for *Wide World of Sports*. *Wide World* was as much travelogue as sports programming. It really did "span the globe to bring you the constant variety of sport," as Jim McKay said each week in the introduction, with images of everything from weight lifting to rodeo to figure skating to a demolition derby flashing on the screen.

The premise of the show worked extremely well at that time. Viewers had never seen cliff diving from Acapulco or wrist wrestling from Petaluma, California. These might have been oddball sports, but there would be a certain curiosity. At that time, obviously, the Internet didn't exist, and satellite technology was in its infancy. Satellite time was so prohibitively expensive that very few events had been broadcast from outside the United States. This was a groundbreaking show. *Wide World* took you to places you'd never seen before. It went behind the Iron Curtain often. And the viewer would get pulled in—and start caring about the competitors and the competition.

In the pre-computer age, every three months, the ABC announcers would receive in the mail a three-page list of assignments—one for each month. From the beginning, when my list came in the mail, I would sit down at the kitchen table and sneak up on it. I would cover up everything on the sheet except the announcer column, and when I'd come upon my name, I'd slowly pull back the paper that was covering the event column to see what my assignment would be. It would vary from A to Z, and could take you anyplace on the globe.

All that said, my first ever staff assignment for ABC was—drum roll, please—the World Barrel Jumping Championships in the Chicago suburb of Northbrook, Illinois. A week later, Chris Schenkel would be covering skiing in Kitzbuhel, Austria, so I would be filling in for Chris—at a Pro Bowlers Tour stop in Florissant, Missouri, just outside St. Louis. I remember thinking as I was going down that first list: *What?* I'd already been to Chicago and St. Louis several times. But then I sneaked up on my third event on the list—and *voila!* I would be covering the World Cresta Run Championships in St. Moritz, Switzerland, in mid-February. Now we're talking.

For as much travel as I'd done in the United States, I'd never been to Europe. It was exhilarating to get on the plane in San Francisco, connect in New York, and then head over the Atlantic Ocean. I couldn't sleep on the New York to Zurich portion of the flight because I was filled with anticipation. On descent, I couldn't wait until we broke out of the clouds and I could see Europe for the first time.

It was a foggy day in Zurich. I collected my luggage, and went straight to the railway station, where I boarded a train for the two-and-a-half-hour ride to St. Moritz. What was the Cresta Run? It was basically a bobsled course traversed by individuals going downhill face-first on small sleds. It's similar to the skeleton competition in today's Winter Olympics. What made it unique was that there were no Cresta Run professionals. Going down this dangerous, icy course were millionaires, royalty, and other men of great wealth. These guys were either rich enough to have winter homes in the area or stay in the ritzy hotels in one of the most exclusive resort cities in the world. It was high society getting its kicks through a life-threatening stunt. At the end of the competition, there was none of the normal beer- or champagne-spraying that you'd see in an American locker room. Instead, these characters, along with their spectacularly bejeweled wives and/or girlfriends (and in some cases, both), would head into town to eat several ounces of Beluga caviar and wash it down with Dom Perignon.

The following weekend, I would go to Norway for the World Ski Flying Championships. Ski flying is basically ski jumping on a larger hill. For the five days between St. Moritz and Scandinavia, I headed to London, where the Cresta Run show would be edited and prepared for my voiceover. Then it was off to Oslo, and an hour's drive to a small town called Vikersund. The ski flying event would take place on that Saturday morning. I had no idea what the actual temperature was. All I knew is that I could not feel a single extremity. Diamond Head was four universes away. It was so insanely frigid that when we were taping the scene set at the foot of the jump, my mouth wouldn't move. Literally. Someone pumped some hot chocolate into me and put some balm on my face, and we barely got the opening done.

Wide World was often a very difficult logistical challenge. Much of what we covered in Europe would be taped and aired on *Wide World* a week or two later (like that Cresta Run show), but there was also the occasional live transmission, and, in other instances, shows that would be taped early in the day to air that afternoon in the States—"same-day coverage," we called it. In those years, satellite time to beam live or same-day coverage of events back to the States for broadcast was very expensive. Live events were ultimately simple—they'd be transmitted as they took place—but for same-day coverage, the network would reserve a finite window of time, and there was a lot of pressure to get the show fully edited to "feed" back to New York during that interval.

In 1981, I would be back again at the World Ski Flying Championships—this time being held in Oberstdorf, West Germany. The event took place in the morning—approximately 10 A.M. to 12:30 P.M. local time—and was scheduled to air on *Wide World of Sports* later that day—4:30 P.M. on the East Coast. The plan was to edit the two-and-a-half-hour event into a half hour of television content—basically, just feature the top competitors, tell their stories, and show their jumps. It was the kind of condensed storytelling coverage that Roone Arledge, the president of ABC Sports, had pioneered on Olympic coverage and *Wide World*. But with quick turnarounds, it wasn't easy.

The producer in Oberstdorf was Doug Wilson. Doug was a very talented and artistic producer who was renowned at ABC for his keen eye and skill at putting together taped shows. On many of those, he typically had days or weeks to edit. In Oberstdorf, Doug only had about seven hours between the end of the event and the window of satellite time that had been booked. Typically, a 60–90 minute window would be reserved to feed a half-hour segment (really closer to twenty minutes when you factor in commercial breaks) from Europe to the United States

My broadcast partner that day was Art Devlin, a former ski

jumper from Lake Placid, New York, who'd competed in the 1952 and 1956 Olympics. Art was ABC's Nordic sports analyst—which meant he worked ski jumping events, cross-country skiing events, and of course, ski flying events for *Wide World of Sports*. I'd first met Art in Sapporo, Japan, in 1972 when I'd made my Olympic broadcasting debut. Art, like me, was one of the nine total announcers NBC had sent over for those Winter Games.

Art and I recorded a good portion of the broadcast "live-to-tape"—as the event was actually taking place. Before the competition began, we recorded our introduction—"the scene set," in television parlance—and right after the event concluded, we did an on-camera close. Whatever we didn't cover from the site we would voice later that evening, once the editing was complete. And the result would (hopefully) be a seamless half hour of network television.

When the competition ended, Art and I went back to our hotel to take a break while the crew, led by Doug Wilson, hunkered down in the edit rooms (which were actually tiny vestibules in trailers near the site). We returned a few hours later to learn that Doug and his gang were behind schedule, still working feverishly with the satellite window fast approaching. The atmosphere was tense—if the show wasn't fed by the end of the satellite window, it would cost the network many thousands of dollars to extend the window, and draw the ire of executives back in New York. And then, of course, there was the additional risk of not getting the show fed to New York in time for the actual broadcast, which would be a total disaster.

Art and I soon got started and voiced over—or "laid down"—most of our commentary. But the satellite clock was ticking. There were still the last couple of minutes of the show to voice over—the final two jumps that would determine the winner. Now there was less than ten minutes of satellite time remaining. Art and I sat in the booth, waiting to get the cue from Doug to resume and finish up. Now there were seven minutes left in the window. Six minutes. Finally, with five minutes to go—and about two minutes of content to record—we were ready to call the next-to-last jumper of the day. I think it was Armin Kogler of Austria, who was in second or third place and needed one more good jump to secure a medal, perhaps even gold.

The tape rolls and as Kogler becomes airborne, Art excitedly shouts, "Oh, it's a tremendous jump and he's well out over the tips of his skis!" Not two seconds after Kogler has left the lip of the ramp, our monitor goes blank. Now we have a technical issue.

In our headsets, Wilson says, "Hang on—it'll be fixed in a minute."

Art took his headset off and opened the door for some fresh air as I waited nervously. Now we're totally up against the gun. Then Art puts his headset back on and we're ready to resume. The tape rolls.

"Oh, it's a terrible jump!" Art bellowed.

Wilson yells, "Stop!"

"Art—it's a *great* jump, what are you doing?"

We were all so exhausted at that point that Devlin thought we were rolling in the next jump by another guy.

"Oh, that's Kogler again? Sorry."

Somehow, someway, we got it all done with thirty seconds of satellite time on the clock. The whole show had been successfully fed. And America got to see Armin Kogler win a silver medal with a final leap that walked a fine line between tremendous and terrible.

MY MOST UNFORGETTABLE *WIDE World* assignment of all came when I was dispatched to an event that been a longtime staple of *Wide World of Sports*: Motorcycles on Ice, in the small town of Inzell, nestled in the Bavarian Alps in what was then West Germany. It featured a large group of Europeans—Poles, Slavs, Austrians, Czechs, Soviets, and East and West Germans—who gathered to race motorcycles on what was basically an outdoor speed skating track. The bikes' tires were outfitted with large spikes. The event started in the early evening but the crowd consisted primarily of fifteen thousand wild and woolly Germans and Austrians—Salzburg was an easy drive away—who had made their way to the site around lunchtime to start tailgating. At that moment, the parking lot had become the Schnapps capital of the planet.

Our producer at that event, Geoff Mason, was always looking for different little twists. His idea on this night was simple: for the scene set, instead of my simply looking at the camera to welcome everybody, I would ride one of the motorcycles down a straightaway, stop at the finish line, take off my helmet, and say, "Hi, I'm Al Michaels and welcome to Inzell, West Germany, for Motorcycles on Ice."

As the new kid on the ABC Sports block, I was trying to make a favorable first impression. You want to be collegial and collaborative and a team player. So I concealed a potentially important piece of information from Mason: The only bike I had ever ridden was a Schwinn. I'd never been on a motorcycle, much less driven one, and I didn't know how one worked or what I was supposed to do. And, oh, by the way, this is all supposed to happen on *ice,* on national television! But I was game.

The first order of business was outfitting me in motorcycle leathers so I looked the part. Somebody on our crew found a Russian rider who hadn't made the cut in the preliminary races and was willing to lend me his. The problem was that the guy was probably five six and weighed 145 pounds. I was five ten, 180. I felt like I was being poured into a straitjacket. Breathing became an issue.

I was flanked by some of the other riders. There was Czech being spoken on one side of me, Russian on another, and German behind me. Of course, I couldn't hear much of anything anyway, because I was wearing a helmet that was scrunched onto my noggin. I had no idea what I was doing—Is this the clutch? Do I turn it or twist it?— and there were thousands of tipsy spectators now watching.

All I know is that at one point I started to rev the engine. Thinking back, I was beginning to let the clutch out, which would have launched me a hundred feet in the air, if not for one of the Soviets, who grabbed my hand and kept the clutch engaged so I couldn't move—and clearly preventing me from taking off and either killing myself or just launching me into space, never to come back.

At that point, Mason decided it was prudent to kill the idea. *Thank you, God.* There's a problem, though. It's 7:20 and the races would start at 7:30. And we needed a scene set, even if it was going to be less ambitious. Quickly it was decided that I'd change out of the leathers—no easy task—and just wear my yellow ABC parka, go over to the finish line, and tape the open.

Except now there was another problem. Our audio crew was working to fix a technical glitch. And so as I stood there in my parka, waiting for the cue, an announcement came over the PA system, followed by whistling and shrieking. Whistling, of course, is the European form of booing. The next whistling sounds I heard were bottles being thrown past my head. I turned to my interpreter. "What the hell is going on?"

He looked straight ahead. "Oh, they just announced that the race is going to start late because the American television production needs more time." Mason had gotten the word to the PA announcer.

"Are you out of your mind?" I yelled to Mason in the truck. He couldn't even hear me. My mike still wasn't working. So there I am, having barely avoided death on a motorcycle with protruding spikes revving up on a blanket of ice—and now I'm going to be sliced open by vodka bottles!

Maybe it was time to go back to the Pro Bowlers Tour.

In the end, as always, we got it done. I delivered my opening (standing, not riding), the races started, and the telecast went well. Somehow, someway, everything on *Wide World of Sports* would work out. Roone Arledge must have known some higher being.

CHAPTER 9

Do You Believe in Miracles?

ROONE ARLEDGE ALWAYS TOOK his time and made announcing assignments later than any of us preferred. So in the fall of 1979, I knew that in February I'd be covering the 1980 Winter Olympics in Lake Placid, New York—but not which events. Figure skating was the domain of Jim McKay and Dick Button, so I could cross that one off the list. Frank Gifford and Bob Beattie were certain to be assigned to alpine skiing. Those characters couldn't get enough of the après-ski scene and Roone, as one of Frank's best friends, was happy to oblige. Speed skating would be a plum assignment because Eric Heiden, a 21-year-old from Wisconsin, was favored to win five gold medals. If a megastar would come out of these Games, it was Heiden. Ski jumping, cross-country skiing, and biathlon held little appeal. As far as hockey was concerned, I thought it would provide a decent story but the Soviets had won the gold medal at every Olympics dating back to 1964, and would be the heavy favorites again in Lake Placid.

When the assignments finally came out a few weeks before the Games, sure enough, I'd been given hockey. Why? Because Dennis

Lewin, one of our producers, recalled that I had called the gold medal game on NBC at the 1972 Games. In addition, Howard Cosell had never called a hockey game. Neither had Keith Jackson, nor Chris Schenkel, nor Jim McKay, nor Bill Flemming, nor anyone else on the staff. So I had more hockey experience than any of the other guys. Sixty minutes worth! And I could explain icing and offside.

I felt good about the assignment—in the Winter Olympics, an indoor role is always good—and the more I learned about the U.S. team, the better I felt. It looked like they would have a decent shot at a bronze medal. I felt better still when I found out my partner would be Ken Dryden, the former Montreal Canadiens goalie whom, almost a decade earlier, I'd watched from the balcony at the Montreal Forum along with Pete Rose, Johnny Bench, and a couple of other Cincinnati Reds. Dryden had just retired at the age of thirty-one, and was just getting started on what has been an eclectic career as a writer, scholar, lawyer, broadcaster, businessman, and politician. As Lake Placid approached, Art Kaminsky, Ken's agent and old friend from Cornell, had pushed ABC to hire Dryden as the hockey analyst for the Olympics. Dryden had always followed all sports, and when the ABC execs asked him whom he might like to work with, he had said, "How about Al Michaels?" They replied, "Great—that's exactly who we were thinking about."

By December 1979, we were ramping up our prep work. In the middle of the month, an event called the Izvestia Tournament, named for the newspaper that sponsored it and featuring the national hockey teams from several countries, would be held in Moscow. Ken and I flew there to watch Finland, Sweden, Canada, Czechoslovakia, and the Soviet Union itself in action. We would be there four days and get to watch somewhere around a dozen games. Dryden flew in from Montreal, I flew in from the Bay Area, and we met at the hotel in Moscow and had dinner the night before the tournament started. We hit it off immediately. Ken was extremely smart, impeccably articulate, and very measured. (To this day, I contend that he should have been the prime minister of Canada.) At the end of the meal, after the table had been cleared, we sat there talking about the difference between the styles of play in the NHL and international hockey. Ken explained the impact of the wider rink in international play, and how the different geometry affected strategy. I found it fascinating, superbly well considered, and brilliantly summarized. After about this ten-minute dissertation, he says to me, "So, do you think this is the type of thing that will interest our audience?"

"Yes. Yes I do," I responded. "But Ken, let me introduce you to the world of television. Can you get it down to eight seconds?"

AGAIN, THE EXPECTATIONS FOR the U.S. team were modest. A bronze medal would be considered a decent achievement. And there was no question about who would win the gold. Dryden had played against the Soviets in the seventies and he and I saw the Soviet team play six or seven games before the Olympics. They toyed with the competition. Three days before the Olympics began, the Soviet team played an exhibition game against the U.S. team at Madison Square Garden. The final score was 10–3, Soviets. It looked more like 20–0.

This, of course, was before the International Olympic Committee allowed professionals to compete. So, in theory, the Olympics were an amateur competition, and the U.S. team was mainly composed of kids in college or those who had recently graduated. Several players were from the University of Minnesota, because Herb Brooks, the American coach, had been the Golden Gophers' head coach. Four players—including Mike Eruzione, the captain, and Jim Craig, the goalie—were from Boston University. A couple of guys were from Minnesota-Duluth, Mark Johnson was from Wisconsin, and Ken Morrow was from Bowling Green. The average age was 22. One player, Mike Ramsey, had just turned nineteen. The grizzled veteran was twenty-six-year-old Buzz Schneider, who had been a member of the U.S. hockey team at the 1976 Winter Olympics in Innsbruck,

Austria. Buzz had played some minor-league hockey, but had then regained his amateur status in time for Lake Placid.

Meanwhile, the Soviet "amateur" hockey players were mostly in their late twenties. I'd always laugh when I saw that their biographies would list them as either students or soldiers. In the Soviet Union, that was an alias for professional hockey player. And this would become all the more apparent in the late eighties, when the Soviets began playing in the National Hockey League and we got to see just how great these players were. Now heading into the Olympics, our relations with the Soviets on the global political stage were tense. They had invaded Afghanistan a few months earlier and we were threatening to boycott the 1980 Summer Games in Moscow (which we wound up doing). But no one was sensing that ice hockey would offer any symbolic battle between the two countries. We just weren't in their league.

The hockey tournament in Lake Placid actually began the night before the Opening Ceremony, with the United States taking on Sweden. The American team was trailing, 2–1, when, with the clock winding down in the third period, Brooks pulled Jim Craig for the extra attacker and Bill Baker scored the tying goal with twenty-seven seconds remaining. There was no overtime, so that was that. The Americans—an underdog in that game—had earned a tie, and gotten a point in the standings. Already we'd had a dose of drama.

What's more, it had already become apparent that because Herb Brooks knew and respected Dryden, we were going to have special access. Brooks had cut off most of the rest of the media to build a wall around his players. His thinking: *If I'm going to deal with one media entity, it'll be the national television broadcaster.* Which, of course, was fine by us. Ken and I had four or five private sessions with Brooks over the course of the Games. Invaluable.

During the Opening Ceremony show, hosted by Jim McKay the next day, I joined Jim to narrate an extensive recap of the action from the night before. I was already getting more airtime than originally thought.

The next night, a Thursday, the U.S. team played its second game. Czechoslovakia, easily the second-best team in the world and likely to win the silver medal, was the opponent. Stunningly, it was the Americans who dominated from start to finish, winning 7–3. And now it was like—*whoa,* what's happening here? A last-minute tie against favored Sweden and a rout of heavily favored Czechoslovakia? And late in the game, there was a moment that epitomized the team and its coach as much as anything. A Czech player leveled Mark Johnson in the open ice, nowhere near the puck, forcing a stoppage as Johnson was attended to. As our camera focused in on Brooks, a microphone picked up Herb's voice. "We'll bury that goddamn shit right in your throat, [Number] Three," he barked. "You're gonna eat that goddamn Koho [hockey stick], Three!" Today, as the saying goes, Twitter would have blown up and the network would conceivably get a fine or at least a scolding from the Federal Communications Commission. That night, though, it just served to paint to the country the quintessential portrait of this intense, no-nonsense coach who was convincing his players that they were as good—and tough—as any hockey team in the world.

Also at that game, a group of fans began to chant *U-S-A, U-S-A.* Years later, I received a letter from a man claiming that he and his friends were in Lake Placid, and that they were the first ones to ever start that mantra. This might sound like one of those unverifiable claims on the order of "I started the wave." But let the record reflect— the USA-Czechoslovakia game *was* the first time I'd ever heard it. And it would become ubiquitous by the end of the Games.

FROM THE START, KEN Dryden and I had a good thing going. It was a very comfortable blend—and Ken had quickly found a way to make relevant, incisive points in eight seconds or less. In football, the analyst can speak for thirty seconds after the play-by-play announcer finishes calling a play in four or five. In hockey, the action is so continuous, it's the reverse. The analyst has to speak in quick bites, get in, and get out, because of the nonstop action that has to be covered. And Ken Dryden understood that immediately.

By the first Saturday of the Games, everything was heating up. Eric Heiden had won his first gold medal. Alpine skiing and figure skating were under way. And hockey was generating this buzz. That afternoon, the United States took on Norway at the field house adjacent to the main arena that had been built for the 1932 Lake Placid Olympics. The venue had the feeling of a high school rink. But it was the Olympics, and in front of a capacity crowd of about two thousand fans (not a misprint), the United States won again, 5–1. And two days after that, they won again, 7–2, over Romania. The Americans were 3-0-1 and in good position to reach the medal round, which would include the top two teams from each six-team bracket.

We were staying at the newly opened Lake Placid Hilton. Dryden had the room next to mine and the late Art Kaminsky, his agent, a terrific guy but a man who took the term *penurious* to new heights (depths?), moved in as his roommate. Art never wanted to look a hotel bill in the eye if it wasn't necessary.

Kaminsky had brought with him one of those push-and-pull table hockey games. You controlled the forwards and defensemen with rods that would go in and out and the goalie with a lever that would move side to side. It was similar to foosball. We played the game for close to an hour every day—Dryden, Kaminsky, and yours truly, as well as anyone else who would wander in. It felt like a college frat house. This entire time—starting with that first night we met in Moscow—Dryden had been schooling me on the wonders of international hockey and its beautiful, elegant cross-ice passing. Now facing me on the other side of the table, with his oversize glasses and looking like a college professor from central casting, all he was doing was jamming the rods in as hard as he could, trying to knock my players off their springs. I was stupefied. "Hey, Kenny, you've taught me this beautiful form of hockey and now you're playing this muck-muck crap. When did you turn into a goon? You've become a goon!"

He just laughed.

On Wednesday, February 20, the U.S. team took on West Germany. At the start of the tournament, it appeared the two teams were evenly matched. As they had in every game apart from the one against Romania, the Americans fell behind early and trailed, 2–0, before scoring four unanswered goals over the last two periods to win, 4–2, and clinch a berth in the medal round. It would be the United States and Sweden from the Blue Division, and the Soviet Union and Finland from the Red Division advancing to medal round over the weekend. The Soviets wound up undefeated in group play with a 51–11 goal differential.

But first, Dryden had some business to take care of. Right after the conclusion of the West Germany game, he got into a car and was driven across the Canadian border to Ottawa, three hundred miles from Lake Placid. Why? He had to take his *bar exam* the next morning. He would pass with flying colors. That was Dryden. In between the game against West Germany and the Friday contest with the Soviets, he passed the bar. I began to think this guy could rescue people from a burning building for three straight days on his lunch break.

WHILE DRYDEN WAS IN Ottawa, a controversy developed over the starting time of Friday's game between the United States and the USSR. The U.S. team would meet the Soviets, and Finland would face Sweden on Friday, the twenty-second, and then on Sunday, the twenty-fourth, the United States would conclude play against Finland with the Soviets matched up with Sweden. The team that accumulated the most points (including those already earned against teams that had qualified for the medal round) would win the gold medal. According to the schedule that was released before the Olympics, the 5 P.M. game on February 22 would match up the second-place team from the Blue Group (which turned out to be the United States) against the first-place team from the Red Group (the Soviets). There would then be an 8 P.M. game that would feature the Blue Group winner (which turned out to be Sweden) against the Red Group runner-up (Finland).

Now what? Clearly, Roone Arledge and ABC obviously preferred that the U.S.-Soviet game be played in prime time in the Eastern Time Zone, 8 P.M., with the Sweden-Finland game then moved back to 5 P.M. So Roone and one of his top deputies, John Martin, along with a young programming executive named Bob Iger, worked to get the games switched. Roone had a lot of juice with the International Olympic Committee and the Lake Placid organizers and just about every other Olympic muckety-muck, but this was a change that would have to be approved by the Soviet Hockey Federation. And even though remuneration was put on the table, the Soviets put up a stone wall and refused. Time was of the essence and the negotiations ended.

So the marquee matchup of the Olympics would start at 5 P.M. on a Friday afternoon. Arledge made the decision to tape-delay the game until eight o'clock.

This scenario could never take place in today's world. Too much would be at stake. Money would win out. But in 1980, in the world of television, dinosaurs were still roaming the earth.

The Hilton was just six blocks from the arena, and Dryden and I left that Friday afternoon at about two o'clock to walk over. Yes, the Americans had become a great story. But our conversation had to be realistic. *If the score can be something like 3–1 Soviets in the middle of the second period, that's about all we can ask for. You're just praying it's not 7–0. If they can keep it close for a period and a half and hang in there against a bunch of NHL-caliber players, that will be more than respectable and keep the audience for a while.* Remember, the Soviet team had toured North America and beaten the New York Rangers, New York

Islanders, and Quebec Nordiques on an exhibition tour the previous year. The U.S. team had been wonderful to watch but again, they were still primarily a bunch of college kids.

The game took place in the Olympic Center, a 7,700-seat multipurpose field house that had been built for these Olympics. A few extra fans would get jammed in that afternoon. Still, there are college teams that play in bigger rinks. There was an intimacy in that building. Even upstairs, you were close to the ice. You could hear every sound echoing from below. You could see the players' faces. The scoreboard was rudimentary. The sound system was simply functional.

Just before the opening faceoff, the crowd was still filing in. We were broadcasting from a makeshift platform in the first two rows of the balcony. On the platform, I was next to Dryden, along with five or six other production people—a statistician, a cameraman, a stage manager, an audio assistant, and another technician. We came on the air and did the scene set. In my on-camera welcome, I said:

The excitement, the tension building. The Olympic Center, filling to capacity. The face value of a top ticket to tonight's game? Sixty-seven dollars, twenty cents. Outside, they're changing hands at three times the face value. . . . I'm sure there are a lot of people in this building tonight who do not know the difference between a blue line and a clothesline. It's irrelevant. It doesn't matter. Because what we have at hand is the rarest of sporting events. An event that needs no buildup, no superfluous adjectives. In a political or nationalistic sense, I'm sure this game is being viewed with varying perspectives. But manifestly, it is a hockey game. The United States and the Soviet Union on a sheet of ice in Lake Placid, New York.

Then I brought Dryden in for his opening remarks. Ken put it this way: "For the U.S. team, it's really discovery time. It's one thing to be young and promising. It's quite another to be good. And in

the next two and a half hours, the U.S. players will go through perhaps the most difficult and demanding, yet exhilarating time of their
lives. They will be playing against a very good team, a team that's
better than they are. And after that time, after it's all over, this team
will find out an awful lot about themselves. They'll simply find out
how good they are."

Early on, the Soviets, in their familiar red uniforms, controlled
the tempo much as we expected they would, and they scored about
halfway through the first period on a goal by Vladimir Krutov. But
then the U.S. team tied it five minutes later on a goal by Buzz Schneider, only to have the Soviets jump ahead again, 2–1, on a goal by Ser-
gei Makarov with 2:26 left in the period. Then—and you could never
make enough of the importance of this—with the period coming to
the end, the Soviets were putting the pressure on and had a chance to
make it 3–1. Instead, the next thing you know, the puck comes out
toward center ice and Mark Johnson scoops it up and beats the Soviet
goalie, Vladislav Tretiak, just as the horn sounds.

For a moment, there was a question of whether the puck had
crossed the goal line before time expired. It did. And now Dryden
and I were thinking, *What a great and lucky break. 2–2 after the first
period. We'll take it.* On the broadcast, Ken was full of great insight
and we felt totally in sync. Later, I'd be asked how I got all those
Soviet names down. Fortunately, most of them ended in *ov.* It was
child's play compared to five Samoans on a fast break. My Hawaii
high school basketball days were paying off in the Adirondacks.

HERE YOU HAD THE United States and the Soviet Union in the
Olympics , but there was only one minimally recognizable celebrity in
attendance: Jamie Farr of *M*A*S*H.* Apparently, there was no A-list
in 1980.

Meanwhile, as the second period began, the Soviet coach, Viktor Tikhonov, made a stunning move, replacing his goalie, Vladislav

Tretiak. Tretiak was considered by many to be the best goaltender in the world at the time, and the U.S. players would later say this had the effect of emboldening the American team. Vladimir Myshkin came in to replace Tretiak. Nonetheless, in the second period, the Soviets were completely dominant. They scored the only goal in the period two minutes in, and outshot the American team, 12–2. Jim Craig, the U.S. goalie, had to make one phenomenal save after another to keep the score close. It was 3–2, but it could have been 8–2. During the intermission, I remember thinking that we'd gotten all we could have hoped for. A one-goal game would still keep an audience. But the thought of actually *winning* the game? A game the Soviets were dominating despite the closeness of the score? No way.

When the third period began, the Soviets picked up where they had left off, still controlling the flow. But then eight and a half minutes in, at the end of a power play, Dave Silk got knocked off the puck, and it slid over to Mark Johnson, who poked it in behind Myshkin. It wasn't the prettiest goal ever scored but the game was now tied with eleven and a half minutes to go. *WHAT?!!* This game—the fuzzy-cheeked Americans against, pardon the expression, the Big Red Machine—is tied in the third period? Because the Soviets had been so dominant for a period and a half, the crowd hadn't had much to get excited about. But now the building was starting to come apart. Just over a minute later, Buzz Schneider tried a long slap shot from just outside the blue line, and off the save, the puck caromed toward the boards. Mark Pavelich would get to it as he was falling to the ice, and send it out to the high slot, thirty feet in front of the net, where—*ERUZIONE SCORES!!! MIKE ERUZIONE!!!! USA 4, SOVIETS 3!!!!!*

There were exactly ten minutes left. Now it was surreal. Our broadcast platform was starting to rock. And the rest of the game would be completely nuts. The Soviets were applying continuous pressure, but they'd abandoned their basic plan and were making desperate line changes, switching up every 20–25 seconds. It was like nothing we'd ever seen from the Soviets, who had always been so poised and clinical. Meanwhile, the U.S. team was playing with great confidence.

As the game wound down, the clock appeared to be in quicksand. The players would later say basically the same thing. You'd sneak a glance at the clock, there would be six minutes left, and then you'd look back to the game and figure a minute had elapsed. But then you'd look back at the clock and it would be, like, 5:43 remaining. Only seventeen seconds had been played?!

Finally, there were under five minutes left in the game. Then four. Now three. Then two. Now we're in the last minute. The crowd is absolutely wild. It's like doing a game in a thunderstorm. The noise is deafening. Chet Forte, the ABC producer, is screaming indecipherable gibberish into my headset. And I'm like a horse with blinkers. *Stay in the game. Stay in the game. Just call the game. Call the game. Don't get swept up by the emotion. The Soviets might tie the game with a goal and you have to be ready for that.*

I've always felt that the hotter the action gets, the cooler you want to stay. You don't want to underplay what's going on, because it *is* exhilarating. But you don't want to be over-the-top either, because when the crowd is out of its mind and the action is intense and the audience is riveted, if you're screaming, you're a nuisance. I want to be brief and let the drama play out. Let the pictures tell the story. Again, it's about that beautiful melody, and not screwing it up with lyrics that don't match.

So, I'm calling each pass and identifying who has the puck. I'm into the mechanics of the broadcast, nothing but the fundamentals. My concentration level is as intense as it's ever been in my career. Next to me, Dryden isn't saying much because anything he'd say would have to be jammed in. I glance up at the clock and there are twenty seconds left. With ten seconds to go, the crowd begins to count the seconds down in unison.

The Soviets are pressuring in the U.S. end but the puck comes behind the net and around the boards and gets cleared out to center ice with about six seconds left.

The game at this point is all but over. Now there are a handful of seconds remaining where I don't have to do literal play-by-play.

I'm like almost everyone in America at this point. *Can you believe this?!*

A word pops into my head—*miraculous.*

A split second later, it gets morphed into a question and answer:

Do you believe in miracles? Yes!

Six words. Through the years I've been asked thousands of times when I came up with the line? That morning? Sometime in the third period? Back in December? When February 22 dawned, in my mind, the United States had no chance to win this game. None. Zero. And even if they somehow did, how would it happen? Would it end with a shot on goal? A flurry outside the net? The line was completely spontaneous and totally in the moment. I had no idea of the impact the words would end up having. This was a time when no one had a home VCR, much less a DVR. No broadcaster made a call thinking, *Oh, they're going to play this back for years.* It bore no semblance to today's world, when anything and everything can be played back through eternity.

Reflecting back, that line came from my heart. This was a unique situation when, as a broadcaster, you could be openly biased: 99.9 percent of the audience is 100 percent with you. I know there's supposed to be "no rooting in the press box," but this was *the* exception. I didn't think about it until much later but it enabled me to say words that were unrestrained and partisan. It was from my inner being. Period. It was written once that this was the nine-year-old boy emerging from somewhere within me. I'll buy that.

Meanwhile, over the following ninety seconds, a million thoughts were racing through my head. *How incredible was this! Where does this rank as a sports upset? What did this mean in the midst of a Cold War?* There was still another game to come Sunday against Finland. But the best thing I could say was nothing. Just let the audience absorb and enjoy the moment. Don't try to tell them what they should be thinking. There'd be plenty of time down the line to examine all the elements. Stay in the moment—just let the scenes play out and allow the audience to form its own thoughts.

The crowd was still going berserk, standing up and cleaving the air with their American flags. The U.S. team had piled on top of each other and on Jim Craig, who was still wearing his mask. The Soviet team stood at its own blue line waiting for the ceremonial handshake. They had a collective look not of shock but of bemusement mixed with envy.

When I finally did speak, all I could say was "No words necessary. Just pictures."

AFTER THE GAME, IT was a scramble. Jim Lampley got an interview with Herb Brooks. The production people had to start editing for a late-night highlight show that would air after the tape of the entire game would run from 8–11 Eastern. And in the arena, they were clearing out the building because the teams from Sweden and Finland were getting ready to warm up for their eight o'clock game and a new crowd, those with tickets for the second game, would be coming in. There was no time for me to reflect. In a few more minutes, I'd be going back to work.

It might seem nutty now but in the television world of 1980, you lived in fear of a technical problem or tape issue or transmission snafu that could become disastrous in a worst-case scenario. Roone Arledge could never have enough backup material as insurance. We'd call it "filling Roone's saddlebags." And on this night, "filling Roone's sad-dlebags," meant that immediately after this incredible, historic upset,

Ken Dryden and I remained in place to announce on tape the entire Sweden-Finland game for the next two and half hours. That's right—while the entire country watched the U.S.-USSR game on tape delay, starting roughly forty-five minutes after it had ended—we were back up on that rickety platform, trying to concentrate on a game that was going to nobody. We called it as if it were live, but it was going nowhere but to a tape machine—unless along the way somehow there would be a technical problem with the airing of the U.S.-Soviet tape.

During the game, I was thinking that a lot of people had kept from finding out the final score of the U.S. game and boy, are *they* in for a treat. It wasn't that hard to keep from finding out the result beforehand. Remember, it was 1980. There was no Internet, no Twitter, no Facebook. ESPN just had started, but it was available in just a small slice of the country. Plus, we had passed the window for the evening news on the networks. Here's how Jim McKay put it that night on the air as he introduced the game: "If there's only one person in this country who doesn't know how this event will turn out, I'm not going to be the one to tell it to him. We've had mail and phone calls from you telling us that's the way you want it." And that's the way they got it.

When the Sweden-Finland game ended, I walked back to the Hilton, alternately exhilarated and exhausted. The first person I ran into was Linda, who was standing with a producer. "*Fantastic* line at the end," the producer said. "Perfect, just perfect!"

"Uh, thanks." I had no idea what I'd said. At the end of the game, the only thing I had been concentrating on was getting the play-by-play perfect.

That night in the Olympic Village, there was at least one American athlete so pumped up from the win that he couldn't get to sleep for hours afterward. Then he *overslept* the next morning—and nearly missed his event. Fortunately, Eric Heiden got to the speed skating track just in time to warm up and go on to his fifth gold medal of the Lake Placid Olympics, the 10,000 meters.

As far as the team was concerned, the guys went back to the Olympic Village that night. How was this getting played back to them? What was the feedback? Maybe a few phone calls, but again, there was no Internet, no cell phones, and a finite number of pay phones. What was the early overall perspective? There was no cable TV. Television coverage was from local affiliates in Burlington, Vermont, or Plattsburgh, New York. If it was possible for an Olympic Games to be relatively isolated, this was the one.

The enormity and the magnitude of what the American team did would be borne out two decades later when *Sports Illustrated* called this game "The Top Sports Moment of the 20th Century." It took time for it all to register. But in Lake Placid, there was more work to be done. The upset of the Soviets has often been referred to as the "gold medal game"—it wasn't. The United States still had a game to play forty hours later on Sunday morning against Finland. And because of the system in which teams carried points earned from the preliminary round into the medal round, if the Soviets had beaten Sweden and the United States had lost to Finland, it was possible that the Soviets could still win the gold, and the Americans would be relegated to the silver or bronze. I remember thinking that if the Americans lost on Sunday, the bloom would not only be *off* the rose, the rose might as well be in a weed patch.

And in fact, the United States would trail Finland that Sunday morning, 2–1, at the end of the second period. The third period was just a couple of minutes away when just before the team headed back to the ice, Herb Brooks looked at his players and delivered a line for the ages: "If you lose this game, you'll take it to your fucking grave." For my money, the greatest pep talk ever. Truer words could not have been spoken.

The team began the third period with a great burst of energy and tied it, 2–2, on a goal by Phil Verchota two minutes, twenty-five seconds in. A little more than three minutes later, Rob McClanahan would score to give the U.S. team its first lead of the game. Five minutes from the gold medal, Verchota would be sent to the penalty box. The Finns had a great opportunity to tie up. But with 3:35 to go, Mark Johnson scored a shorthanded goal to make it 4–2.

As the horn sounded. I exclaimed, "This impossible dream comes *true*!"

On the prime-time Olympic wrap-up show that night, Jim McKay asked me, "How do you think what we've witnessed here will be looked upon down the road?"

I responded, "Whenever something out of the ordinary happens, there's always this immediacy. There's a part of you that wants to say, *'It's tremendous! It's the greatest! We'll never again see anything like this!'* You can't say that right now. We need some time. But I have a feeling this is going to wear pretty well down the line." In my heart, I was certain it was going to wear *really* well.

For years after those Olympics, I would receive letters from people telling me how much the hockey team's exploits had meant to them. At first, I thought, *Why are you telling this to* me? *I didn't play.* Then it occurred to me: these folks couldn't write to the team. People could figure out where to write to me. The team had no such address. When it all ended, the Olympic team disbanded, and the players and coaches went in different directions. (In this case, some to the NHL and professional hockey, others back to school or into the workplace.) So there was no way to reach out to them collectively. They had no single mailbox. I was a conduit, a link to that link—and my address at ABC Sports was easy to find. I still have many of those letters and relish reading them from time to time.

Here we are more than thirty years later and Lake Placid still resonates. Americans of a certain age can recall where they were on December 7, 1941, or when President Kennedy was assassinated, or when the Challenger exploded, or certainly September 11, 2001. And those of a certain age also remember where they were when the U.S. hockey team beat the Soviets in 1980. One huge difference, of course, is that this is a happy memory. Ed Swift covered the Miracle on Ice for *Sports*

Illustrated and wrote in his end-of-year piece when *SI* named the team "Sportsmen of the Year"—"It made you want to hug your television set." Perfectly put.

A good part of what has made that game so enduring and so endearing was the context. The Cold War had been coming and going for years but was pretty frigid at that point. The Soviet Union had invaded Afghanistan. We were threatening—and would follow through on—a boycott of the 1980 Summer Olympics in Moscow. (As quid pro quo, the Soviets would boycott the 1984 Summer Olympics in Los Angeles). In the fall of 1979, you couldn't turn on the news without hearing a menacing report about U.S.-Soviet relations and the possibility of a military confrontation.

At present, it's distinctly different. Among the lessons 9/11 taught us: it doesn't take a country or a huge army to wreak havoc. You can have a small group of maniacal terrorists. Today, who could be our archenemy in an Olympic Games? It's not as if al-Qaeda fields sports teams.

Also of note in February 1980: fifty-two American citizens were being held hostage in Iran. That crisis had started three months before the Olympics and would last until January 1981. To millions of Americans and people around the world, our country looked inept; we were also in a recession and the prime rate was nearing 20 percent (how crazy does that sound today?); in some parts of the country, gasoline was being rationed and long lines at service stations were becoming the norm. All in all, it seemed as if there was a collective malaise from sea to shining sea.

In addition, after the Vietnam War had ended and throughout the seventies, patriotism wasn't considered particularly cool, especially among the younger generation. There was a genuine rift. During the 1976 baseball season, two fans, a father and son, ran onto the field at Dodger Stadium carrying an American flag that they then attempted to light on fire. Rick Monday—the same Rick Monday who was a year behind me at Arizona State, a former Marine Corps Reservist who was then with the Chicago Cubs—ran over and grabbed the flag before it could be ignited.

I remember saying in an interview after Lake Placid that we went from attempts at burning flags to waving flags. That's what Lake Placid did. I'm not alone in thinking that the hockey team, at that particular time, had a lot to do with how we felt about ourselves and our homeland.

There was no way I could have predicted that decades later people would come up to me on the street and say, "I can't tell you how excited I still get when I hear, *Do you believe in miracles?*" (I still often get asked to record messages for answering machines. Al, can you please say, "Do you believe Bob is away from his desk right now? Yes!!!") When they made the film *Miracle,* the director, Gavin O'Connor, told me, "Thanks for giving us the title."

Over the years, I've stayed in touch with a number of the players. There have been dozens of corporate events where I've been brought in to moderate a discussion with some of the guys as part of a program that would often start with a highlight tape. The response from the audience is always terrific and never gets old. A few years ago, I ran into Dave Silk, who along with Mike Eruzione, Jim Craig, and Jack O'Callahan was one of the Boston University players on the team. Immediately before I said, "Do you believe in miracles," I said "Morrow, up ahead to Silk, five seconds left in the game . . ." He told me, "Can't thank you enough for getting my name in there. When people sometimes say, 'You're full of it, you never played on that team,' I tell them, 'Hey, listen—I'm that guy Silk, from 'Morrow, up ahead to Silk!'"

My favorite line, though, might be from the captain, Mike Eruzione. We've stayed close. I was talking to him a few years back and he said, "You know, when I sometimes get a little down, I just pop that tape in. And the greatest thing about it? Every time I shoot, the puck goes in."

CHAPTER 10

Saturdays in the Fall

WHEN I BEGAN WORKING for ABC full-time in 1977, the network had a virtual monopoly on big-time college football coverage. On most weekends from September through late November, college football was my primary assignment. And one of the things I most enjoyed was traveling to, in a manner of speaking, the hinterlands of America. Baseball had taken me to most major American cities. But this was a change of pace—with trips to Tuscaloosa, Alabama; Athens, Georgia; Laramie, Wyoming; and lots of other college towns. And the atmosphere on these autumn Saturdays, when the attendance at these big stadiums would often vastly outnumber the population of the entire town, was special.

ABC's coverage in those days might include, on any given weekend, a national telecast as the second half of a doubleheader with Keith Jackson calling the play-by-play, along with a slate of regional games that would precede it. In 1977, I was normally assigned to the third or fourth most important regional game. Beginning in 1978, I was elevated to the "lead regional," or second most important matchup of the day. But the network didn't want to make an "A" and "B" designation between their two main analysts, so they rotated them each week. That meant that one week my partner might be Ara Parseghian, the fabled former Notre Dame coach, and the next week it might be the iconic former Arkansas coach Frank Broyles, who had remained at the school as its athletic director. I'd also work a couple of games each season with other analysts, including the 1959 New York Giants' number-one draft choice, Lee Grosscup.

In mid-October 1978, I was assigned to do a game that would be played about four miles from our home in Menlo Park. The University of Washington Huskies were coming down to Palo Alto to take on Stanford. My broadcast partner for this one was Frank Broyles. Frank flew into San Francisco the day before the game and we met at about noon at the athletic department office on the Stanford campus. We would have a meeting with the head coach, watch a little film, say hello to a few players, watch part of practice, and then head to our production meeting. Standard procedure would be to have the meeting at the crew hotel but, in this case, since it was a home game for me, I was happy to host the meeting at our house. When our crew of about ten people was ready to leave the campus and head to our home, I told Frank to hop into my car for the ten-minute drive.

For the first five minutes of the trip, we talked about our meeting with the head coach. Broyles, who was one of the most revered coaches in the history of college football, said, "I have never met a more impressive young coach in my life. He is very, very special. What a brilliant mind. He will go on to achieve great things. I just loved listening to what he had to say."

Frank had never before met the coach, whom I'd actually gotten to know a little bit back in Cincinnati. When I was announcing the Reds' games, from time to time the Bengals would have a short afternoon practice at Riverfront Stadium and then vacate the field in time for the Reds, who'd be playing a night game, to come out for batting practice. On a few of those occasions, this coach, then an assistant under Paul Brown, would stick around to watch Rose, Bench, Perez, and company take their swings. He loved baseball. I had three or four conversations with him around the batting cage in Cincinnati.

Now here it was, a few short years later, and he was the head football coach at Stanford—the same man who had just, with his intellect, blown away Frank Broyles. His name, of course, was Bill Walsh—and you know the rest. The following year, he'd be hired by the San Francisco 49ers and would go on to win three Super Bowls over a ten-year run, eventually get inducted into the Pro Football Hall of Fame, and inarguably go down as an innovative genius and one of the great football coaches in history. It had taken Frank Broyles all of about forty-five minutes to figure it out.

So, after Frank had raved about Bill Walsh for half the short ride to my home that afternoon, for some reason—and I can't remember why—our conversation drifted to politics. "You know," he said, "we have this attorney general back in Arkansas who next month will be running for governor, a very bright young man who is something special. I know this may sound kind of crazy but I truly feel that one day he could become president of the United States." That's right. Before he'd even been elected governor of Arkansas (then voted out, and voted back in), Frank Broyles had already turned in his scouting report on Bill Clinton.

A postscript to that story: Fast-forward fourteen years, to 1992. I hadn't spoken with Frank for several years—he had long since left ABC and was still in Fayetteville as Arkansas's athletic director. I was eight seasons into *Monday Night Football*. It was the morning after Election Day and William Jefferson Clinton had just been elected as the next president of the United States. I *had* to get Frank Broyles on the phone.

"Frank," I said when I reached him late that afternoon, "do you remember in 1978 when you told me that Bill Walsh was the most impressive young coach you'd ever met?"

"Did I?" he replied modestly.

"And then you told me how impressed you were with that young attorney general in Arkansas, a guy named Bill Clinton?"

"Well, I remember thinking highly of him," he responded, still trying to play it down.

"Yes, you did," I reminded him. "So Frank, now that Walsh is headed to the Hall of Fame, and Clinton is headed to the White House, I'm calling you for only one reason.

"Who do you like in the fifth tomorrow at Santa Anita?"

I ALSO LOVED WORKING with Ara Parseghian—even if I came into the experience primed for the opposite. In the autumn after I'd graduated from college, in 1966, Michigan State played Notre Dame in another one of those "Games of the Century." Notre Dame was No. 1 in the nation and undefeated; Michigan State was No. 2 and undefeated. It was 10–10 late in the fourth quarter, and on Notre Dame's last drive, Parseghian played it very conservatively and the teams finished in a tie. Each school wound up the season, 9-0-1. (Dan Jenkins of *Sports Illustrated* wrote that Parseghian chose to "tie one for the Gipper.") Watching on television, I hated what I had seen. What kind of coach plays for a tie? So for years after that, I relished watching Parseghian's teams get beat—including one particularly memorable instance in 1972, when USC crushed Notre Dame 45–23, with Anthony Davis, then a sophomore, scoring six touchdowns, including two on kickoff returns. (The *Los Angeles Times* headline the next day: "Davis! Davis! Davis! Davis! Davis! Davis!")

Well, barely more than a decade later, we were paired together in the broadcast booth—and Ara turned out to be one of my all-time favorite partners. Eventually I got around to telling him my feelings when we first had met about what he'd done in that Michigan State game and we laughed about it. Ara gave me the same explanation he gave countless other times—that he didn't think his injury-riddled team could move the ball against the Spartans, and he didn't want to risk giving them the ball back. And that he "didn't *go* for the tie—the game ended in a tie."

One of the great things about this decorated coach who'd won two national championships at Notre Dame was that he had a terrific sense of humor—and that very much included about himself. One time—I believe it was in Ann Arbor, before a Michigan game—we were asked to show up for a dinner the night before the game to shake hands with a bunch of Michigan boosters and ABC sponsors. This was something we were asked to do with some frequency, and we were always happy to help out our sales department. On this particular occasion, I was asked to introduce my broadcast partner. So I took the mike and said, "Ladies and gentlemen, it's a pleasure to introduce my partner, a man who, in the history of college football has few, if any, equals. His record speaks for itself. Nowadays, the term *genius* is tossed around much too often and easily. But when it comes to Ara Parseghian, the *genius* label is a perfect fit. After all, can you think of a coach—any coach—who could possibly limit Anthony Davis to six touchdowns in one afternoon?"

Ara laughed harder than anyone.

OVER THE YEARS, I was also paired many times with Lee Grosscup, who, like Ara, was a fabulous partner. Grosscup had been the first-round pick of the New York Giants in 1959, which is a story unto itself. A quarterback at the University of Utah in the late 1950s, Grosscup utilized the shovel pass—basically a short flip two or three yards forward—in an offense that was advanced for its time. It was a heckuva way to build up your passing statistics. The Utah games, though, were rarely televised then, and NFL teams didn't exactly have intricate scouting networks—plus there was no NFL combine at that time where, as is the case today, every prospect's time in the shuttle run and performance in the bench press would be scrutinized ad nauseam.

In the fall of 1957, Utah played Army at West Point and "Cupper," as everyone still calls him, had a fantastic day. I actually was there that afternoon—my brother and I had ridden up with our father. Utah lost, 39–33, but the next day the *New York Times* had a big, glowing tribute to Grosscup in its game story and in 1959, essentially on the basis of that performance, the Giants drafted Grosscup in the first round. Unfortunately, while he was extremely well liked by his teammates, as Frank Gifford would later recount to me, Lee never would replicate his college success in the pros and wound up playing for teams like the Hartford Charter Oaks of the Continental Football League and the Saskatchewan Roughriders of the Canadian Football League. By the time his playing career was over, he had played for seven teams in four leagues. In Hartford, Lee was a player-coach, and once said that he knew it was time to leave when people couldn't decide if they hated him more as a player or as a coach.

When his career ended, he became an analyst and had a wonderful way with words, supplemented by a phenomenal memory. Lee was my partner for the first college football game I ever worked for ABC—San Diego State at Arizona in Tucson.

Lee also rolled with the punches. On a trip to Jacksonville for a Georgia-Florida game, he and I were asked to speak at a booster dinner the night before the game. The emcee went into a long, detailed, adulatory introduction for Lee, mentioning all of his achievements and honors. And then, the big finish. "Ladies and gentlemen, please welcome . . . Lou Crosscut!" Lee didn't miss a beat as he took the microphone.

Grosscup has a tremendous sense of humor, and we constantly made each other laugh. We had our own code phrases and sometimes dropped references into our broadcasts that only we understood. One Saturday, we worked a UCLA–Washington State regional telecast in Pullman. Washington State is located in what is known as the Palouse, a region of eastern Washington. The name itself can make you laugh.

We decided to ask some locals if they could explain what the Palouse was.

"Sure, there's the Palouse River and the Palouse apples and . . ."

"Right, but do you know what it means?"

We asked eight or nine people at a restaurant the night before the game. No one knew. Turns out it's an Indian word meaning gentle, rolling hills.

Well, as the broadcast started with a sweeping view of the stadium and surrounding landscape, I couldn't resist, fortunately not while on camera, opening with, "I'm Al Michaels and we are in Palouse Country. . . ."

Lee immediately started laughing. And when he started laughing, I started laughing. It went downhill from there. We were laughing so hard that we both had to hit our "cough" buttons—muting our microphones—so the audience couldn't hear us. I tried to start thinking of the worst events in world history to get myself to stop laughing.

Then, just as we were about to recover and get back to the game, our producer in the truck barked into our headsets, "What the hell is going on up there?" Which only made us more hysterical. We eventually got through it. Barely. Here we were—two grown men who might as well have been sitting in the back of a tenth-grade classroom—with the adolescent giggles. Everyone needs one friend like that.

I GOT TO COVER some sensational college football games, including a rivalry game, Georgia versus Florida, played annually in Jacksonville, that due to its legendary tailgating scene is known as the "World's Largest Outdoor Cocktail Party." In 1980, Georgia's big star was freshman running back Herschel Walker. Florida had a senior wide receiver, Cris Collinsworth, whom I'd get to know pretty well, you might say, some three decades later. Walker carried the ball 37 times that day for 238 yards, and the Bulldogs won, 26–21, thanks to a Lindsay Scott 93-yard catch-and-run touchdown with just over a minute remaining. The Bulldogs would go on to win the national title.

There were also a few stinkers. In 1985, I was in Ames, Iowa, home of Iowa State University, for a game between Iowa and Iowa State. Though the two schools were in different conferences, it was a natural in-state rivalry. The visiting Hawkeyes had a great team and were ranked in the top five in the country. It was a monstrous blowout—the final score was Iowa 57, Iowa State 3. On top of that, though the game was in late September, it was a raw, cold, nasty day, and by the third quarter almost everyone had left the stadium. Our sideline reporter was Al Trautwig, who's always had a great sense of humor. With less than a minute left in the game, I sent it over to Trautwig for his final report and he was sitting in the top row of the stadium, in the end zone. The camera started on a close-up of Al and then pulled back so you could see that he was sitting directly underneath the scoreboard.

"You might be wondering what I'm doing here, Al, sitting right beneath the scoreboard," Trautwig said. Then he looks over his shoulder straight at the clock and says, "Well, I just want to be the first person in the stadium to know when this game is over." Classic!

On the flip side, there was a game in September 1982 that I called between Michigan State and Illinois at Memorial Stadium in Champaign, Illinois. Early in the second quarter, the referee, a Big Ten official by the name of Richard McVay, suddenly fell on the field and lay there motionless. McVay was fifty-five, had recently lost seventeen pounds, and had passed a preseason physical. He'd suffered a massive heart attack. The crowd remained silent as the game was delayed for almost twenty minutes while he was attended to. Then, an ambulance drove out to the middle of the field and McVay was taken to a local hospital. On the air, I had to remain very careful. There would be no speculation. There would be no secondhand information. Minutes later, the game would resume. I said something to the effect of "Well, I don't know how anybody—the players, the coaches, the fans, the rest of the officiating crew, anybody—can concentrate on the rest of this game. But it's going to start again."

Meanwhile, somewhere in the south that day, ABC's "A" game was being produced by Chuck Howard, with Keith Jackson doing the play-by-play. Chuck oversaw all of the network football coverage. About a half hour after our game was restarted, during a commercial break, my producer, Ken Wolfe, told me that Chuck had heard that the referee had died.

"How does Chuck know that?" I asked.

Apparently someone on Chuck's crew had spoken to someone at the hospital.

"We can't report that."

Wolfe was in total agreement. How would we know whether this was fact or rumor? But even more important, what if McVay *had* died? Do we know if anyone had contacted his wife and family or next of kin? We certainly didn't. And we knew that he was from Columbus, Ohio, and that this regional telecast would be on the air in his hometown.

Howard told Wolfe that he was instructing Keith Jackson to announce it on their game, which was airing in the South. And that we should do it as well. We refused. Our feeling was, who gives a damn about where an audience hears something first? Here was a man who might have died—or might not have—but there was nothing more important than absolute verification and direct notification of his family and certainly not from television.

It turned out that Richard McVay did die at the hospital. The news would be announced soon enough but certainly not by our crew until we were absolutely certain his family had been informed.

Again, I go back to the "you heard or read it here first" nonsense. The audience and readership doesn't care. It's nothing but a "look at me, look at me" vanity play on the part of broadcasters and newspapers.

That game marked the second time in 1982 I had gone to the Midwest and ended up reporting on a tragedy. In mid-May I'd gone to Indianapolis to cover the time trials for the upcoming Indianapolis 500. My broadcast partners were Jackie Stewart, the legendary Formula One champion; Sam Posey, a very accomplished racer himself; and Chris Economaki, who edited a popular racing newspaper, and had for years been covering the scene in the pits for ABC.

Among those trying to qualify that afternoon was Gordon Smiley, who was thirty-six years old and had finished 25th and 22nd in the "500" in appearances over the prior two years. Qualifying consists of running four laps by yourself around the Indianapolis Motor Speedway at speeds well in excess of 200 miles per hour.

Smiley went out to warm up and on his second warm-up lap, as he exited the long back straightaway and entered the third turn, his car began to oversteer. In a flash, a gradual left-hand turn became a violent right-hand turn, which sent him into the outside wall nose-first at nearly 200 mph.

The car virtually disintegrated and the fuel tank exploded. All you could do was say a prayer.

At that moment, we weren't on the air live. We were taping some of the earlier qualifying runs and we were still an hour or so away from our live show. Our crew then scrambled to build a package about a man who had lost his life, and, among other things, choose which portions of the footage needed to be edited out because they were simply too graphic. I opened the broadcast, reported what had happened, and then brought in Stewart and Posey for their thoughts. Then we went to the pits. Chris Economaki interviewed one of Smiley's crew members. His whole crew was in shock. Frankly, we all were. It was a horrible thing to witness. It took me several days to get some of the images out of my brain. Then it was time to resume our coverage of the qualifying, not that anyone could concentrate.

But I'll never forget Jackie Stewart's description. He said, "This is like an aircraft accident." It was.

Sports are mostly a lot of fun and a diversion, but tragedy occasionally intrudes. And those moments present a large challenge for announcers and production crews. They're almost always completely unexpected and there's no "how-to" guide. I've found that the best way to handle these moments is to let my heart lead me. You're looking at a man who may be dying? It's not a time for acting. Be natural. If you express emotion, or trip on your words a bit, the viewers will understand. And never speculate. Just tell the viewer what you know, not what you think.

And then, if and when the action eventually resumes, echo the mood in the play-by-play. Don't get excited about too much. Realize that the relevance of anything that subsequently takes place is pretty minimal. Just go on and get through it.

Oh, and something to always avoid—the phrase "This puts everything into perspective." I detest that cliché. Everything—and certainly sports—should *always* be kept in perspective. We don't need a tragedy or a disaster to remind us.

CHAPTER 11

The One and Only

THE FIRST TIME I met Howard Cosell, I wound up replacing him. It was in San Antonio in March 1977, at an event called the United States Boxing Championships. ABC had made a deal with promoter Don King and *Ring* magazine to stage a tournament to determine the best American fighter in each weight division. But in fact, after the tournament had gotten under way, signs of improprieties and shady dealings were emerging. (In a Don King enterprise? *Really?*) Sooner than later, it would be determined—in part thanks to the investigative work of Alex Wallau, an ABC executive who would become my best friend not long after, and to this day still is—that King was using the tournament, and the money and exposure coming from it, to sign the best fighters to exclusive contracts. Furthermore, *Ring* magazine was falsifying records and inflating rankings to get a number of fighters into the tournament for King. Word was circulating that the United States Congress (!) was about to launch its own investigation. The night before the next installment of the event in San Antonio, no one was sure of anything, but ABC was leaning toward keeping its best-known boxing commentator—a man who prided himself on a scrupulous set of morals when it came to sports—off the coverage. That announcer, of course, was one Howard Cosell. And so I was flown in at the last moment as the potential replacement. Howard was already in San Antonio.

When I arrived in Texas that evening, I had dinner with Howard and the production crew. It wasn't my first experience in boxing— back in Hawaii, I had announced some small cards put on by a local promoter with the unforgettable name of Sam Ichinose (pronounced "itchy-NOSE-ee"), as well as some cards promoted by Harry Kaba-koff, a real showman from the mainland. To help promote one of those shows, Kabakoff suggested to me a week before the event that I get into the ring to spar with Jesus Pimentel, the Mexican bantam-weight who once fought for a world title. The sparring session was going to be part of a goofy feature piece for my sports report on the six o'clock news. So there I was, climbing into the ring, ready to spar a couple of rounds. At the time, in my mid-twenties, I felt I was in really good shape. This would be fun. Then, after forty-five seconds of dancing with Pimentel, giving and taking some light, gentle jabs, my tongue was hanging out of my mouth, and I was completely out of breath. It became my own version of "No Mas."

Years later, at this dinner in San Antonio, Howard Cosell was very friendly. I was the brand-new kid on the block and it was readily ap-parent that he'd had enough of his other ABC colleagues. With me, though, there hadn't been time for familiarity to breed contempt. Sure enough, the next day, it was decided by the ABC brass that Howard should be kept off the telecast—things were getting too dicey with Congress at bay—and thus, I would be ringside calling the action.

Howard had left a law career in the 1950s to get into broadcast-ing, initially on ABC radio. Later, he'd risen to fame on *Wide World of Sports* with his frequent interviews with Muhammad Ali. But it was on *Monday Night Football* where he became a full-fledged mega-celebrity, possessing a much larger profile than many of the athletes he covered. And then working with him from 1977 through 1985, I learned what a charming, brilliant, bitter, confounding, complex, and maddening figure he could be—sometimes, it seemed, all at once.

Howard never held most of his colleagues in high regard. He would always mock Jim McKay. When the Munich massacre began unfolding at the 1972 Olympic Games, with the hostage-taking of the Israeli contingent of coaches and athletes, Roone Arledge selected McKay for the anchor seat for ABC's coverage. Cosell always deeply resented that he wasn't the chosen one, and he *never* let it go. He'd refer to McKay behind his back as "the diminutive one" and "the one who shouldn't have been there." McKay, meanwhile, would wind up winning an Emmy—for news!

Howard thought that Keith Jackson was bombastic, an announcer of little substance whose legacy was nothing more than terms like "big uglies in the trenches." He had little regard for Chris Schenkel, as fine as gentleman as you could meet. And he basically loathed his longtime *Monday Night Football* partner Frank Gifford. "The human mannequin" was one Cosell description of Frank. He resented everything about him, especially his close friendship with the boss. "Roone's bobo," he'd call Gifford.

While Howard spent a good deal of time excoriating the other ABC announcers, he was okay with me at the time. I think he recognized the Rascal. He saw that I was willing to question authority, and that I wasn't reluctant to offer opinions, even if they sometimes went against the company line. We would wind up having some great times together. I enjoyed his company for the most part, especially in the earlier years. I liked his wife, Emmy. And while Howard irritated plenty of broadcast partners by smoking cigars in the booth, it never bothered me—and eventually I finally figured out why. When my father had taken me to Ebbets Field and Madison Square Garden decades earlier, the air had always been filled with cigar smoke. So that smell took my brain back to my childhood.

When Cosell was on the road, he usually brought only one jacket with him: the Tweety Bird yellow blazer that ABC Sports inexplicably decided would be the signature piece of our on-air wardrobe. And he'd wear it everywhere. Here was one of the most recognizable men in America at the time, going around town with a blazer you could see from the next state over. He'd complain that he couldn't go *anywhere* without being recognized but, *really,* that was the way he wanted it.

Cosell and I worked together on a number of *Monday Night Baseball* games in the late seventies, and then our pairing became more regular in 1981. This was the year that the players went on strike in the middle of the season. Days before the work stoppage, we were in Kansas City, where the Yankees would be playing a Monday night against the Royals. Howard and I both arrived at the Alameda Plaza Hotel on Sunday afternoon. The phone rang in my room, and I heard that familiar, unmistakable voice.

"Alfalfa. *What* are you doing?"

Of course it was Howard calling, using the nickname that Bob Uecker had originally conferred on me. Howard had stolen the moniker and began to believe that he had copyrighted it.

"Nothing," I said. "What's up?"

"DINN-uh," he growled. "Let's go to the Savoy Grill for DINN-uh."

And so a half hour later, we were walking into the Savoy Grill—Howard wearing that hideous yellow jacket, as usual. And par for the course, Howard consumed at least four or five glasses of vodka on the rocks before the food ever came. Howard could hold his liquor very well, but by the end of dinner, he'd had an aquarium's worth.

In those years, the so-called golden years of ABC Sports, ground travel was exclusively by limousine. And in Kansas City, the one company that ABC had utilized for years not only had basic limos, but they were stark white and twice the average size. We also had a regular driver in Kansas City—a woman in her mid-fifties named Peggy, who had been driving ABC personnel for years.

Howard and I finished dinner at around 8:45, and as we walked outside the Savoy, it was still twilight. We got into the backseat as Peggy began to drive us back to the hotel through local surface streets. The route took us through a gritty, inner-city section of Kansas City, and soon we came to a traffic light. On the sidewalk to our left, we saw two kids, maybe sixteen or seventeen years old, in the middle of a serious fistfight, surrounded by a knot of other teenagers egging them on.

Suddenly, Howard opened his door and began to get out of the limo. Peggy screamed, "Mr. Cosell! Mr. Cosell! No!" I tried to grab him. It was too late. He was out of the car and onto the sidewalk.

At this point in my life, I have a wife, an eleven-year-old son, and a seven-year-old daughter. Worst-case scenarios start racing through my mind. *If they jump him, am I really going to fight a pack of teenagers to stick up for Howard Cosell? Do I tell Peggy to drive away as fast as she can?* There are no cell phones in 1981—you can't call a cop.

So now, Howard is standing on the corner—signature toupee on his head, cigar dangling from his mouth, ridiculous yellow blazer making him impossible not to notice. Suddenly the fight stops. The kids are looking at him, dumbfounded—each wearing this look of suspended animation, eyes and mouths wide open. They're incredulous. It's as if everyone, in unison, is saying, "WHAT THE #%$*^&!"

Howard certainly had their attention. And then, he began to speak. Feel free to do your own imitation of his voice here in your head. "Now LISTEN. It's quite apparent to this TRAINED observer that the young southpaw does NOT have a jab REQUISITE for the continuation of this fray. Furthermore, his opponent is a man of IN-FERIOR and DIMINISHING skills. This confrontation is halted POSTHASTE!"

Total silence followed. Then came the moment of truth. "Howard Cosell? Howard Cosell!" one kid said. An instant later, they were all dancing around him like he was a maypole. Somehow, a pen got produced and the next thing you know, Howard was signing autographs and patting the kids on their heads.

Real life had been officially suspended.

Howard then got back into the limo, closed the door, and leaned back against the headrest with total satisfaction. Peggy was still in a state halfway between shock and disbelief. I was just happy to be alive.

What Peggy and I had just borne witness to was so insanely surreal that we were rendered temporarily speechless.

Peggy then drove off, and about a block down the street, she looked back at Howard through the rearview mirror.

"Mr. Cosell," she said. "Excuse me, but I have to tell you something. I have been driving for twenty-five years. I thought I had seen *everything*! I have never seen *anything* like that."

Howard took a long, deep drag on his cigar. He looked straight ahead.

"Pegaroo," he said. "Just remember one thing. I *know* who I am."

OFTEN WHEN HOWARD AND I worked baseball together, we were joined in the booth by Bob Uecker. The concept was that Uecker was supposed to play the role of Don Meredith for the *Monday Night Baseball* telecasts. Johnny Carson, who had brought Uecker on as a guest close to a hundred times, once said that Bob might just be the single funniest man ever. He's certainly in the argument. To this day, almost anything out of Bob Uecker's mouth makes you belly-laugh.

Uecker has always had a collection of great lines, a lot them revolving around how inept a player Bob was during his career in the sixties. ("I signed with the Milwaukee Brewers for $3,000. That bothered my dad at the time because he didn't have that kind of money." Or, "I hit a grand slam off Ron Herbel and when his manager, Herman Franks, came out to get him, he brought Herbel's suitcase.") And

Uecker's always been quick with a rejoinder. That came in particularly handy when he was in the booth with Cosell.

Howard's knowledge of baseball could probably best be described as shallow. He thought he knew everything about the game, but he really knew very little. If Cosell was in the booth for a Monday night Yankee game in May, with the opposing team leading 8–1 in the third inning, he might be expected to say that the Yanks should bring in Goose Gossage to put out the fire. There was little use explaining to Howard that, no, in the third inning, with the Yankees trailing by seven, it would border on insanity to call on their best reliever, a pitcher who would end up in the Hall of Fame. To Howard, the conventional analyst was just another dumb jock. He was Howard Cosell! He knew better.

In the early eighties, the three of us were doing a game at the Astrodome in Houston. At one point, late in the game, Cosell, as he was wont to do, called for a bunt, even though it was a situation in which no one would *ever* bunt. Uecker wanted to mildly chide Howard, but knew he had to be careful. "Well, Howard, I'm not really sure you want to bunt here," Uecker said gently. And he went on to explain why.

Howard responded (and again, try to hear how Howard would articulate this in your brain), "Uecky, I get your point. But you don't have to be so truculent. You *do* know what truculent means, don't you?"

Uecker didn't miss a beat. "Of course, Howard. If you had a truck and I borrowed it, it would be a *truck*-u-lent."

Uecker didn't need a Howard setup to come up with the perfect line. He could also use me as his straight man. Another time, we were talking about Charlie Finley, the eccentric owner of the Oakland A's, and his proposal to manufacture all baseballs the same yellowish orange color as tennis balls. The idea was that the brighter baseballs would be easier for the fans to follow.

"It'll never work," Bob said flatly.

"Why not?" I asked.

"Because," he said in total deadpan, "they could never find enough diseased horses."

NOW IT'S THE LAST weekend of the 1982 baseball season. Three teams were still in contention to win the National League West and make the playoffs: the Dodgers, the Giants, and the Braves. Atlanta held the trump card—while the Dodgers were playing the Giants in San Francisco, the outcome wouldn't matter if the Braves beat the Padres in San Diego—which they did. So Atlanta (managed by Joe Torre) won the division and advanced.

Cosell and I were set to work the National League Championship Series that year, and the third spot in the booth was still to be determined. Roone Arledge was always very big on bringing in someone of the moment, someone topical, someone in the news. So that Sunday night, the call went out from ABC to Tommy Lasorda. Lasorda had come a long way since his days as the manager of the Spokane Indians in the Pacific Coast League—he'd won three pennants with the Dodgers, and a World Series title the previous season. But now, with his club eliminated from the playoffs, would he be interested in a brief sojourn into broadcasting? The answer was yes.

Since he'd "discovered" me in Hawaii, Tommy and I had crossed paths countless times over my years with the Reds, the Giants, and ABC. Now we're together in St. Louis for the National League playoffs. It's the Cardinals versus the Braves. It's baseball in October. Beautiful. Except that Tommy was very nervous. Frankly, he looked petrified. As we rehearsed the opening segment, I had to keep telling him, "Tommy, it'll be okay, you'll be fine."

Cosell opened up the telecast. Then he brought me in. And then I brought Tommy in. We talked with him about the two teams. *The Cardinals do this, the Braves do that. Here are their strengths and weaknesses.* So far, so good. Then Cosell is ready to take us to a commercial.

But before he does—and I'm going to paraphrase here, but not by much—Howard says, "Okay, throwing out the ceremonial first pitch are the children of the late Cardinals third baseman, Kenny Boyer, who succumbed a fortnight ago, at the age of fifty-one, to the ravages of lung cancer. Kenny Boyer fought that insidious disease tooth and nail to the very end. He went to Mexico for laetrile treatments and absorbed more radiation than anyone thought could be humanly possible.

"So when you look at the long and storied history of the St. Louis Cardinal franchise, you can go back and you can have your Rogers Hornsby. You can have your Joseph 'Ducky' Medwick and Jerome 'Dizzy' Dean, as well. You can take Albert 'Red' Schoendienst and, yes, even the Man himself, Stanley Frank Musial of Donora, Pennsylvania.

"Because when it comes to the embodiment of the St. Louis Cardinals franchise, look no further than the countenance of one Kenton Lloyd Boyer. He was a man's man. And we'll miss him."

Howard then lowered his voice another notch. "We'll be back after this."

Know this about Howard. There was nothing he loved more than delivering a eulogy. He would affect a "half-mast" voice. Didn't matter who it was. Cosell wanted to show you how much he knew about the deceased and how well he could put their life into context.

We went to commercial. We turned around. I was sitting on the left facing the field, Howard was in the middle, and Tommy was on the right. We had been using hand mikes—and now we were putting our headsets on. I started jotting something down in my scorebook. Howard, of course, was preening after delivering his Boyer tribute.

Then, I thought I heard sniffling in my headset. Then I heard it again. I looked over at Lasorda—his eyes were moist and I saw little rivulets running down his cheeks. Howard saw it, too, and said, "Tommy! What's the matter?"

Tommy's voice was breaking and he said, "Howard, in the minors, I actually roomed for half a season with Kenny Boyer. I loved him. He was one of my dearest friends. What a man. A tremendous man. Howard, I've never heard a eulogy like that. Only you could do it. That was just beautiful."

There were a few seconds until we were back on the air. Cosell leaned back. He had the cigar going. He looks at Lasorda and then says, "Hey, Tommy, just understand one thing. Kenny Boyer was a *prick*!"

It was quintessential Cosell. Show everyone how smart you are, show that you know every player's middle name—"Stanley Frank Musial, Kenton Lloyd Boyer"—and just make it part of the show.

But it actually calmed Lasorda down. And we went on with the game.

IN 1984, COSELL AND I were in San Francisco to broadcast the baseball All-Star Game. Earl Weaver, who had retired as the manager of the Orioles two years earlier, would join us in the booth. Jim Palmer would be doing dugout interviews. Since Earl had managed in the American League exclusively, he'd not had the pleasure of visiting the dump that was Candlestick Park. It's the day before the game, and the three of us go out to Candlestick for a meeting and to talk to some players. Afterward, in the limo back to the hotel, were Cosell, Weaver, myself, Palmer, and Steve Hirdt of the Elias Sports Bureau. Few people could curse a blue streak in the mold of Earl Weaver. Every third word might be something you wouldn't find in *Webster's*. And this was Earl in the limo: *Jesus Christ, I've never been to a colder fucking place in my life. It's the middle of fucking summer. The wind is blowing forty miles an hour. It feels like it's twelve goddamn degrees. Who built this piece of crap?*

As Earl is ranting, Howard has his eyes closed, and clearly has no interest in any part of the conversation. Or, at this point in his career and life, in any conversation. Howard was worn-out. He didn't want to be with any of us, and we didn't particularly want to be with him. Meanwhile, having worked at Candlestick for several years, I explained it all to Earl. *Back in the fifties, the mayor, George Christopher, knew this developer, Charlie Harney. When the Giants came out here from New York, they needed a new stadium. Harney had this piece of land. What else was he going to do with it? It was basically worthless. He and Christopher were in cahoots. Who knows who got paid what to do what, but it's really simple. Candlestick Park is a monument to political chicanery.*

Howard appeared oblivious.

The All-Star Game is the next night. The telecast wasn't more than a few minutes old when Howard said, as I recall, over a blimp shot, "You're looking at Candlestick Park in San Francisco. Some would say it's a monument to political chicanery. Nevertheless, it is the site of tonight's All-Star Game. . . ."

Howard Cosell could be a lot of things. He could even be a parrot.

Meanwhile, let's talk about Earl Weaver here. Apart from a lifetime membership in the Profanity Hall of Fame, he was a lovable crank. I'd first gotten to know him when I was covering the 1979 World Series for ABC. Earl's Orioles were facing the "We Are Family" Pirates. The Pirates were managed by Chuck Tanner, who, a decade earlier, had been a good friend and mentor as the manager of the Hawaii Islanders.

Before Game 5 on a Sunday afternoon in Pittsburgh, I saw Earl at the batting cage, and he looked rumpled and exhausted.

"Earl, are you all right?" I asked him.

"Jesus Christ. I couldn't get any sleep last night. That fucking hotel we're staying at is so goddamn noisy. Never slept a minute."

"Where are you guys staying?"

"We're staying at a hotel that is so fucking old, they named William Penn *after* the hotel."

An Earl classic.

The Orioles would lose the Series in seven games. Following the

1982 season, Earl retired. (He'd eventually come back for a couple of seasons in the mid-eighties.) Earl was an aggressive manager, rarely relying on small ball but a proponent instead—as he famously put it—of "pitching, defense, and the three run-homer." Earl was intense, lived hard, and had gotten burned-out. He joined us on *Monday Night Baseball* as an analyst for the 1983 season and was pretty good—a little green but full of insight. He was normally very nervous before a telecast. I always figured it was not over the possibility that he'd make a mistake on the air—but that the censors wouldn't have their fingers on the mute button fast enough.

Another thing about Earl: When we would ride out to an airport together the morning after a game, he would always be jotting down a bunch of numbers on a notepad. I figured it obviously had something to do with baseball.

One morning I asked him what he was working on.

Without looking up, he said, "I'm trying to figure out if I have enough money to live on for the rest of my life."

"What?"

"Oh, I do it all the time. I'm just adding in last night's fee."

So here was the legendary Earl Weaver computing his up-to-the-minute net worth. He was a real-time human actuarial table. If there was one of those cartoon thought bubbles over his head, it would have read: *If I lost my job tomorrow, how much longer could I live before the money runs out?*

He didn't need a three-run homer. He needed a winning lottery ticket.

Earl didn't pass away until January 2013 when, at age eighty-two, he had a heart attack aboard a cruise ship. The St. Louis native died on the same day as another legend, Stan Musial.

BY 1983, HOWARD COSELL had reached a new level of surliness. He was choleric and cantankerous, as he might have put it. He'd had enough of *Monday Night Football* and would take himself off the show at the end of that season. In October, at the World Series between the Phillies and Orioles, I met Bob Costas for the first time, before Game 1 in Baltimore. Minutes later, a very youthful Bob also introduced himself to Howard in the press box. "I KNOW who you are," Howard sniffed. "You're the CHILD who RHAPSODIZES about the infield fly rule."

By 1984, Howard was dialing back his schedule, but he'd become the world's biggest pain in the ass. He would arrive on-site in a foul mood and was poisoning the environment. He didn't want to be around people, and people didn't want to be around him. He was threatening not to work the Los Angeles Olympics—he was still angered that, twelve long years before, McKay had been the anointed one in Munich. He'd already announced that he was finished with boxing, so Chris Schenkel would handle that assignment in Los Angeles. Just a day or two before the Opening Ceremony, suddenly Howard showed up but with nothing to do. It was clear to those of us who'd worked with him that he was there in anticipation of a Munich-like event and that *this* time Arledge would see the wisdom of putting him—and not McKay—in the anchor seat. Meanwhile, the Olympics got under way and Los Angeles turned, in a matter of just a couple of days, into Utopia. No traffic, no smog, spectacular weather, terrific competition. Everything seemed perfect and the concern over a terror attack or anything insidious was fading rapidly. Of course, being on the air was like a drug for Howard—so where would he get his fix? I passed him in the hotel lobby on the third or fourth morning of the Games and he muttered something about Schenkel. I heard the word *incompetent*. Typical Howard—just taking another shot at a colleague. Not a day later, of course, Howard showed up at the Los Angeles Sports Arena, the boxing venue. Now we were all hearing that Cosell would announce *some* fights to give Schenkel an occasional breather. Howard was still, at that point, the thousand-pound gorilla. Who was going to tell him "no"?

Need I say more? By the end of the Olympics, Howard would be
calling *every* fight. Schenkel might as well have been on vacation. If
there was a light flyweight preliminary bout between a guy from Ni-
geria and a kid from New Zealand, Howard was your man.

Two months after the Olympics, Cosell, Jim Palmer, and I were
in Kansas City for Game 1 of the American League Championship
Series between the Royals and the Detroit Tigers. Howard came to
town dark and brooding. I love postseason baseball, everyone on that
production crew loved postseason baseball—and there was Cosell
making everyone around him walk on eggshells. The second game
of the series was a four-hour affair, going eleven innings before the
Tigers finally won. At one point late in the game, Howard was calling for a bunt—his favorite piece of strategy. *So what else was new?* To
make matters worse, he'd been in the bar at the Alameda Plaza Hotel
for a couple of hours before we'd even left for the ballpark. And he
had a big plastic cup that was constantly being filled and refilled during the game. It wasn't unusual for Howard to drink during a game,
but this may have been a record.

Palmer and I were attempting to keep Howard from looking like
a complete fool by calling for a bunt in a situation where no manager
would ever bunt. We were working the edges, so as not to embarrass
him on the air—but we couldn't let Howard go on and on. The game
ends and I'm disgusted. We'd had a terrible night. The telecast was
awful, sabotaged by Howard's incessant and often incoherent ram-
blings. Not fifteen seconds after we're off the air, Howard starts to
tell me that he knows far more baseball strategy than anyone, and he
is who he is because he *always* takes a stand. Then, he says to me—
obviously in reference to the fact that I wasn't in agreement with him
on the air—"you need to learn to take a stand."

"Excuse me?" I shouted. "We're protecting your ass. You're sitting
here drinking all night and you've ruined the damn telecast. I'll take
a stand right now, Howard—the next time you're in this shape when

we're doing a game, either you're not going to be there or I'm not going to be there. Is that a good enough stand for you?"

He said nothing and just walked away.

I walked back to the pressroom behind the broadcast booth at Royals Stadium. I'm standing there with Palmer, alternately commiserating and venting, when a sportswriter walks up to the bar and asks the bartender, a woman, for a glass of vodka. As he turns away for a second, she pours him about three drops' worth. When he turns back, he says, "I'll need a lot more than that." At which point she holds up an empty quart bottle of Smirnoff and says, "I'm sorry, sir, Mr. Cosell drank the rest."

The next day, an off day in the series, we got on a plane ABC had chartered to Detroit for Game 3. Palmer and I wanted nothing to do with Howard. We didn't even want to look at him. Thankfully, my old friend Curt Gowdy was broadcasting the series on network radio and we'd invited him to come with us. We also knew that Curt could sit with Howard so neither of us would have to. Also, in the *New York Post* that day, the columnist Dick Young, who'd always detested Cosell, had excoriated him and Howard knew all about it.

We landed in Detroit a little before noon and checked into the Pontchartrain Hotel. An hour later, there's a knock on my door. I open it and there's Howard, cigar burning brightly, walking right past me and settling into a chair. "Alfalfa, I just want to tell you, it was Palmer I was really pissed off at last night. He should have—"

I cut him off. "No, Howard. We were *both* trying to protect you. We were trying to get you off the hook. If Palmer and I think you're totally off base, what are we supposed to do? Are we supposed to say, 'Howard, you're a moron?' We're trying to save you from yourself."

We did the game the next night. The Tigers won and swept the series. I normally want a series to go the distance—more drama. This was the one time I was happy just to get out of town as fast as possible. At the time, the two networks covering baseball, ABC and NBC, alternated coverage of the World Series each year, and it was NBC's turn—so we were done with baseball. Our season was over. A few weeks later, though, with my contract expiring at the end of 1984, I had a meeting in New York with Roone Arledge to talk about a new deal. When we got around to baseball, I told him that it was simple. "Look, I love baseball," I said. "It's been the cornerstone of my career. But I can't share a booth with a guy who doesn't want to be there and prepares for a game in the hotel bar. I can't do it anymore."

Roone said, "I'll promise you this: if Howard does baseball next season, he won't be drinking before the game or during the game." I took him at his word.

I renewed my contract and Howard was back on baseball for the 1985 season and, I must say, Roone's guarantee would hold up. Still, it wasn't a satisfying season. Howard still didn't want to be there. He did half the games, at most, and when he was in the booth, he wasn't Howard anymore. I remember thinking that—to use a line Howard often intoned on the air—he was simply a shell of his former self.

He was, however, nearing completion on a second book about his career. Everyone at ABC Sports knew he was working on it and we were all expecting a hatchet job. In fact, we were all positive about it. In late September, a few days before the book would come out, details began to emerge. Sure enough, Howard was going after everybody at ABC Sports, including, to a certain degree, Roone Arledge himself! Howard might as well have burned himself at the stake. He just didn't care anymore. He gave me a couple of small shots—tweaks, really. But nothing compared to the vitriol he had saved up for most of the others.

That was our year to televise the World Series. But when Cosell's book came out, and his trashing of ABC became public, Arledge had had enough. A week before Game 1 of a World Series that would match Kansas City against St. Louis, he removed Cosell from the broadcasts and replaced him with Tim McCarver. On a personal level, it was the greatest trade in the history of broadcasting.

Just a couple of weeks earlier, Cosell, Palmer, and I had been together for a Sunday afternoon telecast in Minnesota, the Twins against the Royals, that would hardly draw flies, going up against the NFL on CBS and NBC. The crowd was not only small but about half the ABC affiliates around the country weren't even carrying the game. They could make more money with local programming. The rating was minuscule. The game ended and the three of us got into a car to go to the airport in Minneapolis. The dynamic with Cosell all season long had been frosty. Palmer and I headed down one concourse; Howard, stooped over and looking forlorn, down another. We mumbled good-bye to him with a cursory wave.

I didn't know it at the time, but I would never work with him again. In fact, I'd never see him again. Or even speak with him. It was the last time he would ever appear on network television. So think about this: Howard Cosell—this seminal figure in sports television who was larger-than-life, this man who was once one of the most recognizable people in America, who made "just tell it like it is" a catchphrase, and who, two decades after his death, is still being imitated—ended his career with a meaningless Royals-Twins game in September 1985 that got a rating you could only discover with a microscope. That was it. Finished.

We had a lot of fun, especially at the beginning. But Howard always had something eating at him. Even in the good times, no matter the circumstances, it was never enough. If you elected him senator, he'd want to be president. If you made him president, he'd want to be king. If you made him king, he'd want to be God. He ascended to an extraordinary position but never felt the industry was exalted or revered enough for him. Howard Cosell may have known who he was. But he could never be at peace with where he was.

CHAPTER 12

Roone, the Olympics, and the Fight Game

SEVERAL YEARS AGO, *LIFE* magazine named Roone Arledge one of the "100 Most Important Americans of 20th Century." Not just in television. Not just in sports. Most important Americans, period. His influence was wide-ranging. And his mystique—a good part of which was self-orchestrated—added to his legend. Arledge was my boss for my first ten years at ABC. I didn't see him or interact with him very much. But everything we did at ABC Sports—and a lot of what is still done today in television—originated from his philosophy.

For Roone, everything started with storytelling. Storytelling was the tool he used to transform coverage of sports on television. And storytelling was how he elevated ABC—"the third network in a two-and-a-half-network business," as it was once referred to—into a powerhouse. Arledge was also always willing to take chances. Who else would have put demolition derby and motorcycles on ice on *Wide World of Sports*? And who else would have put the polarizing Howard Cosell in the broadcast booth of *Monday Night Football*? Half the audience seemed to love him, half the audience seemed to hate him, but it became must-see TV.

Roone was also the visionary who saw how popular and compelling the Olympics could become as a television event. In 1972 at Munich, under Arledge's supervision, ABC's coverage of the Israeli hostage crisis and tragedy helped to create a template for how breaking news would be covered in the years to come. The network would win multiple Emmy Awards for its coverage.

It was that kind of success that led the network to eventually name Arledge, who had been the president of ABC Sports since 1968, as the head of the news division as well—a move that took place around the time that I was hired by him. And for the ten years that Roone was my boss, he spent 95 percent with the news division. Or at least it seemed that way. Roone was notorious for not returning phone calls—not just calls from nobodies, but from anybody. Meanwhile, no matter what the event was, if it was being covered by ABC Sports, the biggest suite in the best hotel in town was reserved for Roone. Even if it was a Monday night "B" baseball game in Arlington, Texas. Several times I was the beneficiary of that excess. Roone would show up at less than 1 percent of the events. The first time I was assigned to cover the Grand Prix of Monaco, I spent five days getting lost in the eight-room presidential suite at the Hermitage Hotel in Monte Carlo. Roone's secretary was a good pal, and the minute she knew that Roone couldn't possibly make it to an event, she would call me and tell me to check into Roone's room.

My occasional college football partner Lee Grosscup took it as an ironic point of pride that despite announcing close to one hundred games at ABC, he had never met Arledge, his ultimate boss. It became a running joke at the network and throughout college football circles—"Cupper" was going to write a book that would be titled *I Never Met Roone.*

Then in the late summer of 1983, the entire college football operation—producers, directors, announcers—was summoned to New York for a seminar in advance of the season. And Roone, we had understood, would be giving us a pep talk. Well, there goes Lee's book. Lee joked that when Arledge came to speak to us, he would hide in a closet so the title could stay intact.

Then, when we arrived at ABC the morning of the seminar, Chuck Howard, the coordinating producer of college football, stood up and said something to the effect of "Roone apologizes, but something's come up and he won't be able to be here." At which point everybody immediately looked over at Grosscup and starting laughing. *He's saved! His title still works!*

Predictably, Roone was playing golf at Deepdale Golf Club on Long Island. It was quintessential Arledge. Fifty guys are flown in from all over the country to meet with him, and teeing it up with some pals took precedence. Don't get me wrong. Roone Arledge is perhaps the most iconic figure in the history of sports television and deservedly so. But he relished his mystique. In fact, he made it an art form. He might as well have invented "Where's Waldo?"

When your contract would come up, though, Roone would bring you into New York for an audience. You'd meet him at his favorite restaurant in Manhattan, show up at one o'clock in the afternoon, and then have to figure out a way to gracefully leave, because otherwise he'd keep you there until dinner. Even though he was very rarely accessible, when you were in his presence, he could make you feel like the most important person in the world.

As a manager, his approach was this: I'm going to pay my people well, and I'm going to treat them very well. I'm going to have them stay in the best hotels, and provide limousines whenever they're on the road. But I'm going to expect them to do their jobs at the highest level. That way, there will be no excuses when it comes to creature comfort. You'd dine in the best places, you'd sleep in the best hotels, and all Roone wanted was for you to go out and do a great job.

He also let his managers manage. The producers, directors, and production personnel weren't directly under his thumb. He also wasn't opposed to a little office infighting. Sometimes it was unclear whose territory was whose. Then, when a turf war would break out, Roone was usually nowhere to be seen.

Philosophically, he felt this way about sports: A game is a game is a game. But what distinguishes one game from another are the people involved. The players, the coaches, the owners, even the fans. Make the audience care about them. Make the viewer have some sort of emotional attachment to them. That theory still holds up well today.

Dick Ebersol and Don Ohlmeyer were protégés of Arledge. But their styles varied from his. They are hands-on guys. By the time I got to ABC, Roone was not. Yes, in his early years, he was probably the best live producer in the business. But by the time I arrived in the mid-seventies, Roone had become a stranger to the production truck. His limited involvement in sports was exclusively on the business end. The only exception was his first love, the Olympics, where he still "line produced"—meaning that he was the central figure in the broadcast center, and was in the middle of every decision made on the fly. But in 1984, at the Los Angeles Summer Games, I saw firsthand that in live television, even legends can't just parachute in and recapture the magic touch.

The United States had boycotted the 1980 Olympics in Moscow. Now, in 1984, the Soviets and the Eastern Bloc countries were boycotting the Los Angeles Games. Still, there was a lot of excitement in the city where I'd spent my high school years. My primary assignment was a plum—track and field. But the track and field events didn't begin until the second week of the Olympics. So on the opening day of competition, the day after the Opening Ceremony, my assignment was the road cycling races for the men and women.

On each Olympic telecast, Roone would have access to what was known as the "override" button. Each individual sport, like road cycling, had an on-site producer. But with that button, if Roone wanted to talk directly to an announcer, he could override anyone else who had the ability to speak to you in your headset. On that first day of competition, we were live with cycling from Mission Viejo, and there were a number of other events taking place simultaneously—including swimming. One of the featured stars of the Games, the West German Michael (pronounced meek-HILE) Gross, was competing in the 200-meter freestyle, and the plan for our coverage was to show Gross's event on tape in prime time that night. When Gross won the race while cycling was on the air, Roone hit me on the override. "Al, Michael Gross just won his first race. Announce that he's won, and tell the viewers they can see the race in prime time." I didn't say anything—I just continued calling the road race.

Roone then said it to me again—as if he thought I didn't hear him the first time. Again I ignored him. At this point, I was just hoping that Roone was thinking this was a technical issue, and not a case of insubordination. We made it to commercial, and then I hit the talk-back button to respond. "Roone, are you sure about this?" I asked him. "Do we really want to give away the swimming results right now? Don't we want people to tune in in prime time to see the race without knowing who won?"

"You're right!" says Roone. "Great idea."

I'm thinking: *Great idea? Actually, it's pretty fundamental. And since when did Roone Arledge need producing lessons from me?*

The story has always stuck with me. In his prime, Arledge was the best event producer in television, bar none. But apart from the Olympics, Roone had done almost no line producing since the late 1960s. In television, like in most anything else, it's easy to lose your fastball.

A WEEK LATER, TRACK and field got under way, and I was busy around the clock. On the next to last day of competition, I called the women's 3,000 meters along with Marty Liquori, the former middle-distance champion and Olympic runner. This would be the famous Mary Decker/Zola Budd race. Decker, who was perhaps the most famous American female athlete at those Games, and was favored to win, took the lead. Then, about four laps in, Budd, a South African who ran barefoot, and who'd been granted British citizenship to get into the Olympics (remember, South Africa was barred at this point for its apartheid policies), made a move and got to the front of the small lead pack. Decker then made a move to the inside to try to overtake Budd. They clipped heels, got tangled, and in a flash, Decker fell into the infield. She was out of the race, her Olympic dream over, and on the ground crying in agony. Budd kept running, and boos washed over the Coliseum—all aimed at the barefoot eighteen-year-old. She'd become an instant villain.

On the air, Marty Liquori then placed all of the blame on Zola Budd.

As Marty continued, I thought to myself, *He must have seen something that I didn't see. But Marty has had years of international experience. Maybe there's a nuance or arcane rule I'm not aware of.* Still, from my perspective, it didn't appear to be Zola Budd's fault. It looked to me that when Mary Decker came on the inside, Budd had position, and the contact was more incidental than anything. But I regret not pressing Liquori about it on the air. I let it go when I should have been more assertive.

The Decker/Budd rivalry was one of the big story lines *before* the Olympics. And at this moment, it became *the* story of the Olympics. Decker on the ground after four laps, Budd taking the lead, but then fading to seventh place, overtaken by the emotion of the moment, clearing the way for Romania's Maricica Puica to win the race.

The following day guaranteed even more drama at Los Angeles Coliseum on the final day of track and field competition. Headlining the program would be the men's 4x100 meter relay, with Carl Lewis going for a fourth gold medal of these Olympics to tie Jesse Owens's long-standing record. Meanwhile, Marty Liquori had wound up in the crosshairs of the track and field community. Most track and field aficionados did not see the Decker/Budd incident in the way Liquori did. Marty was taking a lot of heat, and so when he got to the Coliseum early that afternoon, he went to Chuck Howard, who was producing track and field, and said that it would be important for us to at some point during our coverage that day take a look back at what had happened the prior night, and allow him to then go through it and provide a better assessment of what had taken place. Chuck agreed.

We were going on the air live at 4 P.M. Pacific Time, with the Carl Lewis race scheduled live for 4:45, or 7:45 P.M. on the East Coast. Every Olympic telecast was always very tightly formatted—there would be coverage of other sports mixed in with track and field, which would also feature the women's 4x100 meter relay, and include a segment previewing the Lewis race, which I would do with O. J. Simpson, our analyst for the men's sprints.

We have a smooth opening to the broadcast. Then, at about 4:10, I do the segment with Marty, and tee him up for his "re-analysis."

Marty was clearly seeing it differently in retrospect, had been able to think about it, and delivered a more cogent and thoughtful analysis about what had taken place the night before. It was a good segment.

But there was a problem that was developing on our end. There was miscommunication somewhere along the line. We had a separate unit at the Coliseum for the track and field production and were feeding everything back into the ABC Broadcast Center in Hollywood, manned by Roone Arledge. The broadcast center was responsible for the overarching format—the responsibility for the flow of the show and the timings being correct. When we had put this extra segment in, there was an assumption that it was being communicated to the broadcast center. Because when we added a four- or five-minute segment, somewhere along the line, before the Lewis race, the broadcast had to drop four or five minutes somewhere else. But for reasons unbeknownst to me to this day, nothing was ever dropped. Either the track and field unit hadn't told Roone that we were adding this apology segment for Marty, or there had been a communication mix-up back at master control. Whatever the case was, as I looked in my "off-air" monitor—the monitor in front of me in the booth that showed me what was on the network—and saw our diving coverage starting on the broadcast, it was becoming clearer and clearer to me that there was a problem arising.

As we moved along, there was another live race we were going to cover—the women's relay at 4:20. I was going to call it with our female sprint analyst, the former champion Wilma Rudolph. She was nowhere to be found.

"Where's Wilma?" I say to the truck.

Nobody knows.

Later we would learn that she hadn't paid attention to the production schedule. She had thought the race was sometime after five o'clock. Whatever. Wilma Rudolph was nowhere to be seen.

"What do you want me to do?" I called down to Chuck Howard.

"Get O.J. in there!" he yelled.

So O. J. Simpson came to the rescue. He hustled into the booth, sat down next to me, put on a headset, and called a race he'd hadn't prepared for. It was chaos behind the scenes but no one watching at home knew, which was what was most important. So we got through that race, but now, I was back to the growing concern over the time schedule.

I'm now looking at my off-air monitor—it's about 4:37ish . . . we're about eight minutes away from the Lewis race. And obviously we're going to need about a four-minute setup to it—to really build it up. I look down at my off-air monitor—and I see it's still the men's 10-meter platform diving preliminaries. *We'll never get out of it in time to get back to track.* 4:38, 4:39, 4:40.

At 4:42—while O.J. and I were supposed to be setting up this big Carl Lewis attempt to win a fourth gold medal—people at home were still watching diving. Is this real? Am I dreaming? *What?* The race was going to start at 4:45. And this was the Olympics, run like a Swiss watch. This was not spring training with the Reds, where Harry Caray could yell down to the field at the umpires to hold up the game.

Now it's less than a minute before the race and Chuck Howard is screaming.

"Start! Start! Start!" he yells in my ear.

"Start what?"

"Just start talking! We'll tape the race."

You'll tape it? Carl Lewis trying to win a fourth gold medal? We're going to tape it? This is nuts.

So thirty seconds before the race, O.J. and I start talking. *Here we are with Carl Lewis, going for another gold medal.* The race starts. We call it. The Americans win in world-record time. And it airs on ABC—fifteen minutes later. This is one of the most anticipated events of the entire Olympics—and it doesn't air live. Today, social media would be all over it instantly. But in 1984, only a few viewers could have figured out that ABC had screwed it up.

It had all started with Marty Liquori's impetuous analysis from the night before. Having to look back at it that afternoon, which added an extra segment to the format, and having it fall through the cracks. Just another story you couldn't make up.

ONE MORE ENDURING MEMORY of the Los Angeles Games came from the first-ever Olympic women's marathon. I covered the race with Liquori and Kathrine Switzer, who'd been the first woman ever to run the Boston Marathon. The race concluded inside the Coliseum—the competitors entering through a tunnel and a little more than a lap before a crowd that numbered in excess of eighty thousand. But because the race spanned 26.2 miles around the city, the best place for us to call a race was from the broadcast center, where we could follow all the action on numerous monitors.

Joan Benoit of the United States, then twenty-seven, won the gold medal. Grete Waitz of Norway took the silver. Then, around twenty minutes later, a Swiss runner, Gabriela Andersen-Scheiss, entered the Coliseum clearly in distress. Beyond exhausted, she was teetering, practically at a 45-degree angle, weaving in and out of the lanes on the track, a baseball cap pulled down low over her face. The fans were going wild, imploring her to finish. Every few seconds, she looked as if she was going to topple over and collapse. This was two years after I'd covered the death of Gordon Smiley, the Indy 500 driver, and Richard McVay, the referee at the Illinois football game. The notion that this woman might die was in the forefront of my mind.

At that point, some security people and several coaches were on the track with her. But if anyone had touched her or assisted her in any way, she would be disqualified. It was a chilling scene—and a real dilemma for the people in close proximity to her.

Meanwhile, we were in the broadcast center, watching this unfold. The pictures were so poignant, there wasn't much to add. The second—and I mean the split second—she crossed the finish line, she was swooped up by personnel and rushed to medical treatment. Fortunately, it all ended up being a heroic moment. And, within minutes, Gabriela was just fine. But it definitely was a challenge to call it live.

AT ITS HEIGHT, ABC'S assemblage of sports was incredibly vast. And once Howard Cosell quit calling boxing around the same time as he gave up *Monday Night Football,* much of our boxing coverage fell into my portfolio.

Boxing has always held a certain fascination for me. There's nothing more raw and basic in sports than two guys entering a ring with nothing but a pair of trunks, a pair of shoes, and a pair of gloves. No teammates. Nowhere to hide. Nowhere to run.

In the eleventh grade, I got into my only lifetime fistfight. I don't even know how it started but it was out on the lunch court at Hamilton High in Los Angeles. If odds had been posted, the other guy would have been a 5-to-1 favorite. But I surprised my opponent with a quick straight left hand to the cheek, and will never forget the feeling of teeth crunching. I scared the hell out of *myself*—and I also ended up causing a five-thousand-dollar dental bill. For a while after that, my friends kid-dingly called me the Toonderbolt (a punch then–heavyweight cham-pion Ingemar Johansson of Sweden had made famous). I soon joked that I would retire undefeated. But it wasn't funny at the time. And that record would have gone down the drain if they'd been scoring my sparring session with Jesus Pimentel a few years later.

At ABC, I did dozens of fights through the eighties, everywhere from Atlantic City to Sarajevo, Yugoslavia, to Caracas, Venezuela, to Dublin, Ireland. There was also a trip to Havana for amateur boxing, where I was told to prepare for a possible visit during the event from El Commandante himself, Fidel Castro. But he never showed up.

And then there was a Saturday afternoon encounter in May 1987 in Port-of-Spain, Trinidad, between the veteran light-heavyweight Marvin Johnson, nearing the end of his career, and Leslie Stewart, who had grown up in Trinidad. Joining me on the air would be my best pal, Alex Wallau, who had made the transition from executive to producer to on-air commentator. Alex knew as much about boxing as anyone on the planet so finally, the ABC powers-that-be figured, why not, let's try him on the air. He would be a perfect fit—he was superb. Years later, Alex would become the president of the ABC Television Network and his business card would be an all-timer: Alex Wallau—President ABC Television Network/Boxing Analyst. And along the way, he would beat stage 4 tongue cancer. Seriously.

Anyway, we couldn't have packed more into our two days in Trin-idad. On Friday night, Alex and I walked to and from a restaurant about a half mile away. It was outstanding. When we got back to the hotel, we asked the desk clerk to recommend a restaurant for the next night. She suggested a spot that was actually next door to the place we'd just come from. And then she warned, "Don't even think about walking there. It's absolutely much too dangerous going through the park after dark." Well, we'd actually unknowingly just walked through that park—the Queen's Park Savannah. My Rolex and two thousand dollars in cash had survived.

The following day, at an outdoor stadium, with the rain coming and going, Stewart wins the fight with an eighth-round TKO. The place goes bonkers. Hundreds of fans storm the ring to celebrate. I'm seated at ringside and get whacked in the back of the head before another guy uses me as a step stool to climb into the celebration. At this point, we're in commercial as I scramble under the ring for safety. My headset is still on as I yell to our producer in the truck, "I'm gonna get killed. Get these animals away. Now!" At the time, even if you weren't on the air, the satellite transmission would pick up everything. So anyone with a dish could hear every word. The next morning, Alex and I had a very early flight to New York and as we boarded, I caught a glimpse of the local newspaper. There I am on the front page under a humongous headline that blared: ABC REPORTER: GET THESE ANIMALS AWAY. That plane couldn't get off the ground fast enough.

That flight to JFK would stop in Barbados. Alex had "discovered" Howard Stern before Howard became the self-proclaimed "King of All Media." At the time Stern was only on in New York and a couple of other East Coast cities, so Alex would tape every show and then send the cassettes to me in Los Angeles. We were his biggest fans. On this trip, Alex had brought along three or four of Howard's most recent shows and we sat there on the plane with dual headsets on, laughing hysterically. On the stop in Barbados, with the Stern tapes still rolling, we notice a small entourage escorting a couple of people onto the plane. We weren't paying much attention. Then we're airborne again, and Alex and I might as well have been rolling in the aisle. We were listening to Stern at his funniest. One row in front of us and across the aisle, a man turns around to see what's going on. We're in convulsions when the man, in clerical garb, smiles. You could tell he was enjoying the fact that we were enjoying whatever it was we were listening to on our earphones. The man was Bishop Desmond Tutu. All Alex and I could think was, *He should only know what we're so hysterical about!* Which, of course, only made us laugh twice as hard. Every ounce of my body ached when we got to New York.

* * *

THEN THERE WAS ANOTHER unforgettable night. April 15, 1985. Thomas Hearns versus Marvelous Marvin Hagler. I called the fight with Al Bernstein. The fight was broadcast live on closed-circuit television, and would then air on tape on ABC several days later. With Mike Tyson's career just beginning, boxing's most compelling stars were the foursome of Sugar Ray Leonard, Roberto Duran, Marvin Hagler, and Tommy Hearns. There had been the Leonard-Duran *no mas* fight. Leonard and Hearns had also staged an epic battle. Hagler and Duran had gone the distance. You had this four-way rivalry and, whatever the combination, you usually had a terrific fight.

So, that night in 1985, it was Hagler and Hearns's turn, with the undisputed world middleweight title at stake. Bob Arum was the promoter, and there'd been a massive buildup. The night before the fight, I remember talking to Alex Wallau, who was producing the telecast, and we both felt Hagler because he wanted it more. Marvin had felt like he had gotten the least respect of the quartet—that he was the Ringo Starr of the Big Four. Sugar Ray was the lead character, Duran was the Latin idol, Hearns was the Hit Man from Detroit. Hagler, who hadn't lost a fight in almost a decade, was from Brockton, Massachusetts, the working-class man with blue-collar appeal, the fighter who wanted to prove he was the best of them all.

There was unbelievable electricity at Caesar's Palace that night, with the outdoor arena erected in the parking lot. The crowd was already in a frenzy when the fighters entered the ring. In all sports—not just boxing—almost always, when there's that kind of buildup, the actual event doesn't equal the hype. Sometimes it doesn't even come close. What still stands out to me about this fight: people couldn't wait for the fight to start, and it totally eclipsed the hype. Some boxing fans felt it might have been the Fight of the Century. Indisputably, Round 1 was one of the great rounds, if not *the* greatest round, of the century.

In most fights, the first round is generally a feeling-out process. One guy might try to sneak in a punch, but it's usually a starter course before the main dish. Not this night. The bell rang and Hagler and Hearns quickly met in the center of the ring and just started whaling on each other. No strategy, no defense, no parrying, no feeling-out process. Just bombs and haymakers.

Am I really seeing this? Fights don't start like this. They were trying to kill each other. This was the purest of back-alley brawls. It took me a good twenty seconds just to wrap my head around what I was witnessing.

And it didn't stop. They kept pounding away. And that night, I saw certain things with the naked eye that were not discernible when I looked at the tape later on. In boxing, sometimes television can't do complete justice to what the naked eye can observe from ringside. Television just can't take you there.

At one point, they were both directly above me. Hearns is on my left, Hagler is on my right. Hearns throws a straight right hand into the left side of Hagler's face. As if in super-slow motion, Hagler's face compresses and contorts and for a split second, I think it's going to cave in. His cheek has become totally concave. The thought flashes through my brain: *He's killed him.* He hit him so hard that it looked like Hagler's whole face would implode.

But then, as in a cartoon, Hagler's cheek popped back into its regular shape, as if nothing had happened. And then Hagler jumped right back on Hearns. I couldn't believe what I was seeing. No one could have absorbed that punch and still be *alive,* much less go back on the offensive. The round ended and my heart—and fifteen thousand other hearts—was beating furiously. I'd just witnessed three insanely exhilarating minutes. Hearns's trainer, Emanuel Steward, couldn't have summed it up better than when he later said that his man "fought twelve rounds in one."

In the second round, which couldn't compare to the first (then again, what could?) but was still a compelling three minutes, Hagler started to bleed badly. As his cornermen worked on the cut after the bell, it became clear that there was a real possibility this fight would soon have to be stopped. If that had happened, the result would have been a technical draw. So Hagler, who in my mind had slightly gotten the better of Hearns so far, knew he needed to finish him off quickly. He moved in for the kill, landed some shots, and Hearns went rubber-legged. At that point, two minutes into the third round, referee Richard Steele stepped in and stopped the fight, and Marvin Hagler had defended his middleweight crown.

I still occasionally look at that fight. This was a case where you had to have the excitement of your voice match the excitement of what you were seeing. But this was a fight that overwhelmed anything anybody had to say. The following week, *Sports Illustrated* featured the fight on the cover. The headline was "Eight Minutes of Fury." A perfect description. Eight minutes no one who was there would ever forget.

HAGLER-HEARNS TOOK PLACE ABOUT a month after Capital Cities bought the ABC network in a surprise deal. One of the first moves the new regime made when they got the keys to the house a little over a year later was to remove Roone Arledge as the head of ABC Sports—he would now hold only one title, President of ABC News (though Roone would negotiate to continue producing the Olympics). In 1986, I was in the first year of a four-year deal. I didn't know exactly what was going to happen, but I wasn't too worried beyond the basic level of anxiety that comes with having a new boss.

Meanwhile, in late 1985, Linda and I decided we would move from the Bay Area to Los Angeles. We had each lost a parent—my father, her mother—in recent years. We wanted to be close to our surviving parents and close to our siblings, and we were both around forty and wanted a midlife change. So we decided to return to Southern California.

Boy, did we pick a hell of a week to make the move. In late January 1986, we moved south, uprooting our teenage son and eleven-year-old daughter in the middle of a school year. In a pouring rainstorm, the moving van arrived twenty-four hours after the Space Shuttle Challenger disaster. And then, just as the truck pulled up to our new home in Los Angeles, I discovered that my new boss at ABC Sports would be a man named Dennis Swanson. Dennis had been running WLS, the ABC affiliate in Chicago, where he'd given Oprah Winfrey her first daytime talk show. Swanson was a former officer in the Marine Corps and had a reputation for being very aggressive—a bull in a china shop kind of guy. So there was a sense that he wasn't going to pay homage to Roone by taking things slowly or being hesitant to shake things up. Still, what came next was a huge surprise.

I'm in my new home in Los Angeles, helping to unpack boxes, when Ken Wolfe, the young producer whom I'd worked with frequently, calls me up. Kenny sounded very excited. "Do you have any idea what's going on here?" he said.

"No."

"Sit down," he said. "You know who is going to do *Monday Night Football*?"

"No. Who?"

"You and me."

"What?"

"I'm going to produce, and you're going to do the play-by-play. You didn't hear it from me—but it's happening."

I was stunned. Howard Cosell had left the show after the 1983 season. Frank Gifford had just completed his fifteenth season as the play-by-play announcer. Joe Namath and O. J. Simpson were the analysts. Was Swanson *really* going to do this?

What I later learned was this: Swanson was a rabid college football fan. He watched games every weekend. One Saturday in 1985, he was watching the "A" game on ABC. The game became one-sided in the second half. So the network switched the game that I was doing to much of the country, including Chicago, where Swanson lived. Swanson later told me he loved the burst of energy and, in his mind, the way I was engaging the audience.

At that point, Swanson knew that down the line, he'd get Roone Arledge's job, and he later told me that then and there he decided that when he moved into that role, he was going to make me his play-by-play man for *Monday Night Football*. If the "A" game had been exciting that day, ABC would never have switched its coverage. Sometimes a little luck goes a long way.

Sure enough, the day after Ken Wolfe's call, I got another call, this one from Dennis Lewin, who was then the head of production. Lewin wanted to come out to Los Angeles the next day to talk with me. We met for dinner. I knew what he was going to tell me, but I had to play dumb. Now it's official. O. J. Simpson and Joe Namath were out. Frank Gifford was being offered the role of analyst, and I would be doing the play-by-play on *Monday Night Football*. That was it. It would be a two-man booth, not a three-man booth.

And away I would go—to what at that time was the most iconic show in sports television history.

CHAPTER 13

Monday Nights

ON MONDAY MORNING, SEPTEMBER 8, 1986, I opened the door of my hotel room in Dallas, Texas, and picked up a local newspaper sitting just outside the door. I pulled out the sports section and found myself staring at a picture of my face. "Can Monday Night Football Be Saved?" read the headline. I laugh at the memory now—that story's been written too many times to count. But back then there was a certain element of truth to it. The ratings had been steadily going down and the perception was that the franchise was sagging. I was supposed to be the *savior*?

A few things had happened since I'd gotten the job seven months earlier. Initially, Frank Gifford resisted the change and made noises about leaving ABC, contending that he could go to CBS and become the co-anchor on the *CBS Morning News*. (At least, his agent did.) I think that Frank considered the switch to the analyst role a demotion. But Dennis Swanson wasn't the kind of person to be held up. In effect, he responded by telling Frank's agent, *If Frank wants to do that, good luck at CBS. We'll find someone else.* Frank eventually agreed to the switch and began his sixteenth year on *Monday Night Football.*

Meanwhile, if moving to *Monday Night Football* was good news, the word was that the not-so-good news was that Swanson was a bottom-line executive who was going to be instituting significant cutbacks being demanded by the new regime. It was made clear that the champagne-and-caviar days under Roone Arledge were history. *Monday Night Football* would not be an exception. Good-bye limos and private planes and hotel suites. Hello, the rumors went, to compact Toyota rental cars and the Embassy Suites. "Congratulations," my friend Alex Wallau said to me. "You got invited to the orgy after the girls went home."

It wasn't quite that severe. Yes, some of the excesses under Roone came to an end, but there was nothing much to complain about. This was *Monday Night Football.* It had been several years since I'd broadcast a few NFL games, so I'd spent a lot of the spring boning up on pro football. In some ways, it's the most challenging sport to stay on top of. In the NBA, there are just a dozen or so players on a roster. In baseball, there are twice as many, but the rhythm of the sport is different. With football, you have fifty-three players on the roster, and, with shorter playing careers, there are more players cycling in and out. (It's not rare for a team to have at least ten or more first-year players on its roster.)

I wasn't exactly starting from scratch. I was a big NFL fan, and I'd been covering college football for years. And this was pre-Internet, pre–NFL Network, pre–Fantasy Football. Fans didn't know as much as they do today, and information and data weren't as easily accessible to them. There weren't wall-to-wall pregame and midweek shows. So the gap between the knowledge of a fan and the knowledge of a broadcaster was much larger than it is today. In any event, by the time the season came around, I felt ready.

Here we go. My opening regular season Monday night broadcast was the New York Giants at Dallas. Tom Landry on one sideline,

Bill Parcells on the other. Phil Simms. Danny White. Tony Dorsett. Lawrence Taylor. Mark Bavaro. Herschel Walker making his Cowboys debut. Texas Stadium. Was I nervous? Well, I started out by welcoming the viewers to the 1976 season, not 1986. On the air, I said to Frank, "It's already been a long year." But then, everything settled down. Dallas won the game, 31–28, with Walker scoring the winning touchdown.

All in all, the season was a lot of fun. Frank and I got along great (Frank even got married in the middle of the season to Kathie Lee). I became more and more comfortable as the year progressed. I thought that the show had regained some cachet—at least the drumbeat of articles about "saving" the show had begun to fade away.

After the season, Swanson decided that we should go back to a three-man booth—that we really needed someone only fairly recently retired to come aboard to provide additional analysis. So we brought in Dan Dierdorf, the six-time Pro Bowl offensive tackle for the St. Louis Cardinals. Frank would remain in the same role but could hopefully share a different perspective. Having worked on *Monday Night Baseball* for a decade, the "adjustment" for me to a three-man booth was fairly simple. Frank, Dan, and I would go on to work together for eleven consecutive years—in this business, a near eternity. Those were very good times.

OVER THE COURSE OF that run, we'd have lots of memorable Monday nights. One of the seminal games came in my second season, on November 30, 1987. The Seattle Seahawks were home in the Kingdome to the Los Angeles Raiders, whose new star was their dynamic running back, Bo Jackson. I had covered Jackson in college at Auburn and his football talent was obvious. His baseball prowess wasn't too bad either—in 1989, he'd be the MVP of the All-Star Game. There have been a handful of athletes who have played multiple sports professionally, including Deion Sanders, who won a Super Bowl ring

with the Cowboys and came close to a World Series ring with the Atlanta Braves. But few, if any, played two sports at Jackson's level. Bo
was just a freak of nature.

That spring and summer, Jackson had been the starting left fielder
for the Kansas City Royals, and then in the fall, had joined future
Hall of Famer Marcus Allen in the Raiders backfield. Bo was electric.
As I said during the game, "Every time he gets the ball, there's a great
sense of anticipation."

The anticipation also came from Jackson's massively hyped
matchup with Brian Bosworth, the Seahawks' brash linebacker, who
promised before the game to "contain" Jackson. Well, at one point
Bo and Boz collided on a short yardage handoff. Bo drove him into
the end zone. Then the real highlight came when Bo ran left, quickly
cut upfield, and sprinted ninety-one yards to the end zone. My call:
"There goes Bo. And nobody catches Bo. Touchdown." He disap-
peared into a tunnel. In thirty more seconds, he could have been in
Tacoma. That night, his twenty-fifth birthday, he ran for 221 yards,
then the Monday night record for rushing, as the Raiders won, 37–14.

Another of my favorites was a game in the middle of October
1994—the Broncos and the Chiefs in Denver, John Elway against
Joe Montana in what would be Montana's final NFL season. It was
a game that had just about everything from start to finish, going
back and forth all night, finally decided on a late touchdown pass
from Montana to Willie Davis. Dan Dierdorf's line at the end of the
game summed it up perfectly. "Lord, you can take me now—I've
seen it all." I'll never forget walking through the Denver airport the
next morning and overhearing virtually everyone I walked by talking excitedly about the game. It was the only topic of conversation—
another reminder of how great *Monday Night Football* could be, and
how popular the NFL was.

The first Super Bowl that ABC broadcast during my tenure followed the 1987 season—Super Bowl XXII, the Washington Redskins
against the Denver Broncos. Yes, I had already called a number of

big events, from the Miracle on Ice to six World Series. But it was still a major rush to wake up that morning in San Diego and think to myself, *I'm going to be calling the Super Bowl today.* The game's prominence had grown almost unimaginably in the twenty-one years since my brother and I had watched the Chiefs and Packers at the Los Angeles Coliseum.

In a way, the Super Bowl is somewhat easier to call than a regular game because you're really concentrating almost solely on the game itself. You don't have to begin to tell the outside stories and work the periphery very much. In the weeks leading up to the game, most of the stories have been told—or frequently overtold—through practically every imaginable media outlet in the world. Fans get inundated with story lines during the buildup, which means there's a different frame of reference than there would be for a regular season game, and even for other playoff games. That also means that one of the keys to broadcasting the Super Bowl is to find the really good stories that few, if any viewers have heard, or, alternatively, find a new context for familiar stories.

On a Super Bowl telecast, one thing you want to do is to start the show cleanly. You want the starting gate to open up and to come out immediately in rhythm. Once you've done that, you're doing what you've done your whole professional life. You come on the air and it's easy to think to yourself, *Holy cow. It's the Super Bowl.* But to me, when I look at the camera lens, all I'm looking into is a piece of glass. To the hundred million fans, I know you're all back there, but, really, it's just me talking to you, one-to-one.

Super Bowl XXII had its moments but 95 percent of them came in the first half. It was John Elway and the Broncos, coached by Dan Reeves, against Doug Williams, the NFL's only African-American starting quarterback at the time, and the Redskins, coached by Joe Gibbs. Denver led 10–0 after the first quarter. In the several years prior to this game, Super Bowls had been very one-sided—routs that didn't live up to great expectations. And so at this point, all our crew was really hoping was that Denver wouldn't win in a blowout—that Washington could keep it close.

They did more than that. In the second quarter, the Redskins went wild, scoring thirty-five points. Williams threw touchdown passes to Ricky Sanders, Gary Clark, Sanders again, and Clint Didier. A rookie running back, Timmy Smith, would break off a 58-yard touchdown run, on his way to setting a Super Bowl rushing record of 204 yards. As we reached halftime, I remember Dierdorf and I looking at each other and thinking the same thought. *What just happened? What the hell happened to our game?*

The second half was tough because there wasn't much of a game left. Any strategy talk went out the window. Washington won, 42–10—another Super Bowl blowout—and Doug Williams was deservedly named MVP. He'd even come out of the game briefly early in the second quarter when he incurred what looked at the time to be a possibly game-ending leg injury, only to lead his team to those five touchdowns before the half.

One other memory stands out from that Super Bowl. The owner of the Redskins was none other than Jack Kent Cooke—the same Jack Kent Cooke who had used me as a sacrificial lamb and then fired me twenty years earlier when he owned the Lakers. In the days before the game, Cooke told a writer that he had provided the launching pad for my career. When I saw the story in print, I couldn't resist calling the writer to set him straight. "Don't for one second believe Cooke's bullshit. That megalomaniac almost *ended* my career."

THREE YEARS LATER, THE next ABC Super Bowl broadcast—Super Bowl XXV, the Bills and the Giants—came under unusual, and even unnerving, circumstances. It was January 1991, barely a week after the Persian Gulf War—Operation Desert Storm—had been launched in Iraq. At Tampa Stadium, unprecedented security measures were being taken. It was the first time I'd ever seen big concrete barriers set up outside a stadium. ABC wasn't allowed to fly a blimp overhead. Meanwhile, the backdrop also gave the pregame ceremonies some added energy—and Whitney Houston turned a memorable rendition of the National Anthem.

Things could also be carried a little too far. We were told the night before the game that some SWAT team members and other security muckety-mucks were insisting that they had to meet with the broadcast crew. So Frank, Dan, and I are in a hotel room listening to instructions on how we needed to react if taken hostage during the game. I'm thinking: *Stop it already. Terrorists are going to invade the broadcast booth and shepherd three announcers to some unknown location?? Puh-leeze!* The meeting ends and when I get Gifford alone, I say, "Frank, you know why these guys were here? All they want is to get into the stadium for free and watch the game." Frank laughed and said, "One hundred percent."

The Bills came into the game seven-point favorites. Marv Levy's team had Jim Kelly, Thurman Thomas, and the K-Gun offense, with Bruce Smith anchoring a vaunted defense as well. The Giants had a strong defense as well, but their offense, with backup quarterback Jeff Hostetler filling in for an injured Phil Simms, wasn't nearly as explosive. In our meetings that week with the coaching staffs, Bill Parcells told us that for his team to win, they had to play clock ball—keep the ball away from the Bills as much as possible. Parcells wasn't above throwing curveballs at you—tell you one thing, then actually do something else in the game. In this Super Bowl, though, that's exactly what the Giants did. They held the ball for more than forty minutes, and squeezed out a 20–19 victory when Bills kicker Scott Norwood missed a 47-yard field goal in the closing seconds wide right.

Another thing about that Super Bowl: About ninety minutes before the game, I was down on the field talking with Phil Simms, who was dressed in street clothes. Phil's year had ended with a foot injury late in the regular season. Parcells walks right by us and says hello to me—we chat for maybe thirty seconds—and completely ignores

Simms. When he walks away, I laconically say to Phil, "Nice greeting." Simms summed it up perfectly—"Hey, in Bill's mind, if you're not playing, you might as well be dead."

The Bills would return to the Super Bowl each of the next three years—and lose each time. They never got closer to a championship than those couple of feet wide right.

WELL BEFORE I STARTED on *Monday Night Football,* dating back to my days on college football, I loved to "sneak" in quick references to the gambling line. It was just a way to let the savvy audience know that I understood *all* the reasons why they might be watching. There was also an assumption on the audience's part that this was the type of thing that was *verboten*. When I make an allusion to the point spread, or the over/under, I know some people catch it, and others don't. And that's fine—it's just another way to have fun, and connect with the fans who do have money invested on the game. I've heard it many times through the years—"Michaels must have a lot of money riding on these games." Let me forever set this straight. The primary reason I love sports is because of its unpredictability. *Nobody* knows who's going to win. I have some otherwise very smart friends who shell out thousands of dollars to subscribe to tout sheets. I keep telling them they're crazy. Or delusional. Very few people could be more wired into information than the broadcasters. We have access to both teams—coaches, players, owners, GMs, anyone who would know anything. And let me tell you that if I had to make my living betting on football, I'd be researching Chapter 11 covenants. I can't remember the last time I bet on a sports event, horse racing excepted. I do love action, though. But I can get my jollies through the greatest game ever invented—Craps. Roll 'dem bones. But I digress . . .

So in January 1995, along came Super Bowl XXIX—the San Francisco 49ers and the San Diego Chargers meeting in Miami. The game featured the biggest point spread in Super Bowl history—early in the week, San Francisco had been favored to win by 19 points, and the spread was 18 to 18½ points on the day of the game.

That Super Bowl marked the only time I was ever asked specifically by a boss to stay away from any gambling references. "Look," Dennis Swanson said to me. "The league is really sensitive about the point spread, and the disparity in this one, so if you can just avoid any of that, that would be great." Very occasionally, the league will reach out in that way to a network. We're independent, not the NFL's public relations arm, and we are not restricted to the degree many people think we are. On the other hand, it is a partnership, there's a ton of money in play, and you want to accommodate each other when possible. It can be a fine line—you don't want to hurt the product, but you want to stay independent and maintain your integrity.

Either way, on that Super Bowl Sunday, the Rascal could only be held in check so long.

The 49ers received the opening kickoff. Three plays later, from the Chargers' 44, Steve Young threw a touchdown pass to Jerry Rice. Referring to the Chargers' other designation, I said, "the Lightning Bolts just got struck by one." And the rout was on. It was the first of six touchdown passes Young would throw that day.

As the game wound down, the score—with that 18½-point spread, mind you—was 49 to 26. Meaning that a Chargers' touchdown could make it a 16-point game. And with just enough time for one final play, the Chargers had the ball near the San Francisco 35-yard line. Stan Humphries was the Chargers quarterback, and he dropped back to pass, looking deep downfield for Shawn Jefferson. "Humphries back to pass," I said, "and all over America hearts are beating furiously as he launches one to the end zone. Incomplete!"

I couldn't help myself.

And everyone across the country who'd bet on the Niners exhaled.

* * *

WHEN I WAS IN high school and my father was involved in the first
AFL television negotiations, he took me with him one morning to
the then–Los Angeles Chargers' training camp. I was introduced to
a young assistant coach by the name of Al Davis. This was 1960. I
remember Davis asking my dad a lot of questions about the television
deal. Davis couldn't soak in enough information about everything,
not just X's and O's. Of course, he'd go on to become the head coach
and eventually controlling owner of the Oakland Raiders. And in the
mid-sixties, he would briefly become commissioner of the American
Football League and help to facilitate the merger between the AFL
and the NFL. Many years later, when I was living in the Bay Area,
I would run into him from time to time. In the late seventies, I was
broadcasting a baseball game in Detroit for ABC on the same Sunday
afternoon the Raiders had a game in Pontiac against the Lions. Davis
invited me to fly back home with the Raiders on the team plane.

Eventually, the Raiders moved to Los Angeles—and not long
after, the Michaels family did, too. So I would run into Davis there
as well. When the Raiders would be preparing for a game on *Monday
Night Football,* I'd show up at their practice facility and get treated
like gold. Davis would give me a thirty-minute private audience on
the sideline. On the one hand, this was contrary to everything you
would hear about the secretive, inhospitable, paranoid Al Davis Raiders. On the other hand, it made sense—Davis thrived on being un-
predictable.

In 1991, I got Davis to agree to tape a rare interview that we
would play during halftime of a Monday night game in Kansas City.
At one point, Davis said, "I want to be known as a maverick." When
we came out of the tape, on the air now with Gifford and Dierdorf, I
talked about Davis's chances for the Pro Football Hall of Fame. From
serving as AFL commissioner and helping to formulate the NFL
merger to hiring John Madden to "Just Win, Baby" to winning multiple Super Bowls, Al Davis's football résumé was overflowing. I then
said, "I'm hearing that one reason he might not be voted to the Hall

was that some voters, mainly sportswriters, had enough of a personal dislike of him to keep him out of Canton." (Plenty of those guys had crossed swords with him over the years.) I concluded by saying if that was true, it was a denigration of the entire process.

Well, Davis got voted in and was enshrined the following year. When he learned that he'd be voted to the Class of 1992, he called me at home. "I just want to thank you. It wouldn't have happened without what you did."

"Wow, congratulations," I said. "That's great. But *you* did it, not me."

"You're the second call I made," he said.

He said the first call was to his wife. I had no idea if he was telling the truth. All I knew was what he was telling me.

But then came the subsequent season. In 1992, the Raiders' star running back—a certain future Hall of Famer in his own right, Marcus Allen—wasn't getting much playing time. Bo Jackson had suffered a football-career-ending injury in the 1990 playoffs, then the Raiders had signed Roger Craig in 1991. In '92 they would bring in Eric Dickerson to do the heavy lifting. It was a mystery as to why Allen was falling down the depth chart and rotting on the bench. It was apparent that this decision went beyond his football skills and that it was being made—for whatever reason—at the top, by Al Davis.

Allen hadn't spoken out publicly about his reduced playing time. But I knew him well, and reached out to ask if he'd do an interview for a Monday night game the Raiders had coming up in Miami a couple of weeks hence. There couldn't be a better platform than *Monday Night Football* to get his side of the story out there. And Marcus agreed. By this point he had had enough of the Raiders.

We taped the interview in Los Angeles—in the family room of my home, actually—forty-eight hours before the game in Miami. And he had plenty to say about Al Davis—accusing the Raiders owner of trying to ruin his career, and stop him from going to the Hall of Fame. And he asserted that the Raiders coach, Art Shell, had told him that the situation was out of his hands. Was Davis holding a personal vendetta against Allen, I asked him? "No question about it" was the answer. "He told me he was going to get me."

We kept the interview tightly under wraps until it aired. We knew there would be a firestorm if the content got out before kickoff. We also knew there would be a firestorm once it was broadcast. The Raiders chartered to Miami on Sunday and there wasn't a peep. I got to Florida that afternoon. The following day—game day—I called Davis in his hotel room around noon. Kickoff would be at 9 P.M.

"Al, you're probably not going to be happy, but I've done an interview with Marcus Allen that we taped on Saturday. I want to read to you a transcript of what will be on the air tonight. Then I want to read you the outtakes, so you know exactly what was said, what we're using, and what we're not using. And we'll give you equal time. We gave Marcus three and a half minutes. You can have three and a half minutes. If you want to respond to this, we can tape something this afternoon. Or we could do it at the stadium. Or we can do it live during the game. Or you can do nothing."

I read Allen's quotes to Davis and asked him what he wanted to do. He said he'd call me back. At around three thirty, he called and read to me a statement that said, in effect, that Marcus was full of shit and a bad guy. I listened to it. I wrote it all down. Then he said, "You have to talk to Art Shell about this, too."

I said, "Why? He's coaching a big game tonight. I don't want to go to Art Shell on the field before the game and have him deal with this. You can deal with Art and broach it with him. I'll report whatever he says." Davis didn't respond to that.

On the field before the game, Art Shell comes over to me. "Al told me what's going on." He was shrugging his shoulders like it wasn't that big a deal.

Then at halftime, the interview aired. Even without the Internet to fan the flames, it was the biggest sports story in the country the next day—far bigger than the game, which Oakland lost. Headlines in every newspaper in the country. *Raiders' Allen Airs Out Feud with Davis. Allen Says Team Owner Is Ruining His Career.* Of course, it completely blew up my relationship with Al Davis.

To Davis, a television partner of the NFL—particularly *Monday Night Football*—shouldn't have been stirring this pot. But again, the show was not a mouthpiece for the league or for his organization. This was a big story and we weren't going to tiptoe around it. People wanted to know what was happening in this wacky scenario, how Marcus Allen felt about it—and we were going to tell them.

Davis never forgave me. I was the enemy now. And he let me know it in typical Al Davis manner. I would cover the Raiders many more times through the years, including a Super Bowl appearance against the Buccaneers. In Denver, a year or two after the Allen interview, I was out on the field an hour before the game and I saw Al glaring at me. I'm maybe fifteen yards away and I could hear him muttering. "I'm gonna get you. I'm gonna get you."

What? He loved to intimidate people but I wasn't going to take any crap from him. "Hey Al," I said. "You're gonna get me? I'm right here. Come and get me." He just kept muttering.

When John Madden was inducted into the Hall of Fame in August 2006, NBC—where I'd just moved—did the game that's played in conjunction with the ceremony. Davis gave a warm induction speech. At the party for Madden, Davis and I happened to come face-to-face. I complimented him on his speech. He nodded and walked away.

Davis ended his relationship with a lot of people this way. If he felt you crossed him, he'd threaten you. He always wanted to be dominating. He loved that word. "We're gonna *dominate* the other team." But he also wanted to dominate people. What a way to go through life. Maybe it's no coincidence that in his years in Los Angeles, one of his best friends was Donald Sterling. You'd see them together at Clipper games. I'm not sure who enjoyed a courtroom more. Especially if they were the plaintiffs. Davis will forever be linked to "Just win, baby." It could easily have been "Just litigate, baby."

In this business, you try to be fair. But you also have to be honest with the viewers. If you lose credibility, you have nothing. And that can mean running the risk of having relationships with friends and sources go through some turbulence. Some relationships can withstand that. But not all.

CHAPTER 14

Two for the Ages

WHILE *MONDAY NIGHT FOOTBALL* would become my calling card at ABC Sports, the network originally hired me for baseball. And from 1976 to 1989, I did every season of *Monday Night Baseball,* as well as five All-Star Games, and some memorable—and unbelievable—postseason series.

In 1979 and 1981, I split the World Series play-by-play with Keith Jackson. Then, in 1983, I broadcast the entire series with Howard Cosell and Earl Weaver. It was the year after Weaver had stepped away from managing, and his Orioles, led by his successor, Joe Altobelli, ended up beating the Phillies in five games. Nineteen eighty-five was the year that Howard Cosell's book got him removed from the booth just before the World Series started. I was delighted when Tim Mc-Carver replaced him. Just before we went on the air for Game 1, I asked Tim if he was more nervous as a player or a broadcaster starting the World Series. Tim looked at me and said, "Are you kidding? Broadcaster!" Then, with the St. Louis Cardinals and the Kansas City Royals facing off in an all-Missouri affair, the Series was marked (or, if you were a Cardinal fan, marred) by umpire Don Denkinger's blown call at first base in the bottom of the ninth inning of Game 6. With the Cardinals up 3–2 in the series, and leading 1–0 in the Game 6, needing just three outs for the title, the Royals' Jorge Orta led off the inning with a grounder to Jack Clark at first base. Clark flipped the ball to pitcher Todd Worrell covering. Denkinger, who was actually one of the better umpires of his time, called Orta safe, even though replays indicated he was clearly out. Kansas City ended up scoring two runs in the inning to win the game.

The next night, in Game 7, the Royals jumped out to a 5–0 lead after three innings and finished the Cardinals off with six more runs in the fifth. In that fifth inning, with Denkinger now umpiring behind the plate, Whitey Herzog went to his bullpen to bring in the volatile Joaquin Andujar, a 21-game winner during the regular season, and one batter later, Andujar charged Denkinger after a pitch had been ruled inside. He was immediately joined by Herzog in a heated argument. Both the pitcher and manager were ejected. After the 11–0 loss, Herzog was asked how a manager could *possibly get ejected* in the seventh game of a World Series. "I'd seen enough," Whitey said.

Today, with the replay system, the call would have been overturned, and Whitey's Cardinals would most likely have won the World Series.

In any event, as exciting as that 1985 Series was, it was eclipsed the very next year by another series—one that featured the most dramatic baseball game I've ever witnessed.

For years, ABC and NBC had shared coverage of the postseason—meaning in odd years, we would do the World Series, and NBC would do the League Championship Series, and in even years it was vice versa. So in the fall of 1986, just as I was only a few weeks into *Monday Night Football,* Jim Palmer and I called the American League Championship Series, featuring the Boston Red Sox and the California Angels, while Keith Jackson and Tim McCarver were paired for the New York Mets and Houston Astros in the National League.

Both series ended up being epic, unforgettable chapters of one of the greatest postseasons in baseball history.

In the ALCS, you had the Red Sox back in postseason play for the first time since losing in 1975 to the Big Red Machine in an incredible World Series—and still chasing the franchise's first World Series title since 1918. Meanwhile, for the Angels, one of the big subplots of this series would revolve around manager Gene Mauch. Mauch had been the manager of the 1964 Phillies team that had suffered one of the most infamous collapses in sports history, squandering a 6½-game lead with twelve games left in the season. Forever after that—with the Phillies, then the Expos, then the Twins, and then the Angels—Mauch was always labeled the best manager never to have won a pennant. That 1964 season would be a permanent albatross.

In 1982, Mauch's Angels won the AL West, and then blew a two-games-to-none lead to the Brewers in the best-of-five ALCS. A few months later, after Mauch's wife, Nina, passed away, he decided to retire. But he returned to the Angels in 1985. And there he was in 1986, with his team winning the division, and facing the Red Sox—managed, ironically, by John McNamara, who'd been Mauch's third-base coach, and then his replacement in 1983 and '84 as the Angels' manager.

Stars abounded in both dugouts. A forty-year-old Reggie Jackson with the Angels, along with two ex-Orioles who'd been All-Stars—Bobby Grich and Doug DeCinces—and an All-Star rookie first baseman, Wally Joyner. The Sox had their own boldface roster—with a future Hall of Famer in Jim Rice, a former MVP in Don Baylor, a twenty-three-year-old 24-game winner in Roger Clemens, Tom Seaver at the end of his career, and a thirty-six-year-old first baseman who'd driven in 102 runs during the regular season despite being significantly hobbled by a bad ankle that would have put a few other guys on the disabled list. I'd first met him when I was in Hawaii, and he played for Tommy Lasorda's Spokane Indians in the Pacific Coast League. His name was Bill Buckner.

The first two games of the series were in Boston. The Angels tat-tooed Clemens for eight runs in an easy Game 1 win. Then the Red Sox won Game 2 with a late onslaught, 9–2. A key play occurred in the second inning when the Angels starter, Kirk McCaskill, had lost sight of a chopper hit back to the mound by Wade Boggs. The game started in late afternoon, and the sun had clearly gotten into McCaskill's eyes. "I don't remember ever seeing a pitcher lose the ball in the sun," he said afterward. But the questions—more and more ridiculous and repetitious—kept coming. Finally, the fourth or fifth wave of sportswriters arrived at his locker. How many times would McCaskill have to answer the exact same questions? Then, in an at-tempt to unearth the Hope Diamond of answers, one guy said, "Kirk, can you tell us *exactly* when you lost sight of the ball?" McCaskill was now exasperated and just wanted to get out of the clubhouse but he rubbed his chin, glanced toward the ceiling, took a deep breath, and slowly intoned—"*Exactly* one and seven-eighths inches below its apex."

Hysterically perfect.

WITH THE SERIES SHIFTING to Anaheim for Game 3, the Angels got to Oil Can Boyd for three runs in the seventh, and went on to win, 5–3. Then, in Game 4, the series was on the verge of being even again at two games apiece. Clemens took a 3–0 lead into the ninth, but then DeCinces led off with a homer. A couple of singles later, Clemens was out of the game and Calvin Schiraldi came in. He then gave up an RBI double to Gary Pettis and with two out and the bases loaded hit Brian Downing with a pitch to force in the tying run. And the Angels went on to win it in the eleventh inning on a Bobby Grich RBI single.

So that put the Angels—and Gene Mauch—up three games to one, and on the brink of a trip to the World Series, with Game 5 the next day—a Sunday early afternoon start in Anaheim. The Red Sox scored twice in the second inning, but the Angels would take a 3–2 lead in the sixth, and then made it 5–2 with two more in the seventh. The Angels' ace, Mike Witt—apart from giving up a two-run homer to Rich Gedman in the second—had been outstanding. Then, in the top of the ninth, he yielded a leadoff single to Buckner, struck out Jim Rice, and then gave up a two-run homer to Don Baylor. Score 5–4, Angels. But next he got Dwight Evans to pop out, and the Angels were one out away from the World Series. Gene Autry, the fabled singing cowboy, had been granted an expansion franchise in 1961. So here was his club in its twenty-sixth season of existence trying to get to the World Series for the first time in its history. The crowd was going wild. Security personnel were stationed every few feet in front of the box seat railings. There were even a few cops on horse-back positioned out by the foul poles. At which point Mauch decided to take out Witt and bring in the lefty Gary Lucas to face the left-handed-hitting Gedman. Mauch will be second-guessed forever for taking out Witt, but in his defense, Gedman had been 3-for-3 against Witt with a single, double, and homer. The crowd gasps when Lucas hits Gedman with a pitch. So now Mauch goes to his closer, Donnie Moore, who'd been dealing with a sore shoulder and receiving corti-sone shots for weeks. In Moore's only other appearance in the series, he'd been shaky—giving up two runs and four hits in a two-inning save in Game 3. Now facing Dave Henderson, who'd been acquired from the Mariners a couple of months before, Moore ran the count to 2–2, and Henderson barely foul-tipped the next pitch to stay alive. Then he fouls off another. And then Moore delivers a slow, flat slider, knee high, over the outside corner that Henderson manages to pull to left. "To left field and deep and Downing goes back," I say, my voice, in disbelief, heading into a much higher octave. "And it's *gone*! Unbelievable! You're looking at one for the ages here." 6–5 Red Sox.

But now the Boston bullpen has to get three outs to send the series back to Fenway. And McNamara brings in Bob Stanley, who gives up a leadoff single to Bob Boone. Ruppert Jones comes in to pinch run and moves to second on a Gary Pettis sacrifice bunt. Joe

Sambito, a lefty, comes in to face second baseman Rob Wilfong. Base hit to right field, Jones scores from second barely beating Dwight Evans's perfect throw. Now the game is tied, 6–6. McNamara removes Sambito and calls in Steve Crawford, the eighth or ninth guy on a ten-man staff, not a pitcher he'd usually rely on in a pressure situation. His ace reliever, Schiraldi, was available but had been lit up the night before and had not pitched well in recent weeks. And sure enough, Crawford gives up a single to Dick Schofield, sending Wilfong to third. Brian Downing is walked intentionally. Bases loaded, one out, pennant standing on third base. Despite everything that's just happened—blowing a three-run lead in the ninth—a relatively deep fly ball will get the Angels and Gene Mauch to the World Series. But Doug DeCinces lifts one to Evans in short right field. Evans has one of the best arms, if not the best arm in baseball, and the Angels can't send Wilfong home. Bobby Grich then hits a broken-bat soft liner back to the mound that Crawford snatches. Afterward, in the clubhouse, the media will ask Crawford to describe those moments in the ninth. "If there was a toilet on the mound," he says, "I would have used it."

In the top of the tenth, Moore is still out there, and gets Jim Rice to ground into a double play to get out of the inning unscathed. In the bottom of the inning, with two out and Jerry Narron at first base and Crawford still on the mound, the count went to 3-and-2 on Gary Pettis. Narron, representing the pennant-winning run, would be going on the pitch. Pettis was a switch-hitter with very little power—he'd hit five home runs in more than six hundred plate appearances during the regular season. With Narron off and running, Pettis drives the pitch to the opposite field, all the way to the warning track in left. Jim Rice is able to reel it in. Rice bangs into the wall as he makes the catch and has to look down into his glove to make sure he's actually caught it. There was the Angels' pennant, sitting in his webbing. Then in the eleventh, Moore, still in the game, gets into trouble, and with the bases loaded, it's Dave Henderson again, this time hitting a sacrifice fly to drive in Don Baylor to give the Red Sox a 7–6 lead. The Angels go down one-two-three in the bottom of the eleventh, with the final out a foul pop to first base, where Dave Stapleton—who came in to pinch-run for Buckner in the ninth—makes the catch. "Popped up, here comes Stapleton . . . Next plane to Boston."

The Red Sox were alive. The Angels were deflated. This was baseball at its drama-filled best. In the ninth inning, I had said that Anaheim Stadium was one strike away from Fantasyland. Now in the space of about an hour, the series had been transformed. And the players who were thrust into the forefront were guys like Dave Henderson and Steve Crawford, supporting actors who would play the greatest roles of their careers.

A couple of other postscripts to an incredible game: I'd known that Reggie Jackson and John McNamara had a great relationship dating back almost two decades. McNamara had been Reggie's manager with Birmingham in the Southern League in 1967. Now here they were on opposite sides. I knew Reggie well, going back to our days at Arizona State and having worked with him on a number of ABC shows, including the old *Superstars* and *Superteams* series. I had asked him about McNamara. Reggie told me that John was his favorite manager ever. And in the tenth inning of Game 5, when Reggie was leading off, I related Reggie's feelings—noting that in a tie game, with one swing of the bat, Reggie had a chance to end his old favorite manager's season. As I'm finishing up the anecdote, the cameraman next to the third-base dugout—Roy Hutchings—was in sync with where I was going and widened out his shot from Reggie in the batter's box to include McNamara in the first-base dugout. It was such a stunning visual touch that it would take a top Hollywood director fifteen takes to re-create it. In my mind, the framing was so spectacular that, on the air, to acknowledge what I'd seen, I blurted out a television term—"great pullback."

Cameramen and women are the unsung heroes of this business. After the game, Hutchings raced up to me in the production compound parking lot. "I can't thank you enough for saying that," he said. "Roy, that was fabulous," I responded. But he kept going. "No, you don't know the whole story," he said. "I'm listening to you tell the story. I did that move on my own, and as I'm doing it, Chet started screaming at me. 'What the fuck are you doing!!?? I'm gonna get your ass out of here.' Then you say, 'Great pullback,' and he shut up. You saved my job."

Chet was Chet Forte, the director. He'd been the incessantly self-aggrandizing director of *Monday Night Football* since its debut in 1970. He'd generally be lionized in the press but they didn't know better. He could ride coattails with the best of them and the Hutchings gem was just the latest example. Hutchings might have even won him an Emmy. Forte was also notoriously abusive to most everyone on the crew and always considered himself *the* focal point of the telecast—not the game itself, not the players, certainly not the announcers or anyone or anything else. He had a huge gambling problem, too, but Roone Arledge had always turned a blind eye toward him. He was one of the "old guard." A few months later, he would be gone from ABC Sports. The new boss, Dennis Swanson, wanted only team players and had a keen eye and disdain for egomaniacal naked emperors.

I also remember driving home with Linda on the Santa Ana Freeway and thinking that that was the best baseball game I'd ever seen. I was very happy with the telecast and felt that Jim Palmer and I were pretty much on top of everything. And then it hit me as downtown Los Angeles came into view—how and why was Jim Rice playing Pettis so deep in left field in the tenth inning? Pettis had no power to the opposite field. But only now, in the car, did it dawn on me that the night before, Pettis had doubled over Rice's head. *That* was the reason. It was never mentioned on the air. And I didn't think about it until we were transitioning to the Santa Monica Freeway.

It was just another reminder. I'll never pitch that elusive perfect game.

* * *

WHEN THE SERIES RESUMED in Boston, Steve Hirdt—the Maestro of Information from the Elias Sports Bureau who'd become not only absolutely essential to every baseball and football telecast I was a part of, but one of my great, great pals as well—had discovered that in the 83-year history of postseason baseball, no team had ever trailed by three or more runs in the ninth inning and won a game. Now, something that had not happened in 648 games had occurred twice within 19 hours.

In Game 6, the Angels scored two runs off Oil Can Boyd in the top of the first inning, but with the bases loaded and two out, Boyd was able to retire Wilfong to keep it close. I remember thinking—and saying—right then what a huge moment that was. The Angels were, after all, still up 3–2 in the series. If Wilfong had gotten a hit, McNamara might have had to go to his bullpen two outs into the game. A huge inning might have turned the monumental Red Sox comeback of Game 5 into just a footnote. Instead, the Sox got those two runs right back in their half of the first, and then knocked out McCaskill with a five-run third. The final score of Game 6 was Boston 10, California 4.

One night later, the Angels went down with a whimper against Roger Clemens. Boston scored three in the second and four more in the fourth. In the ninth inning, we took a shot of the visitors' dugout, with the Angels in a state of total dejection. "As far as I know," I said, "the longest nonstop flight in the world is San Francisco to Hong Kong. But tonight, an even longer flight will be the Angels' trip home to Southern California."

The Red Sox were on to the World Series, where there'd be more unimaginable drama—and ultimately heartbreak—ahead. And where in Game 6, McNamara wouldn't take Buckner out in the bottom of the tenth inning with a two-run lead, even though he'd made that move throughout the ALCS and late in the season in similar circumstances. Remember, Buckner had been playing on a bum ankle with a hairline fracture and was playing with a special shoe. In the years after Buckner's infamous error on Mookie Wilson's grounder, McNamara always took umbrage and got his back up when someone would suggest that he just wanted Buckner to be on the field when the Sox won their first championship since Woodrow Wilson was in the White House. Even if that appeared to be the case.

And then there was Donnie Moore, whose career would never be the same. He pitched in great pain in that series—cortisone shots were his regular friend—but he pitched through it and paid a price. His last major-league appearance would be in August 1988 for the Angels. Not quite a year later, at his home in Anaheim, he shot and wounded his wife, and then took his own life as one of his sons looked on. Some would link it to that Game 5 in 1986. How could anyone possibly know? All I know is it was tragic.

As for Gene Mauch, he'd manage just one more season and then retire. He died in 2005. His *New York Times* obituary read, "Gene Mauch, Manager of Near Misses." He was a very good man and a very good manager. I loved talking baseball with him. He deserved better.

THE CARDINALS GOT BACK to the World Series in 1987 but lost in seven games to the Minnesota Twins in a Series in which the home team won every game. Games 1, 2, 6, and 7 were in Minnesota, and I remember how earsplittingly loud the crowd was. It was like standing next to an airport runway. Later, we'd learn that they'd pumped the sound of the crowd back through the stadium's audio system. Management denied it but they were full of it. The fans screamed all game, every game. As the columnist Scott Ostler put it that week, "the Twins beat the Cardinals before a crowd of 55,245 Scandinavian James Browns."

In 1988, McCarver, Palmer, and I announced the NLCS, when the Dodgers beat the Mets in seven games. That was the Orel Hershiser series—in which the Cy Young winner, who ended the regular season with a record 59 consecutive scoreless innings, started three games, and came in to save another. Then Kirk Gibson's World Series Game 1 heroics would come days later on NBC, sending Tommy Lasorda's team on its way to beating the A's. Oakland, though, would be right back in the World Series the next year on ABC—a series on familiar turf for me.

It was an all–Bay Area affair—the San Francisco Giants and the Oakland A's. The A's were favored, with a potent offense led by Jose Canseco and Mark McGwire, as well as a tremendous pitching staff. The Giants were led by Will Clark and Kevin Mitchell. In my three seasons with the Giants, the *best* team I covered finished 27½ games out of first place. A World Series at Candlestick Park seemed a century away.

The teams' stadiums were about eight miles from one another as the seagulls fly. There would be no flights between any of the games. I could check into one hotel for the duration. But little did I know—I'd be spending seventeen nights there. And this World Series would turn out to be the most unusual ever.

Game 1 in Oakland was played on Saturday night, October 14, with the A's winning, 5–0. Bart Giamatti, the baseball commissioner and former president of Yale University, had just died a month earlier. At the end of the game, I said: "Appropriately, in a World Series dedicated to a late scholar, the first game is all A's."

Oakland won again on Sunday, 5–1, to take a 2–0 lead in the series. Monday was an off day. To Palmer, McCarver, and me, it was feeling like a sweep. The Series resumed Tuesday in San Francisco and, to accommodate prime time in the East, Game 3 was scheduled for 5:30 P.M. local time at Candlestick Park. We would come on the air with the pregame show at five. It was a gorgeous fall day in the Bay Area, ice-blue sky, soft light breezes, 68 degrees. When we came on the air, I made some opening remarks and then brought in Tim McCarver.

In our introduction, we wanted to make the point that although Oakland had won the first two games by lopsided scores, the games had come down to a couple of key plays and misplays. And that set up McCarver to talk through one of those moments from the previous game. As Tim was talking over video of a Dave Parker double in Game 2 that scored Jose Canseco, the broadcast booth shook. It kept shaking. And then there was this thrust that made me wonder if we weren't about to get pitched from the mezzanine into the lower deck. McCarver put a death grip on my left leg with his right hand. (To this day, Tim remembers it the other way around, but I'm sticking to my story. I recall needing three Advil the next morning.)

Having lived in California for many years, I knew immediately what was going on. This was an earthquake. I said on the air, "I'll tell you what, we're having an earthq—" But just as the audience heard the *q*, if not the *u*, we lost power. If you had asked me at the moment how long the quake lasted, I would have said about a minute. When you can't wait for an earthquake to stop, time seems to stand still. In reality, it was finished in fifteen seconds.

When the tremors finally stopped, all we heard was this collective "ooooh" sound from the crowd. There was still plenty of sunlight but all the stadium lights were out. And we had lost all communication with the truck. We knew nothing. Was there damage? Where was the earthquake centered? Live through an earthquake, and you think you're at the epicenter—that *you* are sitting right on top of it. It turns out we were seventy miles north of the epicenter. That's how strong it was.

I didn't know if we were still on the air but I couldn't just throw down the microphone and make a run for it. Once our communication with the truck began to come back intermittently, my monitor showed a graphic that just said "World Series." We still had no idea if we were on the air or not. It turned out we were, for at least a few seconds, and I said, "Well, folks, that's the greatest open in the history of television, bar none. We're still here. We are still—as far as we can tell—on the air and I guess you're hearing us, even though we have no picture and no return audio. And we will be back, we *hope*, from San Francisco in just a moment."

In the booth, McCarver, Palmer (who hadn't even gotten on the air yet), and I were waiting to find out what we would need to do next. There was a phone in the booth and when I picked it up, to my great surprise there was a dial tone. I wound up calling the office of Bob Iger, who had started and worked with me for many years in sports and had just taken over as the head of entertainment for ABC in Los Angeles. "You all right?" he asked me immediately. "Yeah, I'm fine—what do you know?" I asked.

Bob knew more than I did—though ABC had switched, believe it or not, to *Roseanne* (that was their backup programming), Iger was getting his information from the news division and had learned the basic details of the earthquake. As we talked and Bob kept filling me in on what he was learning on the fly, much of the crowd at Candlestick, now over the initial shock and getting restless, started chanting "Play ball, play ball!" They had no idea that a section of the Bay Bridge had collapsed, the double-decker Cypress Freeway in Oakland had pancaked, and that there was a huge, several-alarm fire in the Marina district of San Francisco. On the field, meanwhile, players were milling about, some comforting shaken family members who'd been in the stands. Eventually, after about fifteen or twenty minutes, we were able to get total communication back with the truck. Curt Gowdy Jr., our producer, had me come down to the production compound. Clearly, there'd be no game played on this night. And it would be easier for me to eventually communicate with Peter Jennings and Ted Koppel, who were in New York and Washington, respectively, for any reporting from a location just outside Candlestick Park.

Having lived in Menlo Park for twelve years, I knew the region well. And I'd always loved geography and aerial photography. I could never get enough of those "Above" books—*Above Paris, Above New York, Above San Francisco.* That would come in handy on this night. Our audio guys rigged up a handheld microphone that looked like the kind Sinatra would carry onstage if he were performing in a club—silver and shiny—and I would spend the next eight hours reporting from outside the ballpark. We had a blimp airborne for the game—now it would prove invaluable in allowing me to see what was going on in the area. Through our liaison in the truck, I could ask the blimp pilot to maneuver while I narrated. *We have a fire in the marina. . . . Now we're over the Embarcadero. . . .*

As I spoke, it was striking how irregular the patterns of damage were. Some areas looked normal, while nearby, others were devastated. The freeway in Oakland—where the second deck buckled and collapsed onto the first—was where 42 of the 63 deaths caused by the quake occurred. Then, two blocks away, everything looked fine.

Dusk turned to darkness, and I was very careful that night not to say anything I wasn't certain of. In these breaking crisis situations, there could be temptation to speculate or advance the story. But that's how people get into trouble. At one point someone in the truck said, "Hey, one of the other networks just reported that the Golden Gate Bridge has collapsed." We had already seen a portion of the cantilevered section of the Bay Bridge that had tilted down, but we had seen nothing indicating any problems from the Golden Gate Bridge.

In that scenario, it could be a knee-jerk reaction to say, "So-and-so is reporting that . . ." Or, more likely when people are reluctant to acknowledge the competition by name, "We're hearing reports that . . . the Golden Gate Bridge has collapsed." I said nothing. Then I asked our liaison to ask the blimp pilot to maneuver toward the Golden Gate Bridge. When I could see the shot, sure enough it was clear that the bridge was in good shape, at least to the naked eye. Cars were even traversing it. This was clearly a case of some nonlocal not knowing the Bay Bridge from the Golden Gate Bridge, something every resident of the Bay Area had put up with for years. We got another report that the scoreboard had collapsed at the Oakland Coliseum, where the A's played. That, too, was a false rumor. Misinformation was flying fast and furiously. It's the bane of the news and sports businesses, both electronic and print—"You heard it here first!" Who cares? That's nothing but a vanity play. If it's not right, it's garbage.

Years earlier, in Hawaii, I'd gone through that whole thing about Bobby Valentine getting some cheap hits courtesy of a local official scorer that led to his winning a batting title, when in reality all I had was a little secondhand information. Days later, Valentine had ended up in the hospital for a week with a broken jaw after getting beaned. I hadn't forgotten my sense of guilt for even playing a tiny role in that deal. Now it was a very different scenario—a breaking and developing news story about a natural disaster. But the lesson still held. *Let me see everything I can see and I'll walk you through it. But we're not going to speculate here.* Jennings and Koppel, in my mind, were always the best of the best to begin with. We played it conservatively, and there was no doubt in any critic's mind that ABC had the best coverage of any network that night.

There was a lot of nice press coverage for my work—and I even received an Emmy nomination for news. But I remember thinking how surprised I was by the reaction. *Isn't it understood that just because you're broadcasting sports, you're not blind to the rest of the world?* I'd like to think—in fact, I *know* that many of my brethren see a world that consists of more than explaining holding or pass interference. The same basic principles apply to both sports and news. It's tenth-grade journalism: who, what, when, where, why, how? It's that simple. Reporting is reporting, and many of my colleagues would have been just as prepared to do what I did that day. As I'd later tell an interviewer, "Do they think we're so insular that we know nothing beside 'hit behind the runner' and 'watch for the blitz on third-and-seven'?"

I stayed at Candlestick all night and through an early segment for *Good Morning America*. Finally, at about 6 A.M., I left the stadium exhausted. It was dark, quiet, and eerie on the ride back to downtown—

with the electricity still out and debris in the streets. San Francisco looked broken. This most beautiful of American cities had been hit over the head with a lead pipe. When I got to the hotel, there was no power. Linda was with me and we walked up thirteen flights of stairs to our room.

Even though I'd been staring at these images of devastation for hours, there was still so much we didn't know. Like how many people had died. For all we knew, the death toll could be in the thousands. A lot of information was still sketchy. The toll would end up much lower, but I didn't know it then. In the hotel room, after a sleepless night, the sun was coming up over this city, this area I love, and I started thinking about all the husbands and wives and sons and daughters who must have been waiting up all night for loved ones who weren't going to ever come home. It hit me all at once, and after being in reporter mode all night long, I remember suddenly feeling sad and very melancholy. Eventually, I fell asleep for about an hour.

THEY WERE STILL CLEARING the rubble when the predictable drumbeat started, led by columnists from around the country. "Cancel this World Series. The area needs to recover." (I think they just wanted to go home.) I appeared on ABC News and said just the opposite. "Most people in this region want the World Series to resume. People here are resilient. They want to show that they can get up off the canvas and slowly but surely return to normalcy."

I thought Commissioner Fay Vincent came up with the right solution. There would be a seven-day delay between games. It would wind up getting extended to ten days. And while workers made sure the stadiums were safe and that the roads could handle the traffic and that most things were back in satisfactory working order, the teams went to Arizona for a couple of days to work out. I stayed in San Francisco to contribute reports to *World News Tonight* and *Good Morning America*.

When the World Series finally resumed Friday night, October 27, there was an odd vibe. After all, no one had been down this road before. There was this transition we had to make—from a natural disaster story back to sports. People were going to be interested in the resumption of the Series on a number of levels. Some viewers would be focused on how the area itself had rebounded. Others would be curious as to what the quality of play would be like following a week-and-a-half hiatus. It felt strange to be back at Candlestick Park. In a nice touch, multiple ceremonial first pitches were thrown out simultaneously by many of the earthquake night's first responders.

Game 3 was an Oakland rout. Then in Game 4, the A's were leading 8–0 by the sixth inning. The Giants mounted a comeback to get it to 8–6, and with one on and two out in the seventh, Kevin Mitchell hit a drive to the warning track in left. It would have tied the game but was caught two feet from the fence by Rickey Henderson. The Giants never got any closer, the A's finished off the sweep, and we all finally went home.

Home from the most unusual World Series of all.

IT WAS AROUND THAT time—the end of the 1980s—that sports television began to change in significant ways. The prime example was a decade-old cable network out of a small town in Connecticut, devoted entirely to sports and gaining traction. After years of broadcasting marginal and off-the-wall events, the network was bidding for and gaining rights to some major packages. It was called ESPN—Entertainment and Sports Programming Network—and 80 percent of it was owned by Capital Cities, the parent company of ABC.

There wasn't a lot of intermingling at that time, in good measure because the ABC network had a lot of unionized personnel, especially on the technical side, and ESPN was a nonunion shop. And again, we were ABC, the *network* that went to *every* television home. And the ABC brand, created by Roone Arledge—the entity that carried

Monday Night Football and *Wide World of Sports* and the Olympic Games—well, the feeling was that it couldn't be overtaken or even challenged by some cable network that aired aerobics shows and kick-boxing events and billiards tournaments. At least that was the sense.

Meanwhile, broadcast rights fees for sports properties were soaring and the bidding process was becoming more and more competitive. The two biggest properties that ABC was involved in the bidding for at that point were baseball and the Olympics. The NFL package still had a few years to run.

I loved covering the Olympics. In Sarajevo, Yugoslavia, in 1984 and Calgary, Alberta, in 1988, there had been no miracles or even medals for the United States hockey team, but Ken Dryden and I were reunited and added some more great memories. I was also the play-by-play (stride-by-stride?) announcer for figure skating in Sarajevo and called the gold medal performances of Katarina Witt and Scott Hamilton and the iconic ice-dancing performances of Jane Torvill and Christopher Dean.

Meanwhile in Calgary, this was the first Olympic Games under our "new management." Cap Cities was now in charge but Roone Arledge, despite being solely the head of ABC News but no longer ABC Sports, would executive-produce the Games.

A couple of nights before the competition began, Arledge and some of the new top brass put together a small dinner to introduce the Cap Cities board members and top investors to some of the ABC announcers and event analysts. I was invited along with Jim McKay, Keith Jackson, and a few other on-air folks. I wound up being seated next to none other than Warren Buffett, who at that point, wasn't 5 percent as well-known as he is today.

Buffett was totally interested in every aspect of the broadcast, asking dozens of questions, and at one point was intrigued when I told him how ABC had been able to "influence" the hockey schedule so that the USA-USSR game in Calgary would not be played on the opening night of the hockey tournament, as was originally scheduled.

The Americans, I explained to Buffett, had been lined up to meet the Soviets in the opener because the pairings had been determined by the results of an international tournament that had been held in Europe months earlier. If the U.S. team had suffered a one-sided defeat to the Soviets, it would have severely impacted their chances of advancing to the medal round and, most important for ABC, would have created little or no interest in hockey for the rest of the Olympics, with a concurrent decline in ratings. Instead ABC had worked with (leaned on?) the governing bodies and so a few weeks before the torch would be lighted in Calgary, the schedule came out and the U.S. team would face, in the opener, not the Soviet Union—but Austria. The U.S.-Soviet matchup had been pushed back to Game 3. If there was a line on the game, the United States would have been favored by about five goals. (The United States would win the game, 10–6.)

Buffett was fascinated by this and wanted to know how ABC could have pulled this off. I explained that we had an executive by the name of Bob Iger, whom I'd started with at ABC Sports in the mid-seventies, and who knew how to navigate his way through this complex maze and get the job done. Buffett was impressed. Years later, when we reminisced about this, Iger would tell me that ABC had to provide certain "concessions" to a variety of muckety-mucks to get this done, including guaranteeing an upgrade of certain restroom facilities in Calgary. Hey, whatever it takes! Some two decades later, of course, Bob would become the exalted CEO of the Walt Disney Company, which had bought out Capital Cities in the late nineties.

Anyway, ABC failed to get the rights to the 1992 or 1994 Olympics, but went down to the wire with CBS and NBC in bidding for the rights to televise the 1996 Summer Games in Atlanta. My contract at the time stated that if ABC had won the bid, I would be the prime-time Olympic host. Jim McKay was going to be moving into an emeritus role and I was going to do most of the heavy lifting for ABC. It was a role I coveted, so, obviously, I followed the rights negotiations very closely.

The bidding dragged on and on. NBC made a last bid of $456 million. (Yes, things had come a long way from ABC paying $1.5 million to broadcast the 1964 Olympics in Tokyo.) And this was after NBC had paid $401 million for the Barcelona Games in 1992 and lost money, a reported $100 million. But the thinking was that Atlanta—a domestic Olympics in the Eastern Time Zone—would lead to a bigger buildup, higher ratings, and more advertisers and sponsors.

Still, ABC got last crack—if they bid about $10 million higher than NBC, they would win the rights to the Games. But ABC decided to pass. That one stung. And not just for me. NBC ended up making a nice profit, so, aside from the personal disappointment, it was a mistake for my company. And NBC hasn't relinquished the rights to the Olympics since—though eventually, that ended up serving me well. More on that a little later.

Meanwhile, after the 1989 World Series, CBS had gained exclusive network rights to Major League Baseball—the Game of the Week, the All-Star Game, and the playoffs and World Series—for almost $2 billion. The next year, ESPN got in the mix by making a deal to show regular season games as well. ESPN's deal worked out well. CBS's lost half a billion dollars. So in 1994, ABC and NBC returned to the game—though this time under an odd new venture that was called "The Baseball Network." The idea was that Major League Baseball would share revenue from the deal with the networks. The upshot—particularly when the World Series was canceled in 1994 due to the strike—was another disaster.

Since the Baseball Network was created as part of a two-year deal, with the plan for NBC to host the World Series in 1994, and ABC in 1995, someone had the bright idea after the strike to split the 1995 Series between the two networks. So, as the Atlanta Braves got set to meet the Cleveland Indians, ABC was going to broadcast Games 1, 4, and 5; NBC was going to broadcast Games 2, 3 and 6; and ABC—by virtue of winning a coin flip—had the rights to Game 7.

The competition between the networks could be so juvenile that

ABC didn't want to promote NBC's game and NBC didn't want to promote ABC's telecasts. In the middle of Game 1 in Atlanta, I was handed a promo to read. *Join us here on ABC for Game Four in Cleveland on Wednesday night and for Game Five, if necessary, Thursday.* With no mention of Games 2 and 3 on NBC.

It was ridiculous—and the Rascal couldn't help himself. "By the way," I said after reading the promo, "if you're wondering about Games Two and Three, I can't tell you exactly where you can see them, but here's a hint: Last night, Bob Costas, Bob Uecker, and Joe Morgan [NBC's broadcast team] were spotted in underground Atlanta." When it was NBC's turn, Bob Costas (an honorary first cousin to the Rascal) made a similar reference to our ABC crew.

It was a close, back-and-forth World Series, with every game except one decided by one run. The Braves won the first two games at home. Then the Indians won two of three in Cleveland. It was wonderful to be back doing postseason baseball. Tim McCarver, Jim Palmer, and I were back together and having a blast. Curt Gowdy Jr., the son of my friend and mentor, was our producer. Everyone headed back to Atlanta with the Braves leading three games to two. Game 6 was an NBC game. If Cleveland won, my gang would do the decisive Game 7, which would be a great thrill. If Atlanta won, it was all over.

McCarver, Palmer, and I went the ballpark for batting practice and to schmooze before the game. Then we went back to the Ritz-Carlton in the Buckhead section of Atlanta to watch the game together on NBC and prepare for what we hoped would be our Game 7. Tom Glavine, though, had other ideas. The Braves' lefty pitched a gem, combining with Mark Wohlers on a one-hitter. Dave Justice hit a home run in the sixth, which was all the offense Atlanta needed. The Braves won the game, 1–0, and the Series, four games to two.

By ten thirty that night, it was clear that we wouldn't be calling Game 7 of the World Series. And I was also learning that ABC wouldn't be bidding for the next MLB contract. So, for all intents, my baseball career was most likely over, at least for the foreseeable future. The next morning, I left for the airport to fly to Minneapolis for *Monday Night Football*. The car picked me up at the hotel and cruised down Interstate 75. Within minutes, we were going through downtown. Another minute later, I looked to my left and what did I see? Atlanta's Fulton County Stadium, where I would *not* be calling Game 7 of the World Series that night. Then a few hundred yards south, I looked out the window again and what did I see? The under-construction Olympic Stadium (later to be turned into Turner Field), where I would *not* be hosting the Opening Ceremony of the 1996 Summer Games.

Nobody will ever have to throw me a pity party, nor would I want one. On balance I have nothing to complain about. I've been blessed in innumerable ways. Sometimes, things are just totally out of your control. But when people ask me about any disappointments in my career, I tell this story.

CHAPTER 15

O.J.

BEFORE WE WORKED TOGETHER at the 1984 Olympics I'd met O. J. Simpson a couple of times in passing. I'd be covering all the track and field events and O.J. had been signed on as the analyst for the men's sprints. The venue for track and field was the Los Angeles Coliseum, the same facility where O.J. had starred for USC in a spectacular college football career punctuated by a Heisman Trophy. Simpson had also been a track star, a member of the USC 4x110 yard relay team that had broken the world record in 1967. He came to the Olympic role with great credibility.

O.J. and I worked together in that spring and summer of 1984 at the Olympic Trials in Los Angeles, as well as at another track and field event in May in San Jose, to develop some familiarity with the U.S. athletes and get a chance to work together on the air. It was in San Jose that O.J. introduced me to the young woman he was dating at the time and would later marry. Her name was Nicole Brown.

At the Olympics, O.J. was an excellent broadcast partner. He was professional. He had an easy manner and a winning personality. He was insightful. He was prepared and never showed up a second late. We called Carl Lewis's races—as well as that women's sprint relay on the final day when Wilma Rudolph was nowhere to be found. And beyond working well together, O.J. and I developed a nice friendship that lasted well after the assignment.

Two years later, the family and I made the move from the Bay Area to Los Angeles. After our crazy first week there, things settled down—Linda and I had met and gotten married in Los Angeles, we knew the area, and we'd visited frequently through the years. And when we moved to the Brentwood section of the city, I had a ready-made tennis partner in O. J. Simpson. Before his knees turned him into a golfer, O.J. and I would play tennis two or three times a week, always on the court at his house, which was just a few blocks from ours. Every few months, Linda and I would go out to dinner with O.J. and Nicole. Even when O.J. switched to golf in the early nineties, I was still a regular on his backyard court. Often my new opponent would be O.J.'s former teammate both at USC and with the Buffalo Bills, one Al Cowlings.

People in the neighborhood raved about O.J. He was gregarious, accessible, engaging, and always walked around with a smile. In Brentwood, everyone knew O.J. and he never stood on ceremony or had any airs about him. He might as well have been running for office. Part of what would make the O.J. story so explosive was that it was so totally at odds and dramatically contrary with the image he had worked so hard to cultivate all those years.

On Saturday, June 11, 1994, I was in New York covering the Belmont Stakes for ABC—Tabasco Cat was the winner—and then flew from JFK back to Los Angeles the next afternoon. I got home around six o'clock early Sunday evening. A few months before, I was starting to get smitten with golf and had joined the Bel-Air Country Club. Now, in mid-June, I knew that golf was becoming a very, very serious addiction. Of course, having been on the road for several days, I couldn't wait to wake up on Monday morning and get right out to the course. I needed a game. I called a couple of guys but they wouldn't be available. Then I thought about O.J., who was a member of nearby Riviera Country Club. *I'll play anywhere. I just need a game.* I rang O.J.'s house but hung up when it went to the answering machine. I couldn't wait around for a return call. Good move, as it turned out. A year later, in the trial when they were trying to determine O.J.'s whereabouts that night, any message probably would have been played back in court. No thanks.

The next day, like everyone else in America, I heard the stunning news: Nicole Brown Simpson had been murdered, along with a friend, Ron Goldman. I had eventually gotten a golf game together and after finishing the round was getting information from the Grill Room television set at the club at the same time as most of the country. The initial word was that O.J. was in Chicago on a golf trip. I knew, of course, that O.J. and Nicole were separated and that she had moved into her own place. But I was thinking about O.J., wondering how he had found out Nicole had been killed, and how he was handling it.

THE STORY EXPLODED IMMEDIATELY and there was a nonstop whirlpool of information and misinformation. In fact, it was becoming a cesspool of misinformation. ABC News asked me to help. Not only did I know the area, and not only did I know O.J. and Nicole, but I knew most everyone in their circle of friends. I played tennis with Al Cowlings. I knew O.J.'s good friend Bob Kardashian, and his wife at the time, Kris. (Yes, I had met the Kardashian girls when they were, like, five, seven, and ten.) I knew Bob Shapiro, who would represent O.J. I'd even met Kato Kaelin at one point. He was living in a guest suite behind Simpson's tennis court for a few weeks. (For the record, I did not know Ron Goldman.)

So I was brought in to try to help separate fact and fiction for ABC. I told my old boss, Roone Arledge, the president of ABC News, that I would help but I was in a dicey position. I would clearly become privy to certain information but that I'd have to protect my sources. He understood. And behind the scenes, I was working with Ted Koppel, then the host of *Nightline*. I was able to give Ted specific background information without attribution. And when he would ask, "How do you know this?" I could only respond, "I'm not going to give you a bum steer. You have to trust me here." The fact that we had worked closely on the night of the 1989 World Series earthquake had given him a certain level of confidence in me.

The day after the murder, O.J. flew back to Los Angeles from Chicago and television vans had invaded Brentwood. Rockingham Avenue was now as famous as Fifth Avenue. O.J. was in residence. By Wednesday, there had to be a thousand reporters and another thousand lookie-loos hanging out on Rockingham and the neighboring streets. Every outlet was reporting that Simpson was still in seclusion. "*Would* he be coming out? *When* would he be coming out? What will he say?" Blah, blah, blah. I called Koppel. "Ted, I have to tell you something. O. J. Simpson is *not* in his house. I know where he is. I can't tell you where he is. You have to find another source if you want to use the information with attribution. But don't report that O. J. Simpson is in the house. He's not there."

"How could he get out of his house without anybody knowing?" Koppel wondered. "That seems impossible."

"Here's how he got out of the house," I said. "I've played tennis in that backyard more than a hundred times. There is a gate back there that connects to his neighbor's property, and he can slide out through it and go between two other houses on North Bristol Avenue, which is the street that runs parallel to Rockingham. It's secluded back there. Nobody would have seen him. That's how he got out of the house."

Now, I knew all this because Bob Kardashian was in contact with me, and Bob had told me O.J. was at *his* house. I couldn't give that away. At this point, I knew too much and I had friends involved and I couldn't betray them by going public with information I'd learned in confidence. At the same time, I didn't want my network repeating the same bogus information that everyone else was putting out.

Meanwhile, as it became evident he was being investigated as a suspect, I spoke with O.J. by phone three or four times. He kept saying the same thing to me. "How can anybody think I did this?" Not, "I didn't do it." He just kept saying, "How can anybody think I did this?" "I can't believe what they're saying on the news." In retrospect, that should have been a clear signal to me that something wasn't right.

At first I gave him the benefit of the doubt. And I did this for a number of reasons. For one thing, he was my friend. And who can believe that a friend would ever be capable of doing something so vicious? Second, the early timeline was confusing.

O.J. may have been the guy in those Hertz commercials, racing through the airport concourse to make his flight. But in reality, I knew that like me, he hated being late for flights. We'd talked about it a number of times. Even in the pre-9/11, pre-TSA days, we both obsessed about getting to the airport with plenty of time to spare.

O.J., remember, had an American Airlines red-eye flight from LAX to O'Hare on the night of the murder. (He was supposed to play golf at a corporate outing the next day, and would later say he was told about the murder in Chicago.) The flight left at 11:45 P.M. and the murders occurred around 10:15. Then Simpson was supposed to have gone home, cleaned up, and gotten into a limo sometime after 11 for the twenty-five-minute ride to the airport and in time to check his golf bag. My initial thought: *The timeline doesn't seem plausible. He never would have cut it that close to missing a flight.*

Also, I'd heard that Howard Bingham, Muhammad Ali's personal photographer, was sitting across the aisle from O.J. on that flight to Chicago. To my mind, Howard Bingham, renowned in his profession and with all he's experienced at close range in his life and his craft, is a man who would understand the human condition about as well as anybody. But when a mutual friend asked Howard if he had noticed anything out of the ordinary—if O.J. had been agitated or nervous, whether he had any inkling something had happened—Bingham said, not in the least. Which made me think, *wait a minute. If Howard Bingham didn't see anything he felt was out of sorts even minimally, then how did O.J. murder two people in cold blood, and then, ninety or so minutes later, get on a plane and be completely normal?* In addition, the scene of the murders was in front of Nicole's condo, only twenty or thirty feet from Bundy Drive, a surface street that always generates a fair amount of traffic. Someone *had* to see or hear something. It was such a chaotic story that initially, I didn't know what to think. There was information coming out—and nobody knew what was true and what was total crap—that suggested he did it. And then there was mitigating information that suggested he couldn't have.

By the end of that week, the story was generating headlines worldwide. The plot was twisting and turning every hour. It was a national obsession. And then along came a White Bronco on the freeway early on the Friday evening of June 17, 1994.

IT WAS FIVE DAYS after the murder, and it had been arranged that O.J. would surrender to police late that Friday morning for questioning. He'd be picked up at Bob Kardashian's house. Even though a double-murder charge carried no bail in California, and, potentially, the death penalty, because of the circumstances O.J. was given the opportunity to turn himself in. The cops arrived sometime around eleven. But when they got there, O.J. was gone. He had sneaked out with Al Cowlings. Kardashian didn't even know that O.J. had left the house. Where was O.J.? The dark joke going around that day was that Al Cowlings was driving O.J. to visit Nicole's grave in Costa Mesa, in Orange County. And that when he found out where they were going, O.J. turned to Cowlings and said, "I said Costa Rica, motherfucker, not Costa Mesa."

By 2 P.M., the Los Angeles Police Department sent out an all-points bulletin. And so the search for O.J. began. I got a call at home from ABC News. While most of my work for the network that week had been behind the scenes, I had also agreed to do a couple of short on-camera interviews. So I'd appeared on *Nightline* to lend focus to certain information, talk about some of the principal figures, and discuss what it was like to work with O.J. on the air. But that night, a horse by the name of Barraq would be running at Hollywood Park. Three years earlier, my good friend Dave Leveton, a lawyer, had gotten me to go in fifty-fifty with him and buy my first racehorse. Dave had owned a number of horses and I went along for the ride. We were having a blast. Barraq had been earning his keep.

The producer said to me, "Can you go on *Nightline* at eight forty-five Pacific Time with Ted?"

I explained that I had to be at Hollywood Park—I didn't say why—but I'd be happy to do it if they would send a satellite truck to the track. I told the producer, "I'll do the interview from there." Post time was scheduled around 9 P.M.

Ultimately, the network couldn't work that out, so instead I agreed to tape an interview at the ABC studio in Hollywood at five o'clock and leave from there to go to the track. By the time I got to the studio, O.J. was still on the loose, whereabouts unknown. I did a brief taped interview with Ted Koppel that would run on *Nightline* that night, got up to leave—and then, I hear all hell breaking loose from the newsroom. *O.J. is on the freeway. In a white Bronco.* And a few minutes later—*Al Cowlings is in the driver's seat.*

I'm told I'm not to go anywhere and minutes later, I'm on a set downstairs alongside Bill Redeker, the West Coast correspondent for the network. Judy Muller, another ABC News correspondent, was at a separate location and tied in with us. Now the network was in full "special report" mode, with Koppel in Washington and Peter Jennings in New York. And I'm tethered to our set because O.J. was on a freeway in Los Angeles. I wasn't going anywhere and resigned myself to the fact that Barraq would probably have to go to the starting gate in a couple of hours with his co-owner ten miles up the road.

Almost 100 million Americans were going to watch this play out on one of the networks, captivated by a spectacle that was unlike anything anyone had ever seen. Would O.J. get caught? Surrender? Somehow escape? Or even kill himself right there on live television?

Now it was after six o'clock. Knowing exactly where they were when the California Highway Patrol started its pursuit, I began doing "geography narration"—similar to my role on the night the earthquake interrupted the 1989 World Series. But instead of "there's the Bay Bridge," it was "there's Sunset Boulevard." The slow-speed chase was continuing. The cops were following. People on the freeway were cheering. O.J.'s friends and former teammates were calling into the networks, telling him to turn himself in. Al (A. C.) Cowlings—my tennis partner—was driving. It was all beyond surreal.

Soon we're into the seven o'clock hour. It's ten o'clock in the east on a Friday night, which means it's time for *ABC's 20/20*. So this chase has become not just an ABC News special—preempting prime time programming—but it's now part of *20/20*, hosted, as always, by Barbara Walters. And once that happens, who has to get on the air, somehow, someway? Barbara, of course. It was her show. So now she's in our New York studio. We had Koppel, we had Jennings, we had Redeker, we had Muller, we had yours truly, and a couple of other correspondents out in the field. We had it pretty well covered. But this was developing into a potential crime of the century—so Barbara, of course, had to weigh in.

And how did she? As we continued to go back and forth, covering every aspect of this not-to-be-believed drama with tension building by the second, Barbara jumped in.

"Does anybody know how old O.J. is?"

There was silence. In our studio, I looked at Redeker. He looked incredulous. We rolled our eyes at each other. I couldn't see Jennings or Koppel at that point but I could only imagine the looks on their faces.

Does anybody know how old O.J. is? Seriously?

Somebody answered forty-six. But more important, the question spoke volumes about television—and about how gigantic this story was. Everybody had to get a piece of the action, no matter how marginally relevant. Or irrelevant. Everyone had to be involved.

A little before eight o'clock, Cowlings and Simpson pulled into O.J.'s driveway in Brentwood but stayed in the car. There were a dozen helicopters overhead. There were photographers and cameramen positioned outside the gates, even if they couldn't really shoot over the hedges. So the television viewer was basically seeing the Bronco only from an aerial view. And there was no visible movement in the car.

At this point, there was little but speculation when Peter Jennings said, "Well, we have on the phone a Robert Higgins who lives in the neighborhood and is on the ground and can see inside the van. Mr. Higgins—"

I heard a voice that said, "Ah yay-ess, how ah you?"

I immediately smelled a rat. I knew most of the neighbors. I knew a lot of people in Brentwood and on O.J.'s street. I'd never heard of a Robert Higgins. And I knew that it would be next to impossible for anyone to see into O.J.'s driveway from ground level outside the property. I looked over at Redeker. He knew what I was thinking and nodded.

Jennings hesitated a second and said, "Uh, just about as tense as you are, I assume."

The voice again, "Oh my Lawd, this is quite the tensest."

Now I was certain it was a prank call. "Mr. Higgins" sounded like he was auditioning for the old *Amos 'n' Andy* show. But Jennings kept going.

"What can you see?" he asked in a somber voice.

"Well what I'm a-lookin' at right now, I'm lookin' at the van and what I see is O.J. kind of slouching down and looking very, very upset.

No—looky here, he look very upset. I don't know what he gonna be doin'."

There was an awkward pause but Jennings kept on with the questions. I was in Los Angeles and Jennings was in New York but I was trying to signal to people in our studio to let them know this was a prank.

I could hear through my earpiece someone in New York tell Jennings to "wrap this thing up because we don't know about this call."

"Thank you, Mr. Higgins," Jennings concluded.

But before the control room could him off, the voice said, "And Baba Booey to you all."

It was one of the Howard Stern guys. Of course it was. I immediately figured it was the fabled Captain Janks but sometime later discovered that it was another prankster, "Maury from Brooklyn." Having been a big Howard fan, I obviously knew Baba Booey, Stern's well-known nickname for his producer, Gary Dell'Abate. Peter didn't. He was just confused. And now someone had to say something—to disabuse Jennings and the audience of any notion that it had been a legitimate call, and do so while realizing that whatever was said was going to be played on *The Howard Stern Show* until the day I'd be pushing up daisies. I had to form my words very, very carefully knowing that on Monday morning, Howard and Robin and the whole gang would be having a field day.

Peter went on for another few seconds, and then I jumped in. "Peter," I said, "just for the record, this is Al Michaels—that was a totally farcical call. Lest anybody think that was somebody who was truly across the street—that was not. He used a name in code that was indicative of the mentioning of the name of a certain radio talk show host. So he was not there."

For the record, *lest* and *farcical* are two words I don't think I'd ever used before, at least publicly. But I was too busy parsing every syllable in my brain—*How do I want to say this so that when they play this back on* The Howard Stern Show, *a show I've already been on a few times, it doesn't appear as though I'm trashing Howard?*

Jennings thanked me and added, "We have them [pranksters] on every coast. Not the first time or the last time we'll have been had." So now Barbara Walters was asking how old O.J. was, and Peter Jennings was getting bamboozled. Network news divisions have had finer hours.

A quick digression: Months later I'm a guest on Howard's show in New York, and of course they played the hell out of that clip—"lest," "farcical," the whole deal. That night, I'm at Giants Stadium for a Monday night game. It's four months after that O.J. night of nights. I'm out on the field an hour before the game, and fans are yelling at me. *Hey Al, lest anyone think that was a legitimate call, it was totally farcical!* To this day, twenty years after the fact—and it could be anywhere in the country—I still hear it regularly. "Hey, Al, it's totally farcical!"

O.J. eventually got out of the car and was taken into custody shortly thereafter. My night in the studio was over at a little past nine o'clock.

And then there was my horse, Barraq. His race had been run. My partner, Dave Leveton, calls to say we had a winner. Not only that, but Barraq had held the lead from the starting gate to one hundred yards from the finish when he'd been overtaken. Then, as could be said in horse racing parlance, "he reached deep down and found more." I'd missed it all.

O.J. WOULD SPEND THE next year-plus in jail, and I visited him three times. Don Ohlmeyer, the former *Monday Night Football* producer who had then turned NBC into an entertainment juggernaut and had worked with O.J. on a number of projects, was a regular visitor. You had a couple of hangers-on that were there pretty much all day long—guys who didn't have jobs but had gotten on the approved visitors' list and who just wanted to be able to tell their friends they were with O.J. regularly. On one visit, O.J. told me what pests they had become but he wasn't sure how to get rid of them. It was like a menagerie. On two of my visits, the Menendez brothers, who were awaiting a retrial on charges they had murdered their parents, were sitting in the next cubicle talking to Leslie Abramson, their attorney.

O.J. was on the other side of the Plexiglas and, rather than denying it all, he was still saying, "I can't believe anybody thinks I could have done this," or "How can *they* think I did this?" That was more and more disconcerting for me. He never said, *"I didn't do it!"* Again this is all hindsight, but if you were in jail for a double murder you didn't commit and one of the victims was your wife, wouldn't you be figuratively pounding the walls? Maybe literally, too.

The verdict came down in October 1995 and millions of people will never forget the look on Bob Kardashian's face. He was clearly stunned by the pronouncement, "not guilty." A lot of O.J.'s friends had the same reaction. O.J. would be back home on Rockingham Avenue within the hour.

I look at it clinically now and I look back on it historically. I haven't spoken with O.J. in years, and have no plans to. Obviously, the vast majority of people in this country feel that he did it. A billion words and a million hours of airtime have microscopically dissected every aspect of the murder, the trial, and the aftermath. Adding anything more is ad nauseam redundant. But we'll never hear the end of it.

CHAPTER 16

Diversions

I CAME TO MY LOVE of horse racing at an early age. At the start of the book, I wrote about going to Roosevelt Raceway on Long Island with my parents, publishing my tout sheet, *Big Al at Westbury,* and once correctly picking a 75–1 shot named Algerine to win. Well, when we moved to California, things didn't change much. My mom—the Original Rascal—would occasionally show up at Hamilton High School, seek out the assistant principal, and explain that her son had a dentist appointment and she was there to pick me up. Naturally, the "dentist appointment" was either at Santa Anita or Hollywood Park, depending on the time of year. We made this our little secret and kept it from my father—he took me to the track only on weekends. And Lila Michaels only further sealed her first-ballot induction into the Mothers' Hall of Fame when she started taking two of my friends along with us to my dentist appointments. My buddies had a lot of cavities to fill, too.

Decades later, knowing how much I liked horse racing, Dennis Swanson assigned me to work the Kentucky Derby on ABC in 1986. I was thrilled. (I was less than thrilled when I got to Churchill Downs, this iconic sports venue, and found that it bordered on ramshackle. Plenty of renovations since.) Then, starting in 1987, until ABC lost the rights in 2001, I covered every Triple Crown race—forty-two in a row. An added bonus was that ABC's horse racing producer was Curt Gowdy Jr.

Jim McKay and I would cohost the coverage, while Dave Johnson called the actual race itself. Through the years, we were joined by Charlsie Cantey, Lesley Visser, Hank Goldberg, and various jockeys like Gary Stevens, Chris McCarron, Jerry Bailey, and Mike Smith, who were either injured at the time or without a mount. Robin Roberts was even with us for a couple of races before ascending to stardom on *Good Morning America*. We had a fabulous crew and a lot of good times. People would ask me how we filled all our time on the air—our pre-race window was usually over an hour—when the actual race was around two minutes. The truth is, the hardest part of those broadcasts was condensing all our material and fitting it into the allotted time.

No sport has richer stories—from the owners to the trainers to the jockeys to the horses to the breeders to the railbirds—than horse racing. I'm not sure any other sport reaches such a cross section of society. At a racetrack the upper crust shares the same emotions as folks taking their last dollar to the betting windows. Royalty shares an afternoon with the proletariat. Still, for almost as long as I can remember, there's always been talk about racing's impending death. Some of this is because new locales and new methods for gambling are always emerging. Some of this is because, unlike ballplayers, horses run only for a very short period of time—making it hard to form an attachment with an "athlete" who will be retired and sent to stud after only a couple of years on the playing field. Would a Triple Crown winner transform horse racing and restore the sport to all its past glory? Of course not—the winner would be a big story for a few days and then be shipped to the nostalgia file.

But I don't think the sport will ever completely die. Although just last year, Hollywood Park, one of my all-time favorite tracks, closed its gates for the final time. Horse racing may not be what it used to be, but that's generally because sports are like other businesses. They need to innovate and grow and avoid getting complacent, while making good strategic decisions and reacting smartly to trends. Those that do, grow and succeed. Those that don't are left behind. I never would have imagined that a day would come when you could walk down the street of any major American city and go blocks without anyone knowing the name of the current world heavyweight boxing champion. I also never would have guessed that more fans would choose to watch an NFL preseason game than a Major League Baseball playoff game, and that the NFL Draft would outrate most NBA playoff games. It's a new world order.

IN 1990, IT WAS time for me to take the next step in the world of thoroughbred racing. There's the old joke: How do you make a small fortune in horse racing? Start with a big fortune. I have my own variation of that. In 1990, along with my friend Dave Leveton, who'd owned a number of horses, including one that ran in the Kentucky Derby (Masterful Advocate in 1987), we bought a yearling and named him Ultimate Fantasy. He got sick and died before he ever got to the races. Not the most auspicious start. Then in 1991, we decided to go in fifty-fifty on another horse. We wanted a race-ready animal, one we could send to the track immediately.

Dave knew what he was doing. His trainer, Gary Jones, was one of the best in California. And we didn't want to get another yearling (a horse between one and two years old). So we went to a bloodstock agent who imported horses from Europe, and a few weeks later, bought a four-year-old by the name of Barraq (pronounced just like the first name of the president). He'd already been named by the previous owner, as a play on the name of the horse that had transported the prophet Muhammad from Mecca to Jerusalem. (At that point,

Dave and I laughed and figured he had to be a distance specialist.) He had been bred in Kentucky but had run three or four times in France and fared pretty well. He was an allowance horse, not a stakes horse, which meant he could only run in races that had certain qualifying conditions. And then, after his racing career was over, my goofball dream was that Barraq would become a big-time stallion. The horse cost us $110,000—we each put up $55,000.

He was brought to California from Europe for his first race, at Santa Anita on April 18, 1991. It was a 96-degree day. I'd been to Santa Anita hundreds of times going back to the days of my mother taking me to "the dentist." But never as an owner. Now here I was at arguably the world's most beautiful racetrack in a sports jacket and tie, so nervous and excited and hot that I'm not just sweating through my shirt, I'm not just sweating through my jacket—I'm sweating through my tie. This is *my* horse and he's about to run a mile on the turf course of Santa Anita. Chris McCarron, the jockey who'd won the Kentucky Derby and the Preakness aboard Alysheba in 1987, is riding *my horse!* The superb race caller Trevor Denman will call the race. I'm in Dreamland.

Barraq was, as I recall, the second choice—French import, first race in America. He had a lot of backing and went off at 2 to 1. As they broke from the starting gate, my eyes were pinned on him. He looked like Pegasus, leaping high in the air, a wild horse trying to get out of the bit. His head was turned toward the grandstand at a 90-degree angle. McCarron was fighting for control. Trevor Denman's call went something like this: *And away they go. King Raj on the inside is off to a good start. Indigena is second along the rail. And then there's Barraq. Barraq is rank. Barraq is* very *rank. McCarron has his hands full!* He was also pouring sweat—"washy," as the saying goes in racing. He'd used up the bulk of his energy in the first hundred yards.

At the end, though, Barraq finished second and I was ecstatic. He had broken horribly, McCarron had to fight him all the way, and he still had enough left that he could finish second in an allowance race.

The purse was thirty-five thousand dollars, and with second place worth around 20 percent, we made a few grand. A good day and tremendous fun.

Now, of course, I couldn't wait for his next race. But first, a couple of days later, I got a call from Gary Jones, the trainer. "I'm gonna geld him. He's too crazy."

Castrate Barraq?! No! Why?

"Geld him?" I said, "Gary, this could be the greatest stallion of all-time!"

Jones was never one to mince words. "Don't be nuts," he said. "Ain't gonna happen. The guy training him in France screwed him up. This is the only chance to get him under control."

I was still fantasizing about the millions this horse was going to bring in from the breeding shed. But my dreams of founding the next Calumet Farm would end that night with a scalpel.

So we now had a four-year-old gelding. And what do you know— he winds up winning five races in his career—one at Hollywood Park, three at Santa Anita, and one at Del Mar. He'd have probably won a few more but the problem was he was always out of commission. He was like a kid who couldn't stop from getting sick. Every few races, Gary would call. "Well, we have to put him on the shelf for a while." It was always a lot of fun paying those vet bills while our boy sat in the stall!

Ultimately, we owned him for almost four years. We probably paid out $25,000 each year to maintain him. So we were in for $210,000 and he earned about $180,000. Which meant we were out $30,000, $15,000 apiece, or $3,750 a year. If he had won just one more race, we would have been in the black. All in all, though, a great ride. And a ton of laughs.

After his racing days were over, we sent him up to the University of California, Davis, where they receive a lot of retired racehorses. Then in 1998, we got word that Barraq had died at the age of ten. R.I.P., wild one.

* * *

BY HAPPENSTANCE, IN MARCH of that year, I ran into Bob Baffert, by then already a superstar trainer, at the San Felipe Stakes, one of the prep races for the Santa Anita Derby, which, in turn, is one of the West Coast prep races for the Kentucky Derby. I'd gotten to know Bob well while working on our racing coverage—in fact, the year before, his colt Silver Charm had come up just short of winning the Triple Crown, finishing second in the Belmont after winning the Derby and the Preakness.

Meanwhile, at Santa Anita that day in 1998, Baffert had a horse in the race, and there was an unlikely connection. He sat down at the table for a minute and said, "I'll tell you a funny story. When we were buying him at the two-year-old sale, I'm looking at the bloodlines and I see that his first cousin was Barraq. And I remembered that that was Al Michaels's horse and he had some talent. It wasn't the reason I bought him but it was a positive."

The horse's name was Real Quiet. And Real Quiet finished second in the San Felipe that day. Then he went on to the Santa Anita Derby three weeks later and finished second again. And then Baffert takes the horse to Louisville.

At Churchill Downs, on that first Saturday of May, Real Quiet goes off at 9–1. And with Kent Desormeaux in the saddle—*Real Quiet wins the 124th running of the Kentucky Derby!* At the Preakness, Real Quiet goes off as the favorite—and wins that race, too. So this horse—a first cousin of my Barraq—was now going for the Triple Crown at the 1998 Belmont Stakes. No horse had won the Triple Crown since Affirmed, twenty years earlier.

Baffert's Silver Charm had come up just short a year earlier. Now Real Quiet was going to try to make history in New York. He came out of the gate alertly and settled nicely, conserving energy for the mile-and-a-half marathon. With a sixteenth of a mile to go—110 yards—he had a four-length lead. Belmont Park is going wild. Until, in a flash, Victory Gallop, the second-place finisher in the Derby and Preakness, comes roaring to the finish line. It was a photo finish—and the photo revealed that Victory Gallop had won by a nose. Once again, there would be no Triple Crown.

Meanwhile, I was thinking about Barraq. We had gelded him, and he'd been put to rest, but he was still the first cousin of a near–Triple Crown winner. Earlier that week, I'd told Bob Raissman of the New York *Daily News* that I was thinking of pulling a "Zachary Taylor." Taylor was the twelfth president of the United States, who died in 1850 and whose body was exhumed some 140 years later to determine if he had indeed been fatally poisoned by arsenic. If I could only get Barraq's body out of the ground for a few minutes, extract a little DNA, and . . . who knows? I was kidding.

Sort of.

EARLIER THAT SPRING, I'D gotten a call from an agent friend who'd been asked to contact me about playing a role in a sports comedy film that was created by Trey Parker and Matt Stone of *South Park* fame and would be directed by David Zucker, the man behind *Airplane* and *The Naked Gun*. Eight or nine other sportscasters—Dan Patrick, Jim Lampley, and Kenny Mayne among them—would also be playing various roles. And the idea was to have Bob Costas and me do the play-by-play for the "championship" game. The deal that was being offered was what's known as "favored nations"—all of us, no matter how large or small the role, would receive $10,000. No negotiations. A couple of years before, Frank Gifford, Dan Dierdorf, and I had played ourselves in *Jerry Maguire*—we'd had a fairly extensive role—and the studio had offered us "scale," or a few hundred bucks. I told Frank and Dan the movie would have a budget of $50 million and there was no freaking way we were doing it for scale. We wound up doing it against my better judgment for $5,000 apiece. Frank and Dan just wanted to have some fun and I had to be a team player. *Jerry*

Maguire did $273 million at the box office. Glad we didn't bust their budget.

They sent over the script. The movie was called *BASEketball* and it was a goofy comedy about a made-up sport. I decided to pass on the offer. For whatever reason, it just didn't feel right. Then I got a call from Costas. "I hear you don't want to do this movie," he said. "Come on, we'll have some fun."

I told him I'd think about it. Then I called the agent and said, "They're paying all of us ten thousand dollars. But they're flying in everyone else. I can drive to the location from my house. And Costas and I have far larger roles than any of the other guys." I was still thinking about the *Jerry Maguire* deal and how Frank, Dan, and I had been played as turnip-truck bumpkins by the studio execs. That wasn't going to happen again. I knew the budget for *BASEketball* would be around $25 million. "Get me another five thousand dollars—the five thousand they're saving on travel—and I'll do it, mainly for Bob."

Also, I was committing to only one day, and I was adamant that I was leaving by five o'clock. I knew enough about Hollywood movie nonsense to realize that if I didn't make this clear, I could be brought back for a second day. Or third. Or fourth. The deal got done. I was getting a little more money than the others but the studio was saving on travel.

Costas flew in and our day on the set started at 7 A.M. It turned out that this was the very last day of shooting—there would be no Day 2. They were already behind schedule and needed to get this movie finished. Our roles and dialogue bordered on inane but for the first couple of hours we were having a blast. We had totally bought in. But as the morning wore on, it was progressively deteriorating. Probably the most outrageous line was Bob's. "You're excited?" he asks me after some sort of great play. "Feel these *nipples!*" Bob was reluctant to say it, but they convinced him to give it a shot, promising that if it didn't work, they could just cut it out. He believed them.

As we broke for lunch, it was clear that we were falling behind schedule. We still had all these scenes left to do and I'm thinking, *They'll never get me out of here by five o'clock.* As everyone was scrambling and trying to cut down on the delays, they were humoring Bob and me—or so they thought—by showing us some of "the dailies," the scenes they'd already shot over the past few weeks. We're watching these and most were on the other side of vapid. And we're looking at each other as if to say, *What are we doing here? This is going to be the end of our careers.*

Bob turned to me and said, "Well, at least it's a great payday."

We hadn't discussed anything about money before this. I wasn't turning my nose up at ten thousand dollars, but I got the feeling something wasn't quite kosher. "Excuse me," I said.

"Well, at least it's a good payday," Bob repeated.

"Excuse me."

Uh-oh. Bob looks at me, and now he knows he's said something he probably shouldn't have. We decided to flip a coin and the loser would have to tell the other guy how much he was getting paid.

I lost the coin flip. "I'm getting fifteen grand," I told him. "The ten thousand for favored nations, plus an extra five because I have no travel costs. So fifteen thousand all in."

Now it's Bob's turn. Sheepishly, Bob tells me that he's getting fifty thousand dollars!

I'm now apoplectic. Not because of the money but because *they had lied.* This took me over the edge. Trust me, I'm no prima donna—and this might sound so Hollywood—but I went to the dressing room, called the agent, and told him what had happened and that I was leaving the set and going home. *I couldn't believe I'd fallen off another turnip truck.* There may be no business like show business, but in Hollywood, there's no bullshit like the bullshit in show business.

As the agent tried to get hold of someone at the studio, I knew that I had the upper hand. These remaining scenes were too important for the film. And it was the last day of shooting. The set was closing down in a few hours. There was no one around at that moment to fill the role. Costas and I had already done too much together. "We'll make it right, we'll make it right," was the response when someone on the set got on the phone with the agent. "We'll deal with it later, but you *have* to trust us."

I'm still ballistic. I tell the agent, "How do we know that? 'Trust us'? They've already lied to our faces. I'm out of here at five o'clock."

I go back on the set, and now we're rushing through the scenes. Zucker is hesitant to talk to me because he knows I've unearthed rotten eggs. I can't concentrate on anything except getting in my car and calling a good friend who's a top entertainment lawyer. I'm thinking, *I didn't want to do this in the first place and I just want to get the hell out of here.*

We finished up and I was still whacked out. I called my lawyer pal, and the next morning he was on the phone with someone in business affairs at Universal Studios who'd already been clued in. My guy says, "Bob Costas got fifty thousand dollars. Because of the aggravation factor, Al will get seventy-five thousand."

The guy at Universal came back with an offer of twenty thousand and was adamant the studio wouldn't go any higher.

"Absolutely not," my lawyer says. "You are going to make this right." And hangs up.

My lawyer then calls me and asks: "What's the best result for you? What do want to have happen?"

"The best result?" I say. "That's easy. Get me out of the movie—it's a piece of crap to begin with."

Meanwhile, the business affairs exec calls my lawyer and makes a threat. "If Michaels won't agree to twenty thousand, we're going to take him out of the movie."

"Perfect!" my lawyer said. "You got a deal! Take him out." Click.

Ten minutes later, one of the top executives at Universal takes over. He realizes this is a problem that goes beyond threats from Business Affairs. The movie is already in postproduction and the film has no ending without the scenes with Bob and me.

With my father in the early 1950s in our apartment in the Flatbush neighborhood of Brooklyn. This may have been the only time I've read *Field & Stream*.

Author Collection

In my Little League uniform, 1956. I made the All-Star team, but struck out four times in the All-Star Game. On to broadcasting . . .

Author Collection

With Mom and Dad and brother David, when I was thirteen. Mom pregnant with sister Susan, 1957. *Author Collection*

August 27, 1966, in Los Angeles. Luckiest guy on the planet. *Author Collection*

Ready to open the 1980 Pro Bowl in Honolulu with Howard Cosell and Fran Tarkenton. Howard nixed the aloha shirts. *Author Collection*

Interviewing Gary Matthews of the Philadelphia Phillies before a *Monday Night Baseball* game in the early 1980s. *Author Collection*

With Ken Dryden before the U.S.-Soviet game at the 1980 Lake Placid Olympics. What a night THAT would turn out to be! © *American Broadcasting Companies, Inc.*

With Tim McCarver and Jim Palmer in Oakland before Game 1 of the 1989 World Series. Three nights later, the earth would shake in San Francisco, four minutes after we opened up the telecast of Game 3.

Author Collection

With Alex Wallau, ABC executive and boxing analyst supreme. Nobody's had a better best friend, period. *Author Collection*

A grand time, as always, with the Coach—John Madden, who set the gold standard for analysts. © *2014 NBCUniversal Media, LLC*

More than two hundred *Monday Night Football* telecasts with Frank Gifford and Dan Dierdorf. We had eleven terrific years together. *Author Collection*

It's already been six seasons with Cris Collinsworth on *Sunday Night Football*. We shouldn't be allowed to have this much fun.

© 2014 NBCUniversal Media, LLC

With one of the most spectacular men ever—the incomparable John Wooden, who created the greatest dynasty in the history of college basketball at UCLA.

Author Collection

On the Triple Crown trail in the 1990s with Dave (*"And down the stretch they come!"*) Johnson and Chris McCarron. *Author Collection*

Getting ready for a *Sunday Night Football* game with Cris and my second set of eyes, spotter "Malibu" Kelly Hayes. *© 2014 NBCUniversal Media, LLC*

With Tiger Woods and PGA official Vaughn Moise at "Showdown at Sherwood" in 1999, at the exact moment I told Tiger how much golf I'd played in a recent month. His response: "You play more than I do!" *Author Collection*

With son-in-law Jeff, daughter Jennifer, Linda, and son Steven at the Emmy Awards in 2011, receiving the Lifetime Achievement Award for Sports. *Author Collection*

On the field with longtime NFL coach Tom Moore at the Indianapolis Colts' Lucas Oil Stadium. *Author Collection*

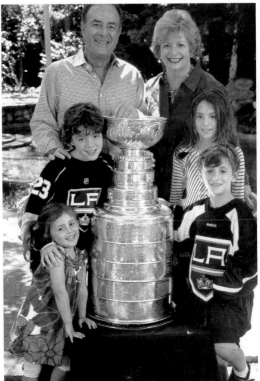

There's nothing like the Stanley Cup winding up in your backyard along with your grandchildren. Thank you, Kings.

Author Collection

And there's nothing like sharing everything together with the love of your life.

Author Collection

I wound up getting the same $50,000 that Costas got, plus $10,000 for my troubles and aggravation. And, of course, the studio paid my lawyer. Actually, this whole craziness could have been a movie itself.

BASEketball came out shortly after and was so bad, it was actually funny. It became a cult classic. Bob and I have had a thousand laughs about that whole experience. And that line about "feeling Bob's nipples"? It wasn't only in the movie—it was in the trailer and played in theaters nationwide for weeks. The movie was a major bomb—$23 million to make with a $7 million gross.

A few years ago someone sent me a *BASEketball* DVD and asked me to sign it. I sent it back with the following message:

"Why did you buy this dreck? All best wishes . . ."

CHAPTER 17

Monday Night Transformations

WHEN I FIRST LOGGED on to the Internet in the mid-nineties, I was immediately hooked. I could read newspapers and periodicals from around the country without having our research folks or team public relations people fax me pages and pages of material. Now I could simply do my homework by signing in. And with email, I could correspond with friends, sources, and work contacts without picking up the phone.

Around that time, I made my first foray into a chat room. I'd heard that people posted their opinions on everything from sports to politics to movies, and figured I'd see what folks thought of *Monday Night Football*. I found a chat room called "T.V. Talk," and used an alias to log in. I posed a question that I figured would start some discussion and give me some feedback. *Hey, everyone, what do you think of* Monday Night Football *this season?* I checked back a few hours later, and there were a few responses but none of them really dealt with the show. And all of them were lewd. Seemed like a reasonable question regarding a show about which there was usually no shortage of opinions. Instead, the only messages I saw were salacious, X-rated comments having nothing at all to do with football. I wrote another post about *Monday Night*, trying to figure out why no one wanted to "chat" about the show. Finally, someone wrote to my alias. "Hey, pal, don't you understand? 'T.V. Talk' isn't television talk. It's Transvestite Talk."

Oops.

Still, it was clear that the Internet was going to be a transformative force. Did I envision a day when I could access the Internet from my phone to watch NFL games live—getting special notifications when teams were in the Red Zone? No. Did I foresee using the Internet to talk to my grandkids, while seeing their faces? Not really. But I knew right away that this was going to have an indelible impact—both good and bad—on the world. *Everything* in the world—sports, politics, business, media, you name it.

Concurrent with the burgeoning of the Internet, another media shift taking place was already beginning to affect me directly: ESPN—the cable channel that was ABC's little corporate sibling was expanding rapidly. In 1996, the Walt Disney Company bought Capital Cities—including ABC and ESPN—for $19 billion. And very quickly, it became apparent that even though ABC was the top-rated network at the time, ESPN was the crown jewel of the deal.

The reason for ESPN's growth was simple: subscriber fees. Just look at your cable or satellite bill. Cable television has a dual revenue stream—subscriber fees and commercials. Network television has only advertising. As I write this, every household with cable pays more than $5 a month to receive ESPN in their basic package. That's over $60 a year. Multiply that by roughly 100 million households that subscribe to cable or satellite. So before ESPN opens up the gate to the parking lot in Bristol, Connecticut, before it sells a single thirty-second commercial, they're already pocketing almost $6 billion a year. It became obvious almost twenty years ago that the playing field was anything but level. And by the way, if you're a great-grandmother in Odessa, Texas, and have not the slightest interest in sports, you're still paying that sixty bucks for ESPN because it's the only way you can still watch your soap operas, your local news, and *Dr. Phil.* Sorry, Granny, you can't have à la carte choices and save yourself hundreds of dollars a year. I've always felt ESPN's Most Valuable Players through the years have been the Beltway lobbyists who've done a brilliant job of keeping Congress confused and at bay.

In 1996, Steve Bornstein, the head of ESPN, took over for Dennis Swanson. Swanson, who'd given me the plum of plums—*Monday Night Football*—was "retiring" at age fifty-eight. In other words, pushed out. And Bornstein would now be running both ESPN and ABC Sports. It was no surprise—I could see it coming from the moment Disney took the deed to the house. A couple of days after he took the job, my new boss called and said, "I want to sign you to a contract extension with alacrity." I laughed at the word and still throw it out on the air every once in a while, a throwback to that phone call. Steve flew out to Los Angeles later that week and said something that was sweet music to my ears. Over breakfast at the Peninsula Hotel, he said, "ESPN is important. But I want to restore the glory of ABC Sports." It never happened.

ESPN was founded in the late seventies. Today the cable industry is more profitable than ever. Which is why the major media conglomerates, and even the leagues themselves, have launched cable sports channels. But Disney had a gigantic head start when it acquired ESPN. And once management had started merging ESPN with ABC Sports, the endgame was clearly apparent: the cable channel was going to be the mother ship. The network sports division would be, sooner or later, swallowed whole.

Monday Night Football started to feel ESPN's weight in the late 1990s. One example among many: to pump up ESPN's *Sunday Night Football* broadcast, the network "borrowed" *MNF*'s exploding graphics and took Hank Williams Jr.'s opening song, "Are You Ready for Some Football?" I was walking through a hotel lobby in Denver with

Dan Dierdorf when we first heard the song blaring out of a television set on a Sunday night telecast. Dan and I looked at each like, "Whoa, what are we doing here? Isn't our game tomorrow?"

Also, in 1998, in the name of "synergy"—then the big corporate buzzword—the *Monday Night Football* kickoff was moved up from 9 P.M. to 8:20 P.M., and each telecast opened with a pregame show at the ESPN Sports Zone restaurant in Baltimore. I often felt *synergy* should be spelled "sinergy." As in sacrilegious. This was just a bald-faced way to promote ESPN's new restaurant chain. It was Frank Gifford's first year out of the booth since 1970 and somebody came up with the brilliant idea to have him fly to Baltimore every week and do a short segment from a glass-enclosed cubicle. He couldn't have looked more uncomfortable. The whole show felt like a cheap carnival act. It might as well have been hosted by Bozo the Clown with a seltzer bottle.

Still, the most dramatic changes for me came in the broadcast booth. At the end of 1997, after a twenty-seven-season run that dated back to the second year of *Monday Night Football,* Frank left the show. His contract wasn't renewed. (He was only offered that small role on the pregame show.) Things were getting so bizarre at the time that Michael Eisner, then the head honcho of Disney, was set to call Frank to give him the word himself. Frank deserved to hear it from the "big boss." But Frank was unreachable (it was later learned he'd been undergoing knee surgery) and after several failed attempts, Eisner had to get on a plane for Europe. So it fell to Bob Iger, then number two at the company, to get the word to Gifford. But Frank was still nowhere to be found and Iger would soon be on a plane himself. Word was starting to leak out that Frank's reign was over and it was important that he'd hear it from the company—and not the press. Meanwhile, even though Bornstein was now heading both sports divisions, a guy named Brian McAndrews had been given a senior management title at ABC Sports. So somehow it was now left to a guy who'd barely been there and would leave soon thereafter to call Frank Gifford. One

thing about Frank—he'd seen it all over the years and could be oblivious to the comings and goings in the executive suite. My phone in the
house rings the next afternoon. It's Frank. He was always the coolest
guy in the room. So matter-of-factly that he might as well had been
talking about the weather, he says, "I think I just got fired by a guy I
never heard of." And thus ended Frank Gifford's incredible run in the
Monday Night Football broadcast booth.

Meanwhile, in one of my first meetings with Steve Bornstein, he
made it clear he wasn't a fan of Dan Dierdorf and didn't want to
renew his contract, which was up the following year. I told him I
disagreed with his assessment, but he was intent on making 1998
Dan's last season as an analyst on the show. And with Gifford now
out, there was an open spot in a three-man booth—a role that would
be filled by Boomer Esiason.

Esiason had gotten to know Ken Wolfe and Craig Janoff, the
producer and director of *Monday Night Football,* while working with
them as an analyst on the World League of American Football in
the early-nineties. They had stayed in contact, and with Wolfe and
Janoff championing Esiason, ABC hired him to join Dan and me in
the *Monday Night* booth in 1998. (This, by the way, all came after a
major push at the time to hire John Madden for *Monday Night*—a
deal that fell apart at the last minute.) Esiason was thirty-seven, and
the year before, had gone back to Cincinnati for a second stint with
the Bengals and started seven games. He could still play but with the
Monday Night opportunity available, he'd decided to retire and make
the jump to broadcasting.

It was a thorny year from the start. Each week, we were coming off that dopey pregame show from Baltimore. Dan pretty much
knew it was going to be his last year. Wolfe and Janoff were—as
they had been for some time—dissatisfied with their contracts, and
bristling at a management team, including executive producer John
Filippelli, that they didn't like or respect. And then there was Esiason in and Gifford out. In our first broadcast—a preseason game in

Canton, Ohio, during Hall of Fame weekend—minutes before the game, Esiason asked me to introduce him specifically as a "Super Bowl quarterback." I told him I thought that sounded awkward—people knew who he was. Then, when I brought him in during the scene set, he immediately proclaimed to the audience, "It's going be a new booth, guys—look out!" Dierdorf and I glanced at each other. Ohhhh-kay.

Dan was let go after the 1998 season—the Pro Bowl was his last game for ABC. Meanwhile, Linda and I stayed after the game in Maui for a vacation. The Broncos had just won their second straight Super Bowl, and the team's coach, Mike Shanahan, owner Pat Bowlen, and John Elway were all staying at our hotel. One morning, I'm playing golf with Shanahan, who'd been a good friend dating back to his brief run as the Raiders' coach a decade earlier. When I meet him at the range, he says, "Did I hear that they fired Dan and kept the *other* guy?" I say yes. He says, "Boy, you're in some business." That night, Shanahan, Bowlen, Elway, and I went to dinner with our wives at Carelli's On The Beach. At this point, Elway still hadn't decided whether he would retire. There were even rumors that perhaps an opening in the *Monday Night Football* booth would entice him to end his playing career and make the transition. At dinner, the topic came up. I asked him if anyone at ABC had contacted him. Elway laughed and said Esiason had come to him and encouraged him to try to get the job. "Come with me," Boomer had told John, "so we can gang up on Michaels together."

Elway retired but passed on any broadcasting opportunities.

Back in New York a month later, I had lunch with the new president of ABC Sports, Howard Katz, who in the 1970s had been mentored by my father at TWI. (Steve Bornstein had been promoted to the head of Disney's Internet group.) At lunch, Howard told me he was concerned about the direction of the show. It was our Super Bowl year coming up—and I told him that after all the tumult of the past couple of years, I thought the smartest thing going forward was to avoid any more changes. I told him I felt the best option might be working with Esiason in a two-man booth. And that's the way it went in 1999.

We did the Super Bowl. The Rams beat the Titans in a thriller in Atlanta that came down to the final play of the game, when Rams linebacker Mike Jones tackled Kevin Dyson at the one-yard line to preserve the St. Louis victory. There would be the regular on-the-field presentations of the Lombardi Trophy and the MVP award and then from the booth, Esiason and I were going to take us off the air with a one-minute recap. But the ceremony ran long—the network wanted to get to some new show on the air that would debut as soon as we were done—and now we'd only have thirty seconds or less. Filippelli, the executive producer, was in the truck and told Wolfe to tell us that we'd only have time for me to say something briefly and take us off the air. There would be no time for Esiason, who then removed his earpiece and left the booth as I was starting the "close." I wouldn't see him again until our production meeting the following Saturday night in Honolulu prior to the next day's Pro Bowl.

By this point, Howard Katz had decided it was time for a big restructuring. And not just in the booth. Wolfe and Janoff were constantly moaning and brooding and had worn him out, too.

WHETHER FAIR OR NOT, as the new millennium approached, there was a perception that *Monday Night Football* was fraying—even if the ratings said otherwise. In the so-called glory years of the show with Howard Cosell, when there was only network television and no competition from cable, *MNF* had generally ranked around 20th out of 54 shows. In the supposedly "flat" period, it was almost always in the top 10 out of 150 shows.

Still, despite all that, total viewership was down simply because of the rise of cable. Instead of just two other options, CBS and NBC, as there were in the seventies, now viewers had a hundred choices. We were now competing against a whole universe of shows, from other sports programming to early-stage reality television to professional wrestling's *Monday Night RAW*. And Howard Katz had a big change in mind. "What would you think," Howard asked me, "if Don Ohlmeyer came back to produce *Monday Night Football*?" Katz and Ohlmeyer were very close. Howard had spent a number of years working at Don's production company.

I'd known Don since the 1970s. He was a disciple of Roone Arledge and had produced *Monday Night Football* in the early years. Don had been supportive in getting me to ABC in the first place, and then had left to run NBC Sports and then, later, NBC Entertainment. He'd made NBC megamillions by overseeing the "Must See TV" Thursday night lineup in the 1990s. Don had retired from television in 1998 at fifty-three years old. He'd been there, done that, and needed a break. But was it temporary or permanent? Even Don didn't know at that point. We were playing golf two or three times a week and I'd never seen him happier.

"You're never going to be able to get Don," I said to Katz. "He's enjoying life too much. He'll never do this. Don't get me wrong. If you could, it would be great. But I just don't see him coming back for a job he already had twenty-five years ago. I just don't see it happening."

Don and I had lunch shortly after that and he told me that Howard had spoken to him about coming back. And then he surprised me.

"I'm thinking about it," he said. "I have some ideas that are totally out of the box, but the only way I'll do it is if I have real autonomy."

Don didn't want the increasing collection of executives and bean counters at ABC and ESPN interfering with his plans. He had big ideas, and wanted the freedom to execute them.

"What do you have in mind?" I asked.

"Number one, Esiason's out. We can find any number of better analysts. But I'd also want to put someone in the booth from outside the football world. Someone who will get people talking.

"I know one thing, though," he continued. "If I ever did this, you'd have to buy in."

I told him the idea was very intriguing. This could range anywhere from sensational to a total bust.

Sure enough, a week or so later, Don Ohlmeyer came out of retirement. That ended Wolfe's fourteen-year run as producer. And he had the autonomy he needed to really shake things up. He sent Esiason packing and hired a new director to replace Janoff. His name was Drew Esocoff, and Don, who'd never met Esocoff, loved the way he had directed that year's Sugar Bowl. How'd *that* hire turn out? Well, Drew and I have now worked together for the last fifteen seasons. Nobody today and nobody ever has done it better than Drew. Ohlmeyer always understood showmanship and had a great sense of what works and what doesn't. He knew a great director when he saw one. And he was never afraid of risks.

However, before Don could start looking "outside the box" for a new guy in the booth, Bill Parcells resigned as the head coach of the Jets. That's when Parcells had that famous quote—"Write it on your chalkboard, I'll never coach again." Of course, three years later, Jerry Jones would help Bill erase that chalkboard. Anyway, Katz, Ohlmeyer, and I figured if we could sign Parcells, we'd go with the more conventional two-man booth. Bill would bring enough to the table. He was a Jersey guy, a New York icon, and a coach who'd won two Super Bowls. I was excited at the prospect.

Katz had dinner with Parcells on Long Island to gauge his interest in the job. Bill said he'd need some time to think about it and, among other things, had a number of questions he wanted to ask me. Over the next few days, Parcells and I had two long phone conversations. I'd known Bill over the years, through covering his teams, as a man who had a lot of answers. Now he was posing the questions. And they were all thoughtful, insightful, and thorough. He wanted to know everything about everything—how would *this* work, how would *that* work, what if we tried this, explain that dynamic to me, and so on. Bill had had a little prior broadcasting experience at NBC and understood the business. The more we talked, the more excited I became. I thought it would be a great pairing. Before we hung up on the second conversation, he said he was going to take a couple of more days to think about it. Among the things that were holding him back was the travel. He hated to fly. Also, I wasn't completely convinced that coaching was totally out of his blood. The last thing I said to him was, "Bill, I hope you'll do this. I think it'll be great and we'll have a lot of fun. But there's one thing I have to say to you—the people who work on this show live and breathe *Monday Night Football*. It's an honor to be a part of. Please don't think of this as a halfway house between coaching jobs. If you take it, we have to know you're all in."

His response was perfect. He said, "I don't know what I'm going to do but I'll tell you this: if I take this job, nobody will work harder and I'll be the best who's ever done it." Now I *really* wanted him to say yes.

But a week later, Parcells passed on the opportunity. He said he really wrestled with the decision, and that he'd gone back and forth multiple times. At that moment, I'd have bet the moon he'd be back on the sidelines at some point. That point would be 2003 in Dallas.

WITH THE PARCELLS DALLIANCE over, it was time for Ohlmeyer to get in full gear. Don decided to replace Lesley Visser as sideline reporter with two reporters—Melissa Stark, in her mid-twenties from ESPN, and the former star running back Eric Dickerson.

Dan Fouts, Steve Young, Nate Newton, and Tom Jackson came in to audition for the role of conventional analyst, and Fouts got the job. In short order, Dan would be in my Partners Hall of Fame. A great guy on every level and the ultimate team player. And you wouldn't have a clue that he'd be on that short list of Greatest Quarterbacks Ever. No false modesty, either. No need to introduce him as anything other than Dan Fouts. Just Dan being Dan—always a joy to be with.

Now it was time to concentrate on our "wild card."

Just as Ohlmeyer figured, he had turned this into a national parlor game. *Who is going to be* Monday Night Football's *new "out of the box" announcer?* USA Today ran a readers' poll with suggestions for the slate of candidates. When there was a conference call to update the media on where things stood, more than one hundred reporters called in.

One Sunday when I was in New York, I was a guest panelist on ESPN's *The Sports Reporters* and was asked who would be in my fantasy booth. The Rascal popped out and I said, "Shania Twain and Maureen Dowd." A few days later in Los Angeles, I opened up a letter. It was a short note: "Al, sounds great to me, too—Maureen."

Because of the way Don Ohlmeyer went about the process, *everyone* was considered. Or thought they were. Don made it clear nobody in the entire country was being ruled out. A couple of radio talk show hosts and a local Los Angeles television anchor on KTLA—a Carlos Somebody—contacted Don and he told them, "Sure, we're considering you." Then they'd go on the air and say they were in the running for *Monday Night Football*. Don and I would laugh our asses off. If Don's barber had thrown his hat in the ring, *that* guy would have been under consideration. We thought about telling all these guys they were only slightly behind Don's dry cleaner on the depth chart.

We actually did bring in Tony Kornheiser for an audition. If there was a guy in the media at that time who we thought could bring us something smart and different, Tony was a legitimate candidate. (Six years later, Kornheiser would join *Monday Night Football* after it had moved to ESPN.)

One morning, Don was driving around Los Angeles and listening to Rush Limbaugh's radio show. Limbaugh said, "I see where Don Ohlmeyer is the new producer for *Monday Night Football,* and he is looking to do things outside the box. I know football. I love football. I'll tell you what would be different—me!"

Leave it to Don. He'd never met Rush but called him within the hour. "Rush, I heard you on the air today. Why don't you come out to L.A. and audition?"

"Is this a joke?"

"We'll see you next Tuesday."

Next thing you knew, here was Rush Limbaugh auditioning.

We wanted to keep everything we were doing under wraps. So David Israel, a good friend of both Don and me who was involved in the recruiting process, found an out-of-the-way studio in the north end of the San Fernando Valley where we'd sneak the candidates in through the back door.

Rush came in and we put on a tape of the Tennessee-Buffalo Wild Card playoff classic that had been played in January—the famed "Music City Miracle" game. We put on our headsets and I did some rudimentary play-by-play. We always wanted to give our tryout folks plenty of room and space to see what they had.

Rush knew a lot about the NFL. It was apparent he was a huge fan and a close follower. And he knew how to connect with an audience. Love him or detest him, he knows how to communicate. You can't possibly have that long a career if you don't have those chops. In the end, though, it was a no-go. It wasn't a question of polarization—Ohlmeyer was never averse to that—it was a question of whether Rush could devote the necessary time to *Monday Night Football* while doing his three-hour radio show five days a week.

Meanwhile, suddenly it was June—nine weeks away from going on the air with the preseason Hall of Fame game. And we still didn't have our wild card.

Ohlmeyer, though, had had his eye on Dennis Miller the whole time. They had friends in common from NBC, where Don had been a top executive and Dennis had spent several years with the cast of *Saturday Night Live,* most famously as the host of "Weekend Update." Dennis had grown up in Pittsburgh loving the Steelers and was a huge football fan. It was time to bring him in for the audition. At this point, we were banking on Miller being "the guy" or . . . who knows what? The clock was ticking.

I'd never met Dennis before. Now Dan Fouts would be there for the audition as well. So the three of us were going back and forth, re-creating a broadcast over a tape of a game and Dennis was off to a good start. He'd gotten off some very funny lines and was trying to demonstrate that he knew football. It was working.

We were calling a tape of a Packers-49ers Monday night game that had been played the previous season in San Francisco. At one point, I said, ". . . and the ball is given to Garrison Hearst over right tackle. Gain of four. Second down and six. The tackle made by number ninety-three, Cletidus Hunt."

"What?" says Dennis. "Who?"

"Number ninety-three," I repeat. "Defensive tackle CLEET-ee-us Hunt."

"CLEET-ee-us Hunt? That's not a player," says Dennis. "That's a raid on a sorority."

Ohlmeyer was sitting behind the glass in the control room with his ever-present cigarette glowing in the dim light. Right then he said, "Let's take ten."

"Taking ten" was the code for me to go outside for a private conference and meet him on the street. So there we are, on Lankershim Boulevard with tractor-trailers and eighteen-wheelers rumbling past and belching smoke. We looked at each other and simultaneously, in complete unison said, "We've got our man."

Then Don and I had a discussion. Could we get away with a line like that on the air? We never reached a conclusion, but Dennis got the job. What would have happened if Dennis had bombed in the tryout? To this day, I don't know. Don was always confident Miller would be "the guy."

*   *   *

TO SHARE THE NEWS with the media—which had been waiting weeks for the announcement—ABC held a press conference call. Ohlmeyer had all of us come to his home in Beverly Hills. Fouts, Melissa, Eric, Dennis, and I all gathered in his den and took our places around this space-age speakerphone. As Don started to make the announcement, he got up and left the room. We all looked at each other. Don continued talking as he walked into a side bathroom. He never missed a beat. Then he walked back into the den, zipped up his fly, sat back down, finished up his introductory remarks, and said to the flower of American sports journalism, "Okay, any questions?" Don always marched to the beat of an entirely different drummer.

The mystery surrounding the buildup had the desired effect. In July, Dennis was on the cover of *Sports Illustrated* wearing eye black above the tagline "Can Dennis Miller Save *Monday Night Football*?" (Where had I heard *that* before?) The question was a hot topic of discussion for several weeks.

A few weeks later, we all convened for our first telecast—the preseason Hall of Fame Game in Canton, Ohio. Don gathered the entire production team on Saturday morning in a conference room at the Cuyahoga Falls Sheraton. There were about forty people in the room: Don, the broadcast team, our new director Drew Esocoff, associate directors, production assistants, runners, the key engineering people, the research folks, and a few others. When Don walked in, he was wearing all white, sucking on one of the 120 cigarettes he would smoke that day. My longtime spotter, "Malibu" Kelly Hayes, leaned over to me and said, "Good God, it's the Great Gatsby."

Don's reputation preceded him. He had a big laugh, a big inventory of stories, and a big personality. He also didn't suffer fools gladly. He had written an expansive handout—a short book, really—about his *Monday Night Football* philosophy and distributed it to all of us. *Here's what we're we going to try. Here's what is going to be different.*

In late morning, it was time for a break. "It'll be a long day for everyone—I'm sending out for some lunch," he said. And with that,

Don reached for a pad and pen and started going around the room. *What do you want? Turkey? Lettuce and tomato? What about you? Ham and cheese? Okay. And what do you want to drink? Diet Coke? Caffeine or no caffeine?* Don took down forty lunch orders and then handed it to a runner. He'd sent a message. *Hey, we're all a team. I may be the boss but I'm also taking food orders. Nobody's going to stand on ceremony.*

That was a year to remember. I love Dennis. Yet he's the ultimate piece of work. He's brilliantly funny but working with a comedian was a different kind of challenge. If you laugh at every line, you sound like a hyena. We were all going down a road never before traveled. Between second down and six and third-and-four, Dennis might drop in a short riff on Sylvia Plath. At times like those, I felt like *my* head was in a bell jar.

The changes went beyond the booth. Don was getting back to producing live sports after a long absence. And we had two new sideline reporters in Melissa and Eric. Ringling Bros. could have bought the rights.

On top of all that, almost every week the games were fantastic. There was drama and suspense deep into the fourth quarter. Or overtime. Blowouts were a foreign commodity on *Monday Night Football* in 2000. Which meant Dennis rarely had the opportunity to just let it hang out in one-sided contests, something we had been anticipating would help to keep an audience from saying good night before the final gun. In a 27–27 game with five minutes to play, the viewers didn't want to hear an obscure joke about the Kennedy assassination or the Green Hornet or whatever esoteric reference came into Dennis's mind.

The most memorable, wackiest game that season was the Jets-Dolphins "Monday Night Miracle," which ended at 1:22 A.M. It took place on an off night between games of the Yankees-Mets World Series. Miami was up 23–7 at halftime. Then Arnold Schwarzenegger visited the broadcast booth and said, with random prophecy, "Wayne Chrebet is going to pull it off. I think as usual the Jets are going to come from behind, you will see. . . . I think the Dolphins have to be terminated."

By the fourth quarter, the Dolphins were leading, 30–7 and half the crowd at Giants Stadium, including Schwarzenegger, was already in the parking lot. But here came Vinny Testaverde and the Jets. Testaverde threw three touchdown passes—the tying one, as Schwarzenegger had somewhat mused, to Wayne Chrebet. Now thousands of fans were making their way back in from the parking lot. However, the Dolphins then got a long kickoff return, and Jay Fiedler threw a 46-yard touchdown pass to Leslie Shepherd to grab the lead right back.

But wait. The Jets marched right back down the field, worked their way inside the Dolphins' five-yard line, and Testaverde threw a pass to offensive lineman Jumbo Elliot on an insane tackle-eligible play with a few seconds left to tie the game again and send it to overtime, where they'd eventually win it.

I called it this way: "Testaverde back to pass and it is juggled and caught by JUMBO ELLIOTT! JUMBO Elliott—who's been in the league for twelve years. It's the FIRST TOUCHDOWN of his career! It's the FIRST CATCH of his career!"

Dennis Miller never missed a beat. "Well," he said, "you couldn't keep him down forever."

During that off-the-charts 2000 season, we had a lot of laughs off the air, too. Christmas Day was a Monday, so we were in Nashville for the Titans and Cowboys. On Sunday night, Christmas Eve, Dennis and I went to dinner at the Palm. It had just opened a week or two before. The décor included caricatures on the walls of a few local celebrities but primarily politicians and all the city councilmen. The manager had heard that Dennis might be coming in, so there was a caricature of him that they'd put up at the last minute. After the meal, the manager asked him to sign the picture.

Dennis said sure, and got up on the banquette to sign his name. But leave it to Dennis—he didn't stop there. He kept going, signing his name on the caricatures of all these Nashville muckety-mucks and country music singers. All the manager could do was laugh nervously. What he really wanted to do was whack him.

We walked out and headed back to our hotel, the Loews Vanderbilt. I had a problem with the phone in my room and the maintenance man came up. "Yeah," he said, "we've had issues with the whole phone system since the election." He went on to explain that Al Gore and his staff had headquartered there on Election Night, a few weeks earlier.

"Wait a second," I said. "When Gore called George W. Bush that night to congratulate him and concede the election—before all hell broke loose and we learned all about hanging chads—he did it from here?"

"Yup," the guy said. "He was in the suite at the end of the hall."

So a few minutes later, I made my way over to the Presidential Suite. And what do you know—the door was slightly ajar. Bud Adams—the Titans owner who'd founded the Houston Oilers of the AFL in 1960, had moved the team to Tennessee in 1997, and had negotiated television deals with my father—would always stay in that suite when he was in town. I knocked but no one answered. I tiptoed in, figuring if I saw Adams, I could just wish him a Merry Christmas. But no one was there. I was envisioning Gore, his team around him, in this room on Election Night. I looked at a coffee table in the living room and assumed I might be staring at the phone that Gore had used to call Bush. He'd probably used a dedicated phone that his team had installed but at least this instrument was in the neighborhood.

Here comes the Rascal, Christmas Eve Edition. I removed the phone from the jack, took it back to my room, and stuck it in my suitcase. With the statute of limitations having lapsed, I will confess that now, in my home in Los Angeles, sits the phone that Al Gore might have used (or at least its first cousin) to as it turned out, prematurely concede the most contested presidential election in U.S. history. It was a Christmas present for myself.

As for Dennis, he'd be with us for two seasons. It was wild and wacky and mostly good fun. Dennis's notes were on a long and narrow piece of cardboard with about eighty lines written on it. I'd say, "Dennis, you're so good, so quick on the uptake. Why do you need this crutch? You hardly use any of these." It was a security blanket.

Dennis's tenure was met with all manner of reviews. If there was one thing that worked against him, it was this: so much of comedy is visual. If Dennis was on *Saturday Night Live* or *The Tonight Show* or his HBO series, you *saw* him. You'd see his facial expressions, his body language. In the middle of a football game, in the midst of the action and with your focus on the field and the crowd roaring, words are often extraneous. The audience might be thinking: *What did he say?* And you certainly couldn't laugh at any of his facial movements—you couldn't see them.

Ohlmeyer would leave after one season and hand the reins to Fred Gaudelli, for my money hands-down the finest sports producer ever to come down the pike. As I write this, Fred and I are in our fourteenth season together. Miller would be out after two. I look back at it this way: he revitalized the show and brought it back into the national conversation. Harder to do than you might think.

After his brief era, though, it was time for the gold standard to come aboard.

CHAPTER 18

Partners

OVER THE YEARS, I'VE worked with more than one hundred broadcast partners, from O. J. Simpson to Arthur Ashe to Johnny Unitas to Don Drysdale to Bruce Jenner. Most of them have been former players or coaches. In a few cases, they've struggled to make the transition. Mark (the Bird) Fidrych, who used to talk to the baseball on the mound, rest his soul, worked one game and decided that the broadcast booth wasn't for him. He actually said to me in the fifth inning—*on the air*—that he had to go to the bathroom. In other cases, the transition has been so smooth that the former athletes end up redefining themselves. Cris Collinsworth, for example, is so good at his craft that fans either forget or aren't even aware that he was once a very good NFL wide receiver who played in two Super Bowls.

Some former jocks approach the commentary role with the mentality *I played the game, I was on the field and you weren't. So listen to what I have to say.* That's usually when laziness blends with arrogance. That won't cut it. I worked with one analyst, a former quarterback, who would constantly say things like "This is what the quarterback is thinking here." The situation didn't matter. I always wanted to say, "Really? *Every* quarterback is thinking the same thing on every third-and-four? Just because you once were a quarterback doesn't mean you know what *all* quarterbacks are thinking in every situation. This is what *you* were thinking, not everybody." The best of the best—John Madden, Cris Collinsworth, and Tim McCarver, to name three of my all-time favorites—worked their butts off to learn what a specific player or coach or manager might or might not do in a specific situation. That's part of what always separated them from the pack.

No one would compare my job to hard physical labor. But it is a lot of work. There are meetings upon meetings. There is a ton of preparation. You have to keep up and stay ahead of everything that's going on that can impact a telecast. You have to be able to anticipate intelligently. Yes, in a small market, a former athlete with a big enough name can make it simply by showing up. He played the game, knows enough people with the team, tells a few stories. You can make a good living doing that. But that's not going to get you to the network level. Or if it does, it won't be for long.

What makes the good ones *really* good? They understand broadcasting and the art of communicating. They don't think of themselves as being in the ex-jock business—they're in the broadcasting business. They understand story lines and flow and perspective. They understand the dissemination of information. They develop a sense of timing and learn how to use their voices and the art of inflection. They know what the seventy or eighty other people on the crew—the unsung people who often make you look a lot better—are doing and respect them. And they are always trying to improve.

And you're never too old. Another of my favorite partners was the former basketball coach Hubie Brown, with whom I did the NBA on ABC a decade ago. Hubie is now in his eighties and still going strong. God bless him. Every couple of weeks, Hubie would say to me, "Tell me how I can get better. Don't hesitate. I want to know. What do you think I should work on?"

Not only was he a great teacher—he was a pretty good student, too.

IN 2002, TWENTY-SEVEN YEARS after I first met with him in his office when he was coaching the Raiders, John Madden and I reunited. ABC had first tried to sign John for *Monday Night Football* at the end of the 1992 season but Fox had just gotten the rights to the NFL and made John a blowaway offer. The network made another push for him when Frank Gifford left after the 1997 season. It was close but didn't happen. Finally, after the 2001 season, Howard Katz, the president of ABC Sports, and Alex Wallau, the president of the network who'd always coveted Madden, made another big play. Pat Summerall, John's longtime partner on CBS and Fox, was soon retiring, and Fox was looking to go in another direction. This time, the timing and fit were perfect. John Madden was moving to *Monday Night Football.*

John and I had crossed paths on a few occasions through the years, and of course had listened to each other hundreds of times. When his move to ABC became imminent, we spoke by phone. Already, there was some skepticism from a few television critics and others wondering if we could "coexist." John and I just laughed about it because we knew there was not a chance in a hundred that it *wouldn't* work.

In one of our initial conversations, I asked John a question. I had remembered watching Super Bowl XXXI on Fox several years earlier—New England against Green Bay. During the lead-up to the game, the question of whether Bill Parcells was going to leave the Patriots was a huge story. Parcells was being totally evasive with the media. Though most of the speculation had him resigning, no one really had the definitive answer and it remained a big mystery. Then, near the end of the game, Madden said on the air, "Well, Bill Parcells will not be flying home with the team."

He had worked the edges of saying *Bill Parcells will not be back with the team next season* without ever actually saying it. To me, it was simple. John knew the real story. Parcells had told Madden of his plans. And Madden had the scoop.

I recounted this to John and he agreed with my analysis of the situation. I said, "That's the kind of thing where, if you and I are working together, I'd want to have a back-and-forth about this. If we have a scoop, I'd want us to dive right in and not skirt the edges or beat around the bush. Would you be comfortable with that?"

He paused and said, "You know, sometimes it's difficult to fly the plane alone." It was exactly the kind of answer I wanted to hear. It was another way of saying "definitely."

John came in a year after Fred Gaudelli had replaced Don Ohl-meyer as the producer of the show. Don had only signed on for a year or two, and felt that he'd accomplished almost everything he'd wanted to in that 2000 season. The truck would now be in great shape with Gaudelli and Esocoff (it still is, to this day)—but now we were rebooting again in the booth. And in a meeting before the 2002 preseason started, Fred asked John and me if we wanted to announce a practice game—pretend we were doing a real telecast over the tape of a game from the previous season. If there would be any kinks, we could work them out in the form of a rehearsal. John looked over at me as if to let me make the decision since he was new to *Monday Night* and I was the incumbent. "No, it's better to just let it happen," I said, and then looked over at John. "We don't need this, do we?"

He said, "I was hoping you would say that."

So our first time ever together in a broadcast booth was at the Hall of Fame Game in Canton in 2002. As confident and optimistic as we were, there's always that tiny inkling of doubt lurking, where you think, *Well, maybe it won't be as good as we think it will and we'll have to work out some bugs.* But before John and I got to the second commercial break, I felt like we'd worked together for ten years. There was an immediate and natural flow. From those first few minutes on, we didn't so much as need eye contact. It felt great. And it would stay that way for the seven years we worked together.

John and I quickly became great pals outside the booth as well. He even indulged my vegetable-phobia. One night, when we were in Green Bay, I ordered French onion soup without the onions—just the broth with cheese and croutons. He was in hysterics. John and I even discovered that we share the same recurring nightmare: we're late for a game and we're stuck on this ring road that surrounds the stadium and can't get to the booth on time.

Part of what made John Madden such a singular broadcaster was the circumstances. So many former athletes and coaches still relish and thrive on competition. Inevitably, they discover that in television, you can't quite re-create the feeling of walking off the field or court and looking at the way the lights on the scoreboard align and knowing for certain if you've won or lost, succeeded or failed. For coaches, in particular, there's no scoreboard to look at when you walk out of a booth after a game. Some viewers might think you did a great job and others would like to see you forever pinned under the wheels of a moving van. Good luck figuring out a final score. For many big names who've transitioned into broadcasting—among them Joe Gibbs and Bill Walsh in football, Pat Riley and George Karl in basketball, Joe Torre and Bobby Valentine in baseball—television was a stopover between jobs, or a coda to a long career to be approached as a part-time pursuit.

Coaching has always been a demanding job. George Halas coached the Chicago Bears for forty years, but even he temporarily stepped away after ten consecutive seasons on four separate occasions. (It didn't hurt that he also owned the team.) Today, the demands on coaches are almost criminal. Sleeping in the office is not uncommon and many devote as many hours to the job in the off-season as they do in-season. Sometimes coaches just need a break, and television can be a way to take what amounts to a leave of absence.

In the case of John Madden, there was none of that. He knew he wouldn't reenter the world of coaching. So he devoted himself to a career in television soon after he left the sidelines. He was only forty when he led the Raiders to victory in Super Bowl XI. He won more than one hundred games as a head coach, and then stepped away when he was only forty-two. He never went back. He *couldn't* go back.

Most fans are familiar with the Madden Cruiser, the made-to-order bus John took from game to game. It fit his image—which was thoroughly genuine—of being a man of the people you'd might have a decent shot to run into some day at an Arby's in Keokuk, Iowa. And it's well known that John rode the bus because he was petrified of flying. I'm not sure people ever realized just how debilitating his fear of flying was.

For starters, John played at Cal Poly–San Luis Obispo in the late fifties. He knew many of the coaches and players on the team plane that crashed in Ohio after a game against Bowling Green in October 1960. Twenty-two of the forty-eight people on board were killed, including sixteen players. Secondly, John has claustrophobia. They'd shut the cabin doors—and John would feel like he *had* to get out. John and I and a couple of others once got stuck between the first and second floors of a large freight elevator at a hotel in San Diego. It lasted only a couple of minutes but it was not a pretty sight.

He had no choice but to endure flying when he coached, but shortly after his retirement from the NFL and early in his broadcasting career, he worked a Thanksgiving weekend game in 1979 in Tampa. He flew there from Oakland, which was home. His return flight stopped in Houston, and on the Tampa-to-Houston leg, he'd had enough. Then and there, on that flight, John made a vow: if he landed safely in Houston, he would get off the plane, walk out of the airport, take a train the rest of the way home, and never in his life get back on an airplane again. Sure enough, that's what happened. And John's "claustrophobia" on airplanes overwhelmed any possibility of his ever returning to coaching—even though there's no question that, for years, he would have been a prime candidate for every job opening.

All in all, life was good for John Madden. He lived at his own pace. His name would be on the best-selling sports video game ever.

He would open a winery and a hotel and an office park. He was a Renaissance man—interested and curious about *everything*. He had a brilliant football mind to begin with and was a natural at communicating and connecting with the viewers. He created a new template for analysts and spawned a bunch of cheap imitators. He was totally committed to his work. No one watched as much film as John. No one was as tapped into the league with as many contacts and confidants. Coaches would seek him out for advice.

One more note on John's last plane ride: This was in the days of paper tickets that gate agents would tear off as you boarded. Somewhere, perhaps deep in the recesses of John's garage, might reside the unused ticket of the Houston–San Francisco portion of that trip. I once told him, "If you ever run out of money, do you realize what that would be worth on eBay?"

JOHN MADDEN HAD A lot of favorite players, but there's no doubt that at or near the top of the list was Brett Favre. So it's fitting that in the four seasons that John and I did *Monday Night Football* together, one of our most unforgettable games centered around Favre.

It was late in the 2003 season, and the Packers were in Oakland. The Raiders were coming off a season in which they'd made it to the Super Bowl (losing to the Tampa Bay Buccaneers) but they were already in steep decline. The Packers, per usual during the Favre era, were headed to the playoffs.

Whenever we'd meet with Brett before games, he was always engaging. You'd get him going and he was very expansive. There were meetings where you'd want to ask twenty questions or delve into a dozen topics, and you'd be there with him for an hour or more. Some answers would go twenty minutes. And John, of course, could talk football with him all day.

Before this game in Oakland, the Packers were staying at the Claremont Hotel in the Berkeley hills. We sat in a third-floor conference room for our meeting. I was sitting to Brett's left and peering through a small circular window that looked out over San Francisco Bay and the Golden Gate Bridge out in the distance. Favre was going on and on and on. And at one point, apparently I began to glaze over a little. Brett, who never missed very much, looked over at me, smiled and asked, "Hey, Al, are you still with me?"

Somehow I came up with this: "Brett, you have to understand something. Look over there. I can look just beyond you and I can see the Golden Gate Bridge. How many times in your life can you look at two American icons in one blink of an eye?"

We laughed, the meeting ended, and then Brett quietly went off to play nine holes of golf at a nearby course with Doug Pederson, the backup quarterback. Pederson had a cell phone with him, and after a couple of holes, it rang. It was Deanna Favre, looking for her husband, trying to reach him to tell him that his father had died. Irv Favre had been driving in Mississippi and suffered a heart attack behind the wheel.

Like any son who loved his father, I thought back to when my own dad had died. He'd been diagnosed with lung cancer in July 1982, and died on February 11, 1983. It was a six-month, straight-downhill deterioration and I was in denial the whole way. Still, when somebody dies like that, you have time to accept it and process it—even though I never really completely did. When somebody dies suddenly, I don't know how you react to that. Here's Brett and there was no chance to say good-bye. You're the son and you're two thousand miles away. I remember thinking when we heard it, *What's going to happen? Will Brett go home? What will he do?*

In our scene set that night, I asked John what he expected would happen. He didn't know because there was almost nothing to compare it to. Nobody knew.

We know what happened. Mike Sherman, the Packers coach, left it up to Brett. And Brett decided to play. And not only did he play, but he turned in one of those one-for-the-ages magical performances. The numbers: 22 of 30 for 399 yards, and four touchdowns. Watching it live made you rub your eyes in disbelief. It seemed like no matter where he threw the ball, it got caught.

One thing I always knew when I was paired with John in 2002—the ride was going to be a lot of fun. I'll say! We worked together for seven seasons—four on Monday nights and three on Sunday nights. If you were to ask me my favorite telecast with John, without hesitation it would be Super Bowl XLIII in Tampa following the 2008 season. The Pittsburgh Steelers rallied late, driving ninety-three yards for the winning touchdown, to beat the Arizona Cardinals in what many people felt was the best Super Bowl ever. It might be my all-time favorite telecast. Fred Gaudelli, Drew Esocoff, and our entire production crew were as good as the game. They didn't miss a shot. You name it—it was brilliantly covered. And I never felt more in sync with a partner than I did that day with John, who as usual, was right on top of everything.

After the game, I wished I would have relished it even more. Why? Because two and a half months later, John would retire. The announcement was sudden and unexpected. I was shocked. John summed it up in quintessential fashion—"It's time." There was one thing, though, that *wasn't* shocking. John Madden went out on top.

IN 2002, THE SAME year John Madden came to ABC, the network made another acquisition: the National Basketball Association. After more than a decade on NBC, the NBA's new television deal meant the Finals would air on ABC—but the majority of games—in both the regular season and playoffs—would be televised on ESPN.

After the first season of the new deal, NBA commissioner David Stern, a man never known to suppress his opinions, was not thrilled with his new broadcast partner. He felt that there was nothing that distinguished the ABC games from the ESPN games. One of the reasons was that Mark Shapiro, ESPN's executive vice president for programming and production, was in charge of the presentation of both packages. Stern had no use for Shapiro, and no interest in dealing with him. The commissioner let it be known to both the ABC and ESPN top brass that he wanted the ABC games to have a special sheen—similar to how *Monday Night Football* on ABC was presented. And one of the several ways he thought that might be accomplished was by bringing me in as the play-by-play voice for the ABC games.

Now, when ABC had originally made the NBA deal, they were contractually obligated to offer me the opportunity to do the games—it was written into my deal that I would get a first look on any new package. It was clear to me that ESPN was going to be the dominant force, so I didn't express much interest. And to top it off, they made me an offer that basically said, "We don't want you." But now in the summer of 2003, David Stern had communicated to Bob Iger at Disney, and George Bodenheimer, the president of ESPN, that he would like me to be a part of the package. In September, an offer came to me—I would announce a half dozen regular season games, several early-round playoff games, and then the Finals. It would be my first experience doing NBA games since my ill-fated and abbreviated few weeks with Chick Hearn and the Lakers, and my first time doing basketball games on a regular basis since UCLA in the mid-seventies. This time, they made me an offer I couldn't refuse. And to enhance the production end, they hired Drew Esocoff, who'd already wowed people in his three years on *Monday Night Football,* to direct the NBA games. I was excited, but also, having been away from basketball for so long, I had a degree of trepidation.

One thing I insisted on in my contract was that I would report to Mike Pearl, then the executive producer of ABC Sports, and a man who had been front-and-center in creating the NBA template at Turner Broadcasting. Even though Mark Shapiro was overseeing the coverage, I didn't want to deal with him. I had dealt with him before, and would come away feeling that with Shapiro, to put it mildly, I couldn't trust what I was being told. One example came in

1998 when he asked me to serve on a select, blue-ribbon panel that would be limited to a "handful" of people who would choose the greatest athletes, coaches, and events for ESPN's SportsCentury project. I later learned that this so-called select panel included well over a hundred media members, mainly sportswriters, who it would turn out had only a cursory role in determining the actual final results, which I also learned had been basically predetermined by Shapiro and ESPN. It was a complete waste of my time, just a transparent attempt to generate publicity for the project by including writers from all over the country. Ironically, Shapiro had gotten his first big break in television from my brother, David, at the 1992 Barcelona Olympics. While I had followed my dreams in the booth, David had become one of sports television's top producers. And in 1992, he had hired Shapiro as one of his production assistants.

Before I knew it, suddenly, it was November. I was in the middle of the *Monday Night Football* season, my second with John Madden. And now the NBA season had started as well, but I still didn't have a partner. The first game on my schedule would be Christmas Day with the Lakers hosting the Houston Rockets at Staples Center. I needed to get in some practice, so Mike Pearl and I arranged for me to do a couple of practice games at Staples Center on nights when the Lakers were playing. We'd have three or four cameras at our disposal, so it was almost like doing a real game, except the broadcast was just going to a control room and a tape machine. Mark Jackson, the former All-Star point guard, had just retired after sixteen seasons in the NBA, and was living in Santa Monica and looking to get into broadcasting. So Mark came down to Staples Center and he and I did a Lakers-Knicks game. Not great, but okay. When I rode with Mike Pearl back to his hotel, I said to him, "Mark is going to be very good someday. He's just very green right now. And I haven't done a game in over twenty years—and I'm green. I think the best scenario is for me to work with somebody with a lot of broadcasting experience."

(Jackson would unretire before season's end to join the Rockets, and ironically, I'd call a playoff game that he played in for Houston.)

Now I was starting to get nervous because Christmas was fast approaching, and I needed a lot more work. Fortunately—at least fortunately for me—there was an NBA team three thousand miles away that had faltered right out of the gate. The Orlando Magic had started 1-10, and their coach, Doc Rivers, had gotten fired.

Rivers had played thirteen seasons in the NBA, and had gotten into broadcasting when he retired. Then, in 1999, he'd been hired by the Magic—with no prior coaching experience—and promptly won Coach of the Year honors, leading an overachieving group to a 41-41 season. However, in 2003–04, Rivers's team got off to that awful start.

Mike Pearl, who had worked with Doc at Turner Sports, called him the day after he was fired to gauge his interest in returning to broadcasting sooner than later. A few days later, Doc was on a plane to Los Angeles to do a practice game with me. And right away, it was obvious—it just worked. I was better with him. He was comfortable with me. Often, it takes time to build chemistry with a partner. Once in a great while, if you're lucky, it clicks from the start.

As Rivers's deal was being negotiated, Pearl asked me if I wanted Doc to come back for another practice game.

"But he's living in Orlando," I said. "I need as much practice as I can get, but I don't want to ask him to fly all the way across the country to do this again."

"Won't be a problem," says Mike. "If it will make you guys better, Doc will do it." And he did. We actually did *two* more practice games. It was an early sign about what kind of a terrific partner Doc Rivers would become.

We made our on-the-air debut on Christmas Day. Yao Ming and the Rockets beat the Lakers, 99-87. We did five more regular season games, including Cleveland rookie LeBron James's first visit to Madison Square Garden. And we had a blast. Doc and I both love golf. He used to play for the Clippers so he knew Los Angeles. We shared a number of favorite restaurants—and agreed that our all-time favorite was Toscana in Brentwood.

So much of the spotlight that season was on the Lakers, who'd won three of the last four titles, and had acquired a pair of future Hall of Famers, Karl Malone and Gary Payton. Some people were expecting them to win seventy games. Instead, they were good, but certainly not dominant. Plus, this was the year that Kobe Bryant had charges of sexual assault in Colorado hanging over his head, and was flying back and forth to court dates in Colorado. And, with Phil Jackson's contract expiring, and with his health of some concern, questions about his future hung over the team. There was a lot going on with the Lakers—good and bad—and it made for great television. The Lakers finished the regular season 56-26 and Doc and I went to Houston to call the fourth game of the Lakers-Rockets first-round playoff series. On the day before the game, Doc called my hotel room and wanted to talk.

He walked in and said, "First, I can't tell you how much fun I'm having doing these games. It's really been great. Exactly what I needed. And I know I've told you that there are only a couple of coaching jobs that I would even think about considering."

"So which job are you taking?"

"Well, Danny Ainge called, and the Celtics have offered me the job, and—"

"Doc, that's great."

I knew that coaching was still in Doc's veins. I was just hoping he'd hold off for a couple of seasons.

Boston needed an answer quickly. Doc accepted right there in Houston. So long, podner.

Still, ABC agreed to let Doc work the rest of the 2004 playoffs. The Lakers beat Houston in five games. Then they met San Antonio in the Western Conference semifinals. The Spurs won the first two games at home. The Lakers won the next two in Los Angeles. Game 5 in San Antonio was a prime time Thursday night game on ABC.

At halftime, I walked out through the tunnel to use the men's room next to the Lakers locker room. As I'm walking in, the owner of the Lakers, Dr. Jerry Buss, is walking out.

"Hey Jerry, what's your coach going to do?" I asked him.

He rolled his eyes, and with a hint of exasperation answered, "I don't know. You know Phil . . ."

And then he added something totally unexpected.

"I'll tell you one thing, though. If your guy hadn't taken that Boston job, he'd have been *my* guy!"

I said, "*Really?*"

He said, "Oh, yes."

Then, as I walked back to our courtside broadcast table, I only had one thought. *Do I tell Doc what I just heard?*

I sat down and realized I couldn't hold back. So about thirty seconds before we go back on the air for the second half, I say to Doc, "Listen, you won't believe this. I just ran into Jerry Buss and he said that if Phil steps away, the job would have been yours."

Doc looked straight ahead. He later told me he was thinking about the beach, playing golf at the Bel-Air Country Club, and ordering his favorite two-sauce pasta at Toscana. And then he said with a twinkle in his voice, "You know, I'm not sure if the ink on that Celtics contract is *totally* dry."

That Game 5 was a classic. The Lakers led most of the way, and then the Spurs grabbed the lead with a little more than two minutes to go. With eleven seconds left, Kobe Bryant hit a jumper to put the Lakers back out in front by a point. On the next possession, the Lakers played great defense and forced Tim Duncan out beyond the free-throw line. Duncan got the ball and had to take an off-balance, going to his left, seventeen-footer that, improbably, went in, to again give the Spurs the lead with four-tenths of a second remaining. Doc presciently noted that 0.4 seconds was the absolute minimum time needed for a player to catch and shoot the ball. Well, with everyone expecting the ball to go to Kobe, Gary Payton inbounded it to Derek Fisher, who threw up a prayer that went in at the buzzer. The Lakers went on to win the series, then beat the Timberwolves in six games to win the Western Conference Finals, too, and now, it was the Lakers against the Detroit Pistons in the NBA Finals.

The Lakers were heavily favored—but in that series, they looked lost. They dropped the first game at home, and needed a desperation three-pointer by Kobe to send Game 2 into overtime, where they won it. But then they went to Detroit, lost all three games, and the Pistons were NBA champions. Larry Brown became the first coach to win an NCAA and NBA title. Chauncey Billups was named Finals MVP for leading a deep, defensive-minded cast that also included Rasheed Wallace, Ben Wallace, Tayshaun Prince, and others.

Meanwhile, the Lakers were about to implode. Not only did Malone and Payton depart, but Shaquille O'Neal was traded to Miami. Phil Jackson ended up retiring but would be back on the Laker bench after one season. And Doc Rivers, of course, went to Boston, coached the Celtics for nine seasons, and won the NBA title in 2008.

Of course, in 2013, Doc finally did get that Los Angeles job—with the Clippers. And his handling of the Donald Sterling insanity may have been his best work ever. It was quintessential Doc: a man of class, style, elegance, and grace. A special man on every level.

CHAPTER 19

Links

WHEN I SIGNED ON with ABC Sports in 1976, one of the first people I would work with was Terry Jastrow. Terry was our primary golf producer but also produced and directed a lot of college football and that was where we first got together. In fact, Terry was the producer of that Stanford game in 1978 when I'd had that unbelievable ten-minute car ride with Frank Broyles regarding the futures of Bill Walsh and Bill Clinton. Later that evening, Terry would swing by San Francisco International Airport to pick up a young lady he had recently started dating. Her name was Anne Archer and the two would be married within a couple of years. Anne was just starting out as an actress and would leave an indelible mark soon thereafter when she received an Academy Award nomination for her role as Michael Douglas's wife in *Fatal Attraction*. The Jastrows and the Michaelses go back a long way.

For years, Terry encouraged me to take up golf. In my twenties and thirties, I played a lot of tennis, much of it with Terry, but in my forties, Terry, a three-handicap, convinced me it was time to take up golf and sponsored me for membership to the Bel-Air Country Club. I resisted but he insisted. Ever since, I've looked at Terry as a drug dealer. He hooked me for life.

There's so much to love about golf. The ambience. Four hours without any phone calls or emails. The constant challenge of trying to become better. You can never master it, but you can always improve. (In my case, *when?*) The competitive aspect. And maybe most of all, the camaraderie. Golf provides great insight into people. It's social and there's plenty of fooling around, and people reveal themselves on the course in various and often fascinating ways.

There are very few things I love more than playing golf, but my golf broadcasting experience is extremely limited. In the late 1990s, ABC had the rights to the Skins Game, a made-for-television big money competition that featured some of the sport's premier players. And in 1997, a young star by the name of Tiger Woods would be making his Skins Game debut. To promote the event for ABC, I interviewed Tiger during halftime of a *Monday Night Football* game. I'd never spoken to him before, and the interview was to be a "two-way" via satellite—with me in Miami and Tiger somewhere on the West Coast. I phoned him that afternoon to go over what we'd be talking about, and mentioned how I'd recently started playing golf, how much I loved it—and my home course. He knew a lot of members at Bel-Air and we had a nice chat, and then I asked him to give me a couple of "swing thoughts." He laughingly obliged.

The following year, Tiger was in the Skins Game again, and once more I interviewed him at halftime on the Monday night before the event. As we had done twelve months before, we spoke by phone that afternoon and I was able to get another couple of tips from him.

Then in 1999, Tiger competed in another big-money show on ABC, titled *The Showdown at Sherwood*. It was a live, prime-time special in August that pitted Tiger against his biggest rival at the time and the number-one player in the world, David Duval. It took place at the Sherwood Country Club in Thousand Oaks, an hour's drive from downtown Los Angeles. As it would start at 5 P.M. Pacific Time, the last four holes of the course were lighted. I was assigned to cohost the telecast with Mike Tirico.

Tiger had been at the PGA event at the Firestone Country Club in Ohio that weekend, and had flown into Southern California, landing about three hours before the match got under way. Woods arrived at the Sherwood course at three o'clock and went out to the practice green at around four fifteen. I went over to meet him for the first time in person.

"How's your game?" Tiger asked as he greeted me.

"Frankly, pretty bad right now."

"Well," he said, "with your schedule you probably don't get to play very much."

"Tiger, let me confess that's not an issue." I said. "My greatest fear is that someday, my ultimate boss, Michael Eisner, who's also a Bel-Air member, will show up at the club. If he looked at the handicap sheet and saw I was a fifteen, that wouldn't give him pause. But if he looked under the 'rounds played last month' column, he'd see the number twenty-six."

Tiger was in the middle of taking his putter back and came to a dead stop. He looked up and said, "*You* play more than *I* do!"

Guilty as charged.

ONCE IN A WHILE, I've played golf with my heart beating out of my chest. In 2008, I was invited to play in the AT&T PGA tournament at Pebble Beach. My pro partner was Joe Ogilvie, a Duke graduate with a degree in economics. Between shots, we would discuss day trading. We had a blast. The other twosome included Les Moonves, the president of CBS, a longtime close friend and one of the great media moguls of this—or any other—era. His pro partner was Justin Leonard.

Now, I've done any number of telecasts throughout my career

where tens and occasionally—as with the Super Bowl—even hundreds of millions of viewers are tuned in. In those situations, because of experience, I'm at home. But I never knew fear until I stood on the first tee at Pebble Beach with five thousand spectators lining the fairway and heard my name being introduced. I could barely put the tee in the ground. I wasn't really thinking about killing someone with my opening shot, though that was in the back of my mind. I was thinking about something equally horrific. As I addressed the ball, the only thought enveloping my brain was *Please, God, don't let me whiff!* All I wanted to do was hit the ball and get out of there. I must have taken the shortest, fastest backswing ever and wound up hitting my drive about 140 yards into the left rough. At least I avoided complete disaster.

Once you get away from the first tee, things settle down, and I played decently for the next couple of hours. And then I got to the fifteenth tee, home of the fabled Club 15. There are bleachers just off the tee box that hold about a thousand spectators and there's a sign above the last row that says, PROFESSIONAL HELP FOR THE AMATEUR GOLFER. The same characters have sat there for years and they know everything about every amateur in the field. Forget Clint Eastwood or Jack Nicholson or Bill Murray. If you're a State Farm agent from Omaha, this gang can tell you how many policies you've sold in the last three years.

So as I walk up to tee off, they've already recited most of my career back to me and now I see that CBS is going to take my drive on live national television and David Feherty is thirty feet away with a hand mike, ready for a post-shot interview. I can't even feel my legs. The crowd goes absolutely silent and I'm standing over the ball totally frozen. At that point, all I could do was back away from the ball. I looked at the gallery and said, "Does anyone have a Valium?" It got a good laugh, which relaxed me, and I was able to quickly set up again and wound up launching one of the greatest drives of my life. It was my Walter Mitty moment. Of course, the postscript would be, with a chance to get on the green in two and have a birdie putt, I wound up on the green in three and three-putted for a double bogey. What else is new? That's golf.

OVER THE YEARS, I'VE been fortunate to play golf with people from many spectrums. About four years ago, my friend Brad Freeman invited me to fly with him to Las Vegas to play at Shadow Creek in a fivesome that included George W. Bush. The president greeted us on arrival and not only had arranged the teams but insisted on keeping score, which can be complicated. It's two "in the box" against three, the pairings vary, you have to factor in handicaps, and so forth. The president had already set up the scorecard.

We had three carts, and the four of us took turns riding with the president every couple of holes. We walked off the eighth green and I slid in next to him. He was at the wheel already at work. He had the card and his pencil and he was doing the math and making sure everything was perfect. I said to him, "You're just like Ben Bernanke."

Without missing a beat, he looked at me and said, "Better."

And continued with the scorekeeping.

He was very competitive, but also had a great sense of humor—it was a joke fest the entire day. I pulled out my iPhone after he had made a long putt for a birdie and started to interview him as if he had won the Masters. He played right along and it was hysterical. President Bush can play, too—a legitimate seven or eight handicap.

I've also played about a dozen rounds with an erstwhile presidential candidate—one Donald J. Trump. Trump, of course, doesn't only play golf—he also owns a collection of courses around the world. I first played with Donald when my good friend Skip Bronson brought him out to Bel-Air. On the par-five eighth hole, he hit his second shot into the middle of a pond to the left of the green, creating an Old Faithful–like geyser. Then, as he's preparing to hit his next shot, all of a sudden he's hitting a ball that's right *behind* the pond with a perfect fluffy lie and telling us that he lies two. Skip says, "How is that possible?" Donald replies, "The tide brought it over."

The upshot: When you play with Trump, if you're not his partner, you have no chance. Though it might cost you forty or fifty dollars to be on the other side, think of it as a cover charge: $12.50 an hour for great entertainment.

A few years back, Donald bought a course in Palos Verdes, just south of Los Angeles, right on the Pacific Ocean. We've played there a handful of times, and on each occasion, all throughout the round, Trump would keep saying, "This is the number-one course in California, hands down. Every golf magazine has it at the top of the list. Nothing even compares, not even Pebble Beach." Finally, one time, on about the fifteenth hole, Donald proclaimed, "Al, let me tell you why this is better than Pebble Beach. Look right out there—what do you see?"

"Of course, Donald, the Pacific Ocean."

And then he said, "And you've played Pebble Beach. What do you see from that course?"

"Well, that's Monterey Bay."

And then as only Donald J. Trump could sum it up—"You see what I mean! They have a bay. I have an ocean."

At which point, I couldn't resist.

"Donald," I said, "we're both New York kids, so let me ask you. Is Monterey Bay connected to the Pacific Ocean by the Gowanus Canal?"

He might have heard me. I don't know. He just kept on selling. Donald the Irrepressible.

SOME OF THE WORLD'S greatest athletes are also fanatical golfers. In the summer of 1998, I was vacationing on Maui with the family, and Michael Jordan was staying at the hotel next to ours on Wailea Beach. At this point, he had retired from the Chicago Bulls for a second time. I'd never met him but we ran into each other on the beach and started to talk about golf. "I'll give you a call," he said. "We'll play." Sure enough, the next morning there was a voice mail in my hotel room from Michael inviting me to play that afternoon at Wailea.

I met him at the course and he introduced me to the other members of the foursome he had assembled: the head pro from Wailea and his friend—Joe Morgan. "Have you guys met?" he asked. *Have we met?* Joe and I laughed. We'd known each other since 1972 when he was traded to the Reds, and then we'd worked together at ABC for a number of years. That he'd be on Maui at the same time was a nice coincidence.

Anyway, as we started the round, it was clear that Michael had an interesting quirk. He didn't just play from the back tees. He played as far back as he could go. If there were twenty yards available behind the back tees, that was where Michael would tee off. He wanted the course to play as long as possible.

At one point he was in a fairway bunker and hit a five-iron from about 205 yards out that landed within three feet of the cup. He hit a number of other terrific shots that day, making six or seven birdies. He was also great company—collegial and funny and excited to talk about all sports, mainly the NFL.

After the round, we went into the clubhouse restaurant and sat down. It was in the middle of the 1998 home run chase that had captivated the country and we started talking about Sammy Sosa and Mark McGwire and whether either or both could break Roger Maris's record. Jordan, remember, was only a few years removed from playing minor-league baseball—the conversation interested him as much as it did Joe and me. Above the bar, there was a small television set— maybe twenty-seven inches—and it was probably fifty feet away from us, a little shorter than the distance from the plate to the pitcher's mound. It was late afternoon in Hawaii, which meant it was night-time on the East Coast and *SportsCenter* was on. The screen displayed the results of the Cubs game from earlier in the day and a lot of other information about the game that we would have needed a telescope to decipher.

Morgan and I got up from the table to take a closer look and to see if Sosa had hit a home run. But Michael started reading the information on the screen from his chair. *Cubs won, 5–4, Sosa was two for four with a double and a walk.* He read everything on the screen. Morgan and I looked each other dumbfounded. Later, as we walked out to the parking lot, Joe and I figured that Michael must see in 4-D, not 3-D. The same way they used to talk about Ted Williams's incredible eyesight, clearly Jordan had something similar going on. With his eyes, just imagine how that rim must have looked from eighteen feet out.

AND FINALLY, IT'S THE NFL off-season in the early summer of 2012. Peyton and Eli Manning were out in California, and came to Bel-Air as my guests. I invited my buddy Skip Bronson and we played a match: Peyton and Skip against Eli and me. I think we put forty or fifty dollars on the line.

Now, Eli may have his two Super Bowls and Peyton may have his one and numerous MVP awards and both have had magical careers. But that day, the big brother/little brother dynamic was completely in evidence. They absolutely wanted to beat each other and Peyton was squirming as Eli and I got off to a very good start and built a fairly significant lead by the fifteenth hole.

But then the lead began to fray. Still, as we teed off on 17, Eli and I knew we only had to halve one of the final two holes to clinch the win. Then on the seventeenth green, Bronson makes a forty-foot snake for a birdie. And I then proceeded to miss a three-footer for a par, which would have been a net birdie—leaving Eli and me with an even slimmer margin. Then on 18, Bronson sinks another long bomb but I'm still in position to tie the hole and win the match with another three-footer. Which, of course, I lipped out. Choke City.

I had cost Eli the match.

I was distraught and all the more so when I saw how ebullient Peyton was. He was hugging Skip for making the putts and laughing about the fact that he was going to collect from his brother. Eli was gracious and a good sport but I couldn't blame him if he wanted to kill me. All I could do was put my hat down over my eyes. I didn't want to look at him.

A few months later, the *Sunday Night Football* opener would be played in New York. We went to meet with the Giants a couple of days before and I put my hat down over my eyes again as soon as Eli walked in the room. I said, "I can't even look at you."

He said, "Nah, you got a bad read on that one."

There's your perfect teammate.

CHAPTER 20

A New Home

TELEVISION BUSINESS DEALS HAVE always interested me. It started with my father exposing me to the inner workings of the business during his time at MCA and Trans World International, and has continued to this day. I've always been fascinated with the back-room intrigue and the deal making.

So I understood almost everything when I wound up with an inside look at one of the landmark deals in the history of sports television.

It's October 2004. I was in the middle of my nineteenth season on *Monday Night Football*, and my third with John Madden. We were in Cincinnati for a game between the Bengals and the Broncos, and on the afternoon of the game, I had a cup of coffee in the lobby of our hotel with Broncos owner Pat Bowlen. Pat was a longtime friend, and also, at the time, the chairman of the NFL owner's committee that negotiated television rights. The league's eight-year deals with its broadcast partners were set to expire after the 2005 season, and already the wheels had been set in motion for negotiations to renew the packages. As it stood, CBS had the rights to AFC games, Fox had the NFC, ABC had *Monday Night Football,* and ESPN had the Sunday night game. CBS and Fox had quickly re-upped with the league, but Disney—the owner of both ABC and ESPN—was slow-playing it, despite having the chance to continue to control both the Sunday and Monday night games. And Bowlen, knowing that I could get the word back to the home office, wanted me to deliver a message.

"Your company is asleep at the switch," he told me. "The number is $1.5 billion." That was the number it was going to take, per year, to lock up the rights to both of the prime-time games.

Then Bowlen gave me one more piece of information to pass along: "Despite what your people might think, the NFL does have another bidder."

Fifteen minutes later, I was back upstairs in my hotel room and on the phone with Bob Iger, who was months away from succeeding Michael Eisner as the head of Disney. When I passed along what Bowlen had said, he told me he thought the NFL was most likely bluffing, setting up a stalking horse to drive up the price. I agreed. Neither of us could identify a serious bidder. NBC was totally in the dumps and hemorrhaging money—to us, they didn't figure—and Turner Broadcasting seemed like too much of a long shot. No well-run company wants to be fooled into bidding against itself. We hung up but one thing was still gnawing at me; I'd known Pat Bowlen to be gruff and to be tough, but also to be a straight shooter.

With a deadline approaching, Disney decided to pass on paying the $1.5 billion. So the league pulled the offer off the table and set a rebid for the spring of 2005. And when Disney returned to the negotiating table, sure enough there was another player—hungry to make a deal, and get back in business with the NFL. It was, in fact, NBC.

In 2005, NBC was a last-place network with a struggling prime-time lineup. But they did have a legendary executive running their sports department, Dick Ebersol. Dick had first worked for Roone Arledge as a researcher on ABC Sports' Olympic coverage. Then he helped create *Saturday Night Live* and later became the head of NBC Sports. But on Thanksgiving weekend of 2004, Dick's life changed in an instant. He had been flying out of Montrose, Colorado, when his private plane crashed on takeoff. Dick had to be pulled from the wreckage by his son Charlie, but his youngest son, thirteen-year-old Teddy, was killed. Dick sustained serious injuries and recuperated for months but continued to work on the NBC deal.

Before the tragedy, Ebersol had been quietly talking with the league's most powerful owners—among them, Bowlen, Robert Kraft of the Patriots, and Jerry Jones of the Cowboys, as well as others in the NFL office—as a forerunner to putting together an offer to bring the Sunday night games to NBC. Clearly, NBC had been that "other" bidder. Ebersol wanted to make *Sunday Night Football* a cornerstone of NBC's prime-time programming. And he was terrific at selling his vision to the league. Sunday nights on NBC would look and feel special. It was a continuation of the philosophy Dick had first learned from Arledge. The show would be for everyone—hard-core fans and casual viewers, men and women, young and old, any and all demographics. Come one, come all.

So, in April 2005, after a final meeting in New York City, the packages for Sunday and Monday nights were split. Ebersol and NBC won the rights to *Sunday Night Football* for $3.6 billion over six years, which included two playoff games each season, and two Super Bowls, as well as something else innovative: scheduling flexibility—the ability to move bad matchups late in the season out of prime time and replace them with better games. Disney, meanwhile, retained *Monday Night* for almost twice that—$1.1 billion per season (with no playoff games, no Super Bowls, and no scheduling flexibility), and proudly announced the package would, after thirty-six seasons, be moving from ABC to ESPN.

How could ESPN be happy with that deal? It all went back to the dual revenue stream: cable fees and advertising. Adding *Monday Night Football* continued to give ESPN more leverage with cable companies to jack its fees up even higher. And, by the way, someone who knew that better than anyone was now a key executive for the NFL—Steve Bornstein. My onetime boss and the former president of ESPN had been fired by Disney and then had landed with the league, where he'd be put in charge of the new NFL Network. Now, in an imperfect storm for Disney, he was on the other side of the negotiating table from his old employer, understanding how to suck every Disney dollar out of the ESPN pipe.

That very night after the deal was completed, I ran into an ABC executive at a restaurant in Los Angeles. ESPN was celebrating—but this executive was flipped off. The deal would mean that the entertainment division would be losing its number-one-rated prime-time show and would now have to program an entire night of prime time against *Monday Night Football* on ESPN. "I can't believe it," he said to me. "Most of ESPN's shows are howling jackasses braying at the moon, but it doesn't matter—because a chimpanzee could run that operation. With those cable fees, they can't fail. And now they think they're creative geniuses. Un-fucking-believable!"

In that new television landscape, the NFL on TV had been transformed. And for me personally, the drama was just beginning.

THE DAY THE DEAL was finalized in April 2005, I got a call from my boss, George Bodenheimer, who was heading both ABC Sports and ESPN. He wanted to personally talk to me about the deal and the future now that Disney had only one package. He told me that he wasn't sure what the company was going to do with regard to the broadcasting teams, because as he saw it, "we have two very good teams—John Madden and you on Monday night, and the Sunday night team of Mike Patrick, Joe Theismann, and Paul Maguire on ESPN." By the end of the call, I was already developing an ulcer.

Then George made the same call to John Madden. An hour later, I called John and he was angry. He related to me the same thing that

Bodenheimer had told me about "not being sure" and "the two good broadcast teams." Madden then said he'd already called his agent, Sandy Montag, to tell him to make a deal with NBC. That wouldn't be hard, as Ebersol loved Madden and would have put a full-court press on to begin with. Madden also knew ESPN wasn't going to fight his departure—because he knew that Mark Shapiro, who had been given full autonomy by Bodenheimer to oversee the new *Monday Night,* wanted him out the door anyway—the sooner the better. Now I was really getting sick. I'd spent four great years with the most iconic analyst ever and had been looking forward to many more when a grenade had been tossed in.

I've never been a big fan of Internet or newspaper polls about sports announcers, but over the years, there was one thing consistent about the polls that dealt with football analysts. John Madden was *always* the runaway winner. By a huge margin. And now he's being pushed out? Insane!

So, in June 2005, two months after the NBC deal was announced, John Madden signed a deal to move to *Sunday Night Football* for the 2006 season. And not long thereafter, when it appeared I'd remain on *Monday Night Football* after it moved to ESPN, Shapiro announced the hiring of Joe Theismann for the *Monday Night* analyst role. I got a call from the owner of the Patriots, Bob Kraft, a good friend and, as a key member of the NFL broadcast committee, a man I spoke with regularly. He asked me to explain what was going on. I said it's simple—it's like you trading Tom Brady for a seventh-round draft choice.

Around that time, ESPN also announced that its Sunday night production team would be taking over *Monday Night Football* when it moved to cable the following season. Now it wasn't just John leaving—Fred Gaudelli and Drew Esocoff were being shoved out by Shapiro as well. Upset, I called Bodenheimer. He said that much of the decision had to do with "loyalty." I told him I didn't understand.

Fred and Drew had been longtime ESPN employees who had been *promoted* to work on Monday nights on ABC. They'd been under the same umbrella longer than the current ESPN guys who were now being named to take their places. So how in hell did replacing them have anything to do with loyalty?! That move told me all I needed to know. It was never clearer that, to the people running things from Bristol, Connecticut, if you were an ABC character, you might as well be wearing a scarlet letter.

I was no fan of Mark Shapiro, a self-promoting and self-anointed wunderkind, and the feeling was mutual. But he was told by people above him that, like it or not, I was going to remain as the play-by-play announcer on *Monday Night Football*. Along the way, months earlier, when there had been an unflattering article written about me in the *New York Post* that included the exact details of my NBA contract, I asked a colleague in the ABC PR department to look into it, and he traced the leak directly to Shapiro's office. Nothing like the enemy within.

Of course, right after naming Theismann the new analyst, and pushing Fred and Drew (and indirectly, John) out, guess who walked away from ESPN in the fall of 2005? Shapiro. He'd taken a job with Redskins owner Dan Snyder to run the Six Flags amusement parks operation. So he'd never even be around for a single ESPN *Monday Night Football* telecast. As one colleague so adroitly put it, "Bodenheimer gave Shapiro the keys to a shiny, brand-new Ferrari and the kid crashed it into the wall. And then walked away from the scene." Some business, huh?

Meanwhile, the 2005 NFL season would be a lame-duck year on ABC. Even though I knew I could stay with the new *Monday Night* package in 2006, my contract was expiring and I obviously was interested in going with John to NBC when the season concluded. And it appeared I'd have until the end of 2005 to make a choice. Dick Ebersol had already been in contact with my agent and wanted me to come over. But the initial offer was one I couldn't accept. I was being asked to take a significant cut in salary and I knew that, in addition, I would almost certainly have to give up the NBA, which I was really growing to love. Then, all of a sudden, while on vacation in Hawaii in July, ESPN told me they wanted an answer immediately. They'd clearly gotten the word that NBC was talking with me. I had less than forty-eight hours to make my decision. The NBC offer wasn't palatable. So, after three gulps of Pepto-Bismol, I called George Bodenheimer to say I was staying. It was announced the next day.

Sure enough, 2005 was an awkward year. John was going to NBC, Fred and Drew were in career limbo, and I was rolling around in bed every night trying to figure out the rest of my career. The last few years had been too much fun and now I was going off to some "foreign" operation without my buddies, who just happened to be the best in the business. In October, Bodenheimer came to a *Monday Night* game in Indianapolis. An hour before kickoff, we walked onto the field together. I told George that I was hearing from my sources in the league office that beginning next season *Monday Night on ESPN* wasn't going to get the same schedule of premier games that the ABC version had gotten. George said no—Mark Shapiro had assured him the schedule would still be the same. I had better information, and I told George the litmus test would be when the schedule came out the following spring. In all my years doing *Monday Night Football* except one or two, the reigning Super Bowl champion had appeared the maximum number of times on Monday night—three. If that was the case again, then that would be the sign the schedule was of the same quality. But if the champion played just twice, or conceivably only once, that would be a sign that Monday night's reign as the NFL's premier game was a thing of the past. I told George I was hearing there would be not three, not even two, but *one* appearance only. And that *Sunday Night Football* on NBC would feature the champions three times. And could "flex" them in even more.

The schedule for 2006 would come out that next April. Sure

enough, the Super Bowl champion Steelers would appear only once on the *Monday Night* schedule. Week two. At Jacksonville.

I wouldn't be there.

LATE IN THAT LAME duck 2005 season, Dick Ebersol visited a *Monday Night Football* game in Baltimore, and watched Fred and Drew produce and direct part of the game in the production truck. He later compared it to "watching the frickin' ballet." Minutes after the game, Dick signed Fred—who was being cast aside by ESPN—to produce *Sunday Night Football* the following season. Ebersol had already signed Drew to direct the new *Sunday Night*. So now I was the last of the Mohicans. Meanwhile, Ebersol still hadn't chosen a new play-by-play announcer for the package.

Finally, at the end of December, I had to at least explore the possibility of getting out of my ESPN deal. In my mind, it just wasn't going to work. I was learning too much about their "new" approach to *Monday Night Football* and I was going to be the wrong guy in the wrong place. I knew Madden, Gaudelli, and Esocoff were politicking Ebersol to get me over with them. I wanted to go there in the first place but couldn't accept the offer. Word began to get out that I was looking to jump to NBC. I knew it would look like I was trying to "break" my contract. One columnist to whom the information was leaked wrote exactly that. I wanted to say, "Hey, pal, nobody *breaks* a contract to take a forty percent pay cut!" But I had to stay quiet. I just knew it had to get done.

Quickly, agents and more executives got involved. This was going to happen. Disney got some concessions from NBC for releasing me from my deal—including rights to broadcast additional Ryder Cup programming and to extended highlight packages from other NBC properties, including the Olympics. Right after the Super Bowl, in which the Steelers beat the Seahawks in Detroit, 21–10, the deal was 99 percent done. But it had already been a headache for ABC's and

ESPN's public relations departments. For several weeks they'd had to deal with the lame-duck statuses of John, Fred, and Drew, plus rumors of my possible departure. At one point in Detroit during Super Bowl week, I personally apologized to the PR people for the distraction. Then, though, a wacky plan was hatched to make their jobs easier when the deal was announced.

In the 1920s, before he'd created Mickey Mouse, Walt Disney's original cartoon creation at Universal Studios was a character named Oswald the Lucky Rabbit. But Walt Disney hadn't been able to hold on to the rights when he left the studio—and all these years later, Universal (NBC's corporate sibling) still owned Oswald, even though no one had any idea who Oswald was. Some Disney heirs had asked Bob Iger for years to try to bring Oswald "back home." This was hardly a high-priority issue for Bob. Then someone came up with the idea that if we included Oswald in *this* deal, the press would lock in on that aspect of the story and it would overshadow any suspicions of nefariousness. And that's exactly what happened. Even though the deal had already been done pre-Oswald, still, to this day, I'll occasionally see or hear a story that says I was traded for a cartoon rabbit—normally written or told by someone who should be traded in a two-for-one deal for Dopey and Goofy.

There was a much bigger story, though. Within a year, *Sunday Night Football*, with the old *Monday Night*'s producer, director, announcers, and about forty of the best technicians and production men and women in the country, would be one of the top few shows on television—with the best games and matchups and 50 percent more viewers than ESPN's "new" *Monday Night Football*. It might not be an over-the-top exaggeration to say that this deal saved NBC. That sentiment was echoed throughout the network.

THE FIRST THREE SEASONS of *Sunday Night Football* were an extension of those wonderful last four years of the *Monday Night Football* we'd been a part of at ABC. Then, when John Madden retired after that epic Steelers-Cardinals Super Bowl, Cris Collinsworth was waiting in the wings. As I've said many times, I felt like I went from Joe DiMaggio to Mickey Mantle.

I first crossed paths with Cris when I covered three or four of his University of Florida games. In 1988, when I was calling the baseball All-Star Game in Cincinnati, and he was nearing the end of his NFL career with the Bengals, he'd stopped by the booth before the game to ask if we could announce on national television that he'd be getting engaged to the beauteous Holly Bankemper before the night was done. We couldn't. But I loved his chutzpah. In 2006, Dick Ebersol had brought him over from Fox to work the *Sunday Night* pregame show along with Bob Costas, making him the obvious candidate to replace John Madden when he retired. It was the perfect choice.

It isn't just that Cris has superb insights and it's not just that he sees every aspect of the game—and I mean *every* part of the game. As with all the top-of-the-pyramid analysts, he knows how to communicate and connect with the viewer. You turn off the vast majority of the audience when you get too technical. Walk down the street and ask 100 people to define a "three-technique tackle," and 99 of them would look back at you like zombies. Cris has mastered the art of taking complex points and explaining them so lucidly that *everyone* can understand.

One great example of Cris's uncanny prophetic ability came at the end of a game in October 2012. The Chargers were playing the Saints in New Orleans, and the Saints were up by a touchdown in the final minute. San Diego had the ball, and on second and ten, Philip Rivers threw an incomplete pass. And then Cris explained there was more to the story. During the replay, Cris pointed out that the Chargers' left tackle, Jared Gaither, had been beaten by Saints defensive end Martez Wilson, which led Rivers to have to release the ball early to avoid a sack. Cris went on to say that Gaither looked hurt, and warned that if the Chargers didn't adjust, Wilson was going to have a sack to end the game. Well—what happened on third down? Wilson beat Gaither, sacked Rivers, stripped the ball, and recovered it. Game over. As perfectly and succinctly predicted by Cris Collinsworth.

Cris also has always been very candid, unafraid to say things that might not sit well with the people he's talking about—players, coaches, even owners—but that are true. And he does it all without making a show of himself. Cris is not one of those "experts" who figuratively jump up and down and scream to the world, "Listen to me! Look at me!" He just tells it as it is.

When we started together in 2009, it was seamless—exactly like working with John Madden or Doc Rivers. And then, apart from being a sensational partner, Cris also became a great friend. A couple of years ago, he arranged something that was going to put me, in a manner of speaking, over the moon. He arranged for me to meet the one human being who topped my list of "the one person you'd never met whom you'd most like to have dinner with."

At one time or another, I've covered almost every sports star of the last four decades. I've gotten to know many of them well. I've been fortunate enough to meet presidents, inventors, renowned authors, and a veritable "Who's Who in America" (and elsewhere). But the one man I always wanted to break bread with was Neil Armstrong. I'm not entirely sure where it came from—it's not like I was ever an astronomy buff. But as a child, at least as a child in my generation, flying to the moon was the be-all and end-all. And then, in 1969, it happened!

Not to diminish winning a Nobel Prize or batting title or Super Bowl or Oscar. But, come on! Neil Armstrong was the first human to walk on the moon. Trump that.

Well, in 2011, at dinner one night, Cris Collinsworth finds out about my fascination with Neil Armstrong. "If I could have dinner with one person," I tell him, "it would be Armstrong."

As it turned out, Cris—a prominent figure in Cincinnati, which was where Neil Armstrong lived—knew Neil and had played several

rounds of golf with him. It also turned out that—no surprise, really—
Neil loved sports. And Cris arranged that a couple of nights before
the Steelers at Bengals game in October 2012, we would be having
dinner with Neil Armstrong! If there was a game on our schedule I
couldn't wait for, *this* was the one.

In August—two months before that game—Collinsworth and
I were in New York preparing to do a preseason game. As we drove
back from the Jets' practice facility, the radio was on. And we hear the
report: *Neil Armstrong has died of complications from coronary artery
bypass surgery.*

R.I.P. forever, Mr. Armstrong.

FOR YEARS, THE FOOTBALL season would start with articles predict-
ing the impending doom of *Monday Night Football.* It's now only been
around for forty-five seasons. I spent twenty of those in the booth and
they went by in about twenty minutes. And now it's Season Nine of
NBC's *Sunday Night Football* and they've gone by just as rapidly. For
the last two years, it's been the highest-rated show in all of television.
All of us on the package know that the games, the matchups, and
the superstars are the central part of the show's appeal. But there are
more than a hundred people who devote a major portion of their lives
working to make *Sunday Night* the very best presentation of a football
game ever.

It starts with Fred Gaudelli and Drew Esocoff and the standards
they set. But their passion and drive envelop everyone on the broadcast. There are a lot of people who make Cris and me look better every
week—"Malibu" Kelly Hayes, my longtime spotter, who once lived
in Malibu but moved to Aspen many moons ago; George Hill, my
statistics maven with the wit of a genius—some of the best lines at-
tributed to me have actually come from notes passed by George; Ken
Hirdt, son of Steve, our head of research; Melissa Horton, our stage
manager ("kennel keeper," I like to say), who keeps everything flow-

ing seamlessly; Audrey Mansfield (could there be a better name for
a makeup artist?); Andy Freeland, who came to the party when Cris
came aboard and could wind up some day as the all-time *Jeopardy*
champion. And downstairs and around the stadium, Fred has put
together the best of the best. Cameramen and women, tape opera-
tors, production assistants—you name it—it's an all-star team. And a
character by the name of Vinny Rao, whose job description is "whatever." Every company in America should have a Vinny Rao. You need
something—*anything*—to get done, Vinny somehow gets it done. Always. And never takes any credit for it.

A fairly sizable number of viewers and even a few sports television
executives tend to minimize and even denigrate the importance and
value of the sideline reporter. I strongly disagree with that assessment.
I've worked with the very best—Lesley Visser practically invented the
genre and is one of the great characters of all time, with a boundless
sense of humor. Andrea Kremer was with us for the first five years of
the NBC *Sunday Night* package and her work on HBO's *Real Sports*
is simply spectacular. I'll put them up against any sports reporters in
the country, print or electronic. On the air, they ask smart, concise
questions that often trigger thoughtful responses. They're not afraid
to broach tough topics. And their value extends off the air, as well.
Because of their proximity to the field and the sidelines, they can
see things that we, from the booth, can't. We can talk to them during commercial breaks or they can communicate with the production truck. And they're like the postmen—neither snow, nor rain, nor
heat, nor gloom of night (nor fans screaming at them from the stands)
can keep them from their appointed rounds.

And then there's our current sideline reporter, the supreme Michele Tafoya. I first worked with Michele on our NBA coverage on
ABC. One of her most memorable postgame interviews came after
that classic Game 5 of the Western Conference semifinals in 2004
between the Lakers and the Spurs. After Tim Duncan had hit his off-
balance seventeen-footer to give the Spurs the lead and Derek Fisher

answered with his crazy, not-to-be believed shot at the buzzer, the Lakers sprinted off the court—"The officials will review it but the Lakers are already on the tarmac," I said on the air. The only guy who couldn't race away from Michele? Let's put it this way—conditioning always seemed to be an issue with Shaquille O'Neal. So Michelle corrals him and asks him to describe the end of the game. Shaq smiles and says, "One lucky shot deserved another." Perfect.

Two years ago in Baltimore, the Patriots met the Ravens in a Sunday night game less than twenty-four hours after the nineteen-year-old brother of Ravens wide receiver Torrey Smith had died in a motorcycle accident. Smith hadn't slept a wink but still played and had a tremendous game, catching six passes for 127 yards and two touchdowns. Michele interviewed him only moments after the Ravens had pulled off a dramatic 31–30 win. A sideline reporter cannot have a tougher task yet, as always, Michele pulled it off perfectly with the exact balance of sensitivity, compassion, and journalism.

Before that season was over, we were back in Baltimore, where the star of that night's game was Jacoby Jones, who ended his interview by saying to Michele, "Thanks, gorgeous." Take a guess what her new nickname became.

More recently, we had a scary situation develop at the end of the first half on a *Sunday Night* game when Gary Kubiak, then coaching the Houston Texans, collapsed as the teams went to the locker room. It was a frightening moment. Michele was right there and kept the audience apprised of what was happening without speculating. Fortunately, Kubiak would be okay. And once again, Michele totally nailed it.

I've called two Super Bowls on NBC—and both have gone down to the wire: the Steelers and Cardinals with John Madden in 2009 and then the Giants' upset of the Patriots with Cris Collinsworth in 2012. Ten months before that game in Indianapolis, Linda and I had made a trip to Israel that had been organized by Patriots owner Robert Kraft and his wife, Myra. We experienced six amazing and memorable days. The Kraft family has been intimately involved with Israeli charities for many years and to witness firsthand the adoration and love that entire country had for Myra Kraft was mind-blowing. She had been deeply and personally involved with hospitals, schools, child-care centers, small businesses, and a dozen other institutions. At the time, she was also in remission from cancer but it had resurfaced and at the end of the trip Bob told me that she'd be going back into the hospital as soon as they returned to Boston. Myra never said a word about it and I will never forget walking six or seven miles back and forth around the Old City in Jerusalem with Myra as our tour guide. It's something she'd probably done a hundred times but her passion and enthusiasm never waned in those four hours. It was likely her last really good day on earth. She'd be back in the hospital two days later and would die in four months. God bless Myra Kraft.

That Super Bowl was also the first overseen by the new chairman of NBC Sports, Mark Lazarus, who took over for Dick Ebersol in 2011. Mark has been the best kind of boss to work for. He puts the right people in the right spots and lets them do their thing. And he supports them. You can't ask for more. He makes it easy for all of us to keep waiting all day for Sunday night.

A Miracle Revisited

I SIGNED ON WITH NBC to do only *Sunday Night Football*. But then in late 2009, Dick Ebersol asked me if I'd host the daytime studio show for the 2010 Vancouver Winter Games. It had been about fifteen years since I'd missed out on the chance to host the 1996 Atlanta Olympics—and it was something that still had a lot of appeal. So shortly after the football season, it was off to Canada.

I had a great time. And since I was hosting the daytime show, I was finished each day at 6 P.M.—giving me the chance to go out and play spectator almost every night. The majority of time the hockey arena was my venue of choice. I always took Cris Collinsworth with me and turned my Florida-born partner into a hockey maven. And what we watched was some of the greatest hockey ever played—the NHL broken up by countries, two weeks of pulsating games. It was all capped off by that dramatic finish in the gold medal game, with Zach Parise of the United States tying it with less than a minute to go in regulation, and then Sidney Crosby winning it for Canada with a golden goal in overtime. I hosted the first two periods in the arena and then had to leave to get ready to cohost the Closing Ceremony at B.C. Place with Bob Costas. I watched the end of that game with

Bob in a small room at the stadium where we were preparing for the show. The feed to our television monitor was on a brief delay—and the thousands of people who had already come into the stadium for the Closing Ceremony were watching it live on the big overhead screens. So, in overtime, when we felt the stadium shake, accompanied by a huge roar, we knew the Canadians must have won it—just a few seconds before we saw Crosby's actual goal.

In London in 2012, I was the daytime studio host again and loved it. The Summer Games have almost three times as many events as the Winter Games, and I saw several of them in person. Being in the Olympic Stadium when the British long-distance star Mo Farah won the 10,000 meters, and feeling that crowd erupt when he took the lead on the final lap, was spine-tingling. And Usain Bolt's performance—winning repeat Olympic gold medals in the 100 meters and 200 meters—provided another shot of electricity. One of the greatest things about sports is the dosages in which the thrills come. You can get a double-overtime hockey game that keeps you riveted for four hours. Or in Bolt's case, two unforgettable memories in fewer than thirty seconds, *total*!

And then there was Sochi 2014, the Winter Olympics. It was an event that was overshadowed beforehand by threats of terrorism. Fortunately, nothing materialized. And then within days of the Closing Ceremony, Russia would invade Crimea and set off a confrontation with Ukraine. But during those two and a half weeks, the athletes, as is always the case with the Olympic Games, turned in a number of remarkable performances. And once again, the hockey tournament was near the top of the list. Though neither would wind up winning a medal, the game between the United States and Russia in group play was spectacular. It went all the way to a shootout with T. J. Oshie of the St. Louis Blues scoring four times to win it for the Americans (international rules, unlike NHL rules, allow coaches to reuse shooters as often as they wish), while Jonathan Quick—the goalie who three months hence would be leading my Kings to a second Stanley Cup in three seasons—made a series of terrific saves to hold off the Russians.

The next day, Quick came to our NBC compound in the International Broadcast Center to be interviewed by Dan Patrick on NBCSN. He wasn't the only star goalie on the premises that afternoon. For our daytime show on NBC, we'd also booked a guest whom I'd never met but wanted to talk to for thirty-four years. His name: Vladislav Tretiak. He was the Soviet goaltender on three gold-medal-winning Olympic teams and was also on the Soviet team that had lost to the United States in Lake Placid in 1980. He's still so heroic in his homeland that he was chosen to light the cauldron for the Opening Ceremony in Sochi. Many consider him the greatest goalie ever.

I met Tretiak when he arrived. We talked for a few minutes and then he went into a room to get some makeup put on before we would start taping. Meanwhile, as I walked out into the hallway, I ran into Jonathan Quick. On a whim, I asked him if he'd ever met Tretiak. He said no. And then I said, "Would you like to?" Wide-eyed and emphatically, he said, "Yes!" I said to come with me and fifteen seconds later I felt as if universes were intersecting and I was introducing Derek Jeter to Babe Ruth. It was a wonderful thing to witness.

A few minutes later, Tretiak and I sat down to do the interview. Vladimir Posner, the Russian commentator who had appeared on *Nightline* often during the Cold War years and was now working for NBC in Sochi, was also on the set to serve as a translator. But when I began asking him questions, starting with his thoughts on lighting the cauldron in the Opening Ceremony, Tretiak answered in English.

We then talked about the U.S.-Russia game from the afternoon before. We talked about the pressure Russia was under to win the gold medal (they wouldn't), and then I transitioned to what I really wanted to ask him about. Lake Placid, 1980.

First, I wanted to know more about what may have been the biggest turning point in that game. How did his coach, Viktor Tikhonov, tell Tretiak—the best goalie on the planet—that he was taking him out of the game after the first period? Tretiak said he was told in the locker room and he was stunned. It was the first time in his life that

he had ever been pulled. And he also noted, with a small smile, perhaps of satisfaction, that Tikhonov later wrote in a book that it was
the worst mistake of his career. They were still friendly, though—
"Coaches make mistakes sometimes, too," Tretiak said wryly.

Then, I got to the question I'd wanted to ask him for thirty-
four years. He had played on a team that was so dominant—and so
great—that winning was always expected and had become routine.
So when the game ended—as Tretiak watched the U.S. team, basically a bunch of college kids the Soviets had crushed, 10–3, just three
weeks before, go crazy, literally falling over themselves on the ice, and
as he waited with his teammates along the blue line for the ceremonial
handshake—what was he thinking about?

For the first time in our interview, Tretiak switched to Russian.
He wanted to make sure he had the right words. Posner translated.

"I saw the happiest people in the world. And they deserved it. And
I was a little bit envious of them. Because we could have been in their
place. But they showed they were tough. Their character."

Then he added this. "Today in America," he said, "the juniors, the
youngsters, play very good hockey—and it's thanks to those boys."

With that, I shook Tretiak's hand, thanked him, and ended the
interview. More than three decades later, I'd gotten his answers to
questions I'd wanted to ask.

It's been an incredible and amazing ride. No day goes by without
me thinking, How did I wind up *here,* and then wind up *there,* and
meet and get to know some of the most interesting and accomplished
men and women of the late twentieth and early twenty-first centuries?
And have a ton of laughs along the way. And still get into the games
for free. And work with the best people to ever come down the pike.
And be blessed with the most wonderful family.

If the law of averages does have me wind up in that Mongolian
sulfur mine in the next life, I'll still be ahead of the game.

I also know Curt Gowdy would be proud.

I've never gotten jaded.

ACKNOWLEDGMENTS

A major, major shout-out and thank-you to Aaron Cohen, my NBC colleague, who was the most valuable player in facilitating the transition from the spoken word to the written word. The road from my voice to the pages of a book proved much trickier than I could have imagined and Aaron worked his magic. Just the fact that you're looking at this right now doesn't happen without Aaron Cohen.

Another NBC colleague, Bruce Cornblatt, made an immeasurable contribution. Bruce is not only a terrific television producer but a book producer as well. He's always known how to keep me focused and on point and took me to the finish line in just the manner I wanted.

Combo platters don't come any better than Cohen and Cornblatt.

I didn't meet Marvin Demoff until 2008 and he's represented me since. He's a brilliant man, a treasured friend and wonderful company who always has his clients' best interests forefront. Just ask John Elway or Dan Marino, two men he's guided for over thirty years. If I could have a do-over, I'd had been with Marvin further back than John or Dan.

You're a lucky man if you can have one longtime friend with

whom you can share absolutely everything. I have three—Alex Wallau, whom you'll meet on several occasions in this book; Joe Cohen, who's been a major part of the sports and television landscape since 1970; and John Shaw, who was the guiding force behind the Rams, both in Los Angeles and St. Louis, for three decades. Not that I'd ever want to abuse the privilege but I know those guys would always be there 24/7.

On *Sunday Night Football*, I work with the best and most dedicated people in the history of sports television. They form my extended family and the ensuing pages will make that abundantly clear.

And finally, to Richard Abate of 3 Arts Entertainment, David Highfill of HarperCollins and my collaborator, Jon Wertheim—I had no idea what this project entailed. If someone had told me that writing the book I wanted would involve the equivalent of going in for fifty root canals along the way, I would have been long gone. We don't get here without you guys.